BIKES AT BROOKLANDS
in the pioneer years

BIKES AT BROOKLANDS

in the pioneer years

PETER HARTLEY

GOOSE & SON
PUBLISHERS

First published in 1973
by Goose & Son Ltd Publishers

ISBN 0 900404 20 5

All rights reserved. No part of this publication may be reproduced or transmitted in any form or by any means, electronic or mechanical, including photocopy, recording, or any information storage and retrieval system, without permission in writing from the publisher.

© Peter Hartley 1973

Printed in Great Britain by
H. E. Warne Ltd
St. Austell and London

CONTENTS

	List of illustrations	page 7
	Foreword	9
	Preface	11
1	The origins of Brooklands Track	13
2	1908—The adventure starts	22
3	1909—The birth of Bemsee	27
4	1910—The tuner finds his feet	53
5	1911—An Indian Summer	85
6	1912—Two, three or four wheels?	126
7	1913—Speeds mount	163
8	1914—Calm before the storm	205
9	1915—The Military take over	234
	Index	241

ILLUSTRATIONS

Brooklands Race Track as it appeared in 1910   *pages* 16-17

PLATES

1.	W. Gordon McMinnies on his 476 cc Triumph	*facing page* 32
2.	Charlie Collier after setting new hour record, 1908	32
3.	Harry Bashall and Frank McNab	33
4.	Will Cook on his 16-20 hp NLG-JAP	33
5.	W. D. Chitty, winner of the 1909 Autumn Handicap	48
6.	The official Matchless-JAP racing team for 1909	48
7.	Billy Wells and his team of Indian-riders, March 1910	49
8.	The start of the 1910 June Handicap	49
9.	Harry Martin on his 344 cc Martin-ASL-JAP	80
10.	Oliver Godfrey and his new 994 cc Indian	80
11.	Victor Surridge on the new 499 cc Rudge, May 1911	81
12.	Jake de Rosier, American track-racing champion	81
13.	Jack Haswell with his 499 cc s.v. Triumph	96
14.	Harry Martin at the start of the first Cyclecar Race	96
15.	The ill-fated Arthur Moorhouse	97
16.	Charlie Collier, winner of the 1000 cc "Car Challenge" Scratch Race, in 1912	97
17.	George Brough, at the MCC Race Meeting in 1912	128
18.	The start of the Junior Brooklands' TT Race, 1912	128
19.	Jack Emerson on his 490 cc Norton	129
20.	Sydney Garrett with his 499 cc Regal-Green-Precision sidecar	129
21.	Les Bailey with his special 349 cc ohv Douglas	144
22.	Freddie Barnes, winner of the Sidecar Handicap, April 1913	144
23.	A. J. McDonagh with his 499 cc Rudge	145
24.	G. E. Stanley, winner of the Benzole Handicap, June 1913	145
25.	The start of the Six-Hour Race, July 1913	176
26.	E. F. Remington on his 986 cc Matchless-JAP	177
27.	Tommy Greene and Cyril Pullin	177
28.	Jack Emerson, the first rider to exceed 80 mph on a machine of under 500 cc capacity, January 1914	192
29.	F. G. Ball on the new 349 cc ohv Douglas	192
30.	Charlie Franklin with his 994 cc eight-valve Indian	193
31.	A. J. Luce, winner of the 3-lap Sidecar Handicap, April 1914	193
32.	Kenneth Holden, who won the Senior Brooklands' TT Race, April 1914, on a 499 cc BSA	208
33.	Jimmy Cocker carrying out track tests early in 1914	208
34.	Bert Haddock awaits starter's orders on his 348 cc AJS	209
35.	Bert Le Vack with his mentor, Oliver De Lissa	209
36.	W. A. Jacobs, winner of the 350 cc Handicap, July 1914	224
37.	E. B. Ware with his 740 cc Morgan-JAP, July 1914	224
38.	Lieut. A. Lindsay with his 490 cc Norton, August 1915	224
39.	Sergeant Arthur Milner on his 349 cc Diamond, September 1915	225
40.	A competitor climbing the Test Hill, October 1915	225

FOREWORD

IT was with great pleasure that I first learnt that Mr Hartley was writing a two-part history of motor-cycle racing at Brooklands. This first book, *Bikes at Brooklands—in the pioneer years*, brings back to me many happy memories of those carefree days at the track before the First Great War, when amateur and professional riders were able to compete on more or less equal terms.

Living fairly close to Brooklands, I was able to watch the building of the track in 1906 and competed there regularly during the pre-war days, first in 1908, on my Triumph and BAT-JAP machines, and later on Humber and Douglas twins. The Douglas was one of my particular favourites and it was a machine of this marque that took me to victory in the 1912 Junior Tourist Trophy Race in the Isle of Man, over the then Mountain Circuit.

Not many people today realise what it was really like at Brooklands before the Great War. We riders formed a small coterie, such that even a mere novice could meet and chat with star riders of the day. It was a friendly, informal atmosphere that pervaded the racing and this comes over well in Mr Hartley's book, which with its wealth of detail will fascinate all those interested in the early days of motor-cycling.

HARRY BASHALL
Haslemere, Surrey

PREFACE

It is difficult to believe, as one looks out of the train window at the British Aircraft Corporation's site just past Weybridge, that here was once the famous Brooklands Motor Racing Circuit.

The track came into being during the Edwardian Era, yet served so well the purposes of its creator, Mr H. J. Locke-King, as a race and test rack, that it was in use right up to its closure in 1939 at the outbreak of World War II. Its motoring and aviation histories have been well documented, but its motor cycle racing side sadly neglected. This is despite the fact that more motor cycle events than any other type, took place during the twenty-eight years in which motor cycles were raced at the track.

This book describes the pioneering days of motor cycle racing at Brooklands, before World War I. It was then that many of those who were to become in later years the technical pacemakers of the British motor and aviation industries, were learning the tricks of their trade there on two-wheelers.

Brooklands enabled the full-throttle running of machines hour-after-hour, such that engines and cycle parts could be tested to destruction; this, under conditions difficult to forecast and hence to produce in the laboratory. Thus really reliable and efficient motor cycles could be developed and Britain's early reputation for motor cycle design excellence be established.

The obtaining of information about those early days has been no easy task, mainly due to the destruction of the official BMCRC track records by enemy action in World War II. It has entailed the combing of early copies of the motorcycling journals, much correspondence, and interviews with many surviving pioneer motorcyclists. In this connection, I should like to thank: Mr Harry Bashall, Mr Vincent Horsman, Mr Percy Brewster, Mr Sydney Garrett, Mr Gordon

McMinnies, Mr Bob Dicker and Mr Bill Ellis, without whose help this work would have been impossible. I should also like to thank my father, Laurence Hartley, who first suggested the idea of a Brooklands book to me and who has helped me enormously with background material. Others who should be mentioned include: Harry Louis, Editor of *The Motor Cycle*, and his staff; and Bill Banks, Head of the Photographic Department of IPC, and his assistant Mrs Mary Smith; all of whom have been so helpful during my research for this book.

Finally, but by no means least, I should mention my wife, Josephine, whose encouragement and help with the editing of the manuscript have proved invaluable.

My hope is that this book will go some way towards providing a picture of the problems and difficulties with which the early pioneer racing men had to contend, and which they so magnificently overcame.

Cuxton, Kent,   PETER HARTLEY
December, 1972.

I

THE ORIGINS OF BROOKLANDS TRACK

IN England at the turn of the century, the motor vehicle was frowned upon. The Motor Car Act of 1903 imposed a speed limit of 20 mph on road-going vehicles in the United Kingdom. Although a great improvement on the Motor Car Act of 1896, which restricted speeds to under 12 mph, it proved a severe handicap to pioneer vehicle designers wishing to prove their brainchildren.

In contrast, on the continent, the motor vehicle was received with much enthusiasm. It was in 1896, in fact, that the *Automobile Club de France* was founded with the avowed intention of promoting international events and motor racing. To appreciate the situation, it must be realised that Britain at that time was essentially a horse-transport-dominated society—the internal combustion engine being regarded as a somewhat dirty, if not actually dangerous, toy, not to be taken too seriously.

By 1905 the continental countries were making enormous advances in developing cars and motor cycles, not the least resulting from the lessons gained from racing. France had the advantage of long straight roads, a heritage from Napoleon's day; Italy had excellent test facilities in the form of hill climbs, in her northern provinces; and in Germany the military were taking more than an unbiased interest in car and motor cycle developments and were themselves organising races.

In Britain, sporting activities in the motoring world were mainly restricted to long-distance road trials and to short-distance speed events on private property—such as sprints and hill climbs. In this respect motor cycles had an advantage over the cars, in that they were able to compete in races on the several small cycle tracks around the country, usually a third-of-a-mile to the lap. True car racing, however, was only possible for those rich enough to take part in continental events, and money and engineering acumen were not necessarily synonymous. If the British vehicle designers were to have any hope of competing successfully in world markets against continental firms, a British high-speed test track was a necessity.

All of this was clearly seen by a certain Mr H. J. Locke-King, wealthy hotelier and owner of the large Brooklands estate near Weybridge, in Surrey. By 1906 he had fully resolved to do something positive about the situation. The owner of a large Itala car and a keen motorist, Locke-King had made extensive tours of the continent and was well able to appreciate the advantages of long straight roads for high-speed testing.

Building of the track

In September 1906, a meeting was arranged with some of the leading motorists of the day, including Charles Jarrott and S. F. Edge, to ascertain their views on a new project. At this meeting Mr Locke-King's associate, Mr E. de Rodakowski, outlined a proposal by Locke-King to convert his vast Brooklands estate into a banked motor circuit for sustained high-speed testing and racing.

Agreement on the details was eventually reached and Colonel Holden RA, designer and builder of the Holden motor cycle, drew up plans for the scheme. Under the direction of a Mr Donaldson, a skilled railway engineer, the $2\frac{3}{4}$-mile track began to take shape towards the end of the year. By April 1907 the vast concrete circuit was completed, at a cost to Mr Locke-King of more than £150,000. A revolution had taken place in that quiet Edwardian countryside. Soon the rural calm was to be shattered by the open motor exhausts of S. F. Edge whilst averaging more than 60 mph for 24 hours, in accordance with a promise made at the earlier meeting. This was to have repercussions throughout the track's history.

In plan the circuit was almost oval, the longer axis running approximately north-east to south-west. The longer banked southern curve (the *Byfleet Banking*) was struck at a mean radius of 1550 ft and had a mean super elevation of 17 ft. Moving round the course in an anti-clockwise direction, this banking fell away before the track crossed the River Wey at the southern (Cobham) side of the circuit. There was then a reverse curve around the already-existing branch works of the Fabbrici Automobili Itala, replaced in 1915 by the aeroplane sheds of Vickers Ltd—a nasty hazard for racers to negotiate in the years that followed. This curve then linked with the start of the track's northern curve (the BARC *Members' Banking*) which was more acute than the Byfleet Banking—being struck at a mean radius of only 1000 ft. Its negotiation was assisted, however, by the steeper inclination which had a mean super elevation of 32 ft.

The two curves were linked on the western side of the track by the *Railway Straight*, which as the name suggests, ran roughly parallel to the main railway line from London to Woking.

Finally there was the *Finishing Straight*, which ran as a chord to the eastern end of the Members' Banking, in a rough north-south direction. At its southern end, the straight diverged from the main or *Outer Circuit* at a point just opposite the Itala car works. Known as the *Fork*, the area between the start of the Finishing Straight and the start of the Members' Banking, became a spectator vantage point, as did the *Members' Hill*—the island of high ground cut off by the Finishing Straight and the Members' Banking. The Members' Hill was linked to the outside of the track, from its highest point, by way of the *Members' Bridge*.

The Finishing Straight ran flat for 991 yd from the Fork to the *Long Finishing Line* where, with the competitors' paddock, clubhouse and the administrative buildings on its western flank, it acquired a gradient of 1-in-12. This was intended to slow the faster cars and motor cycles, but it gradually became apparent that the few hundred yards remaining were insufficient for this purpose, and as time went by more and more races were both started and terminated at the Fork. In the early days described in this book competitors entered the Finishing Straight on their final race lap and after crossing the Long Finishing Line, turned left on to the Outer Circuit for a short distance and then left again into a slip road leading to the paddock. Anti-clockwise travel round the circuit was rigidly enforced, except for the occasional short-distance record attempts, where advantage was taken of the prevailing south-westerly winds blowing up the Railway Straight.

The accuracy of the initial Outer Circuit lap measurements was confirmed in 1909, by none other than the Director General of Ordnance Surveys: it was 2.767 miles on the 50-ft median line.

Entrance to the track was via a tunnel under the Members'

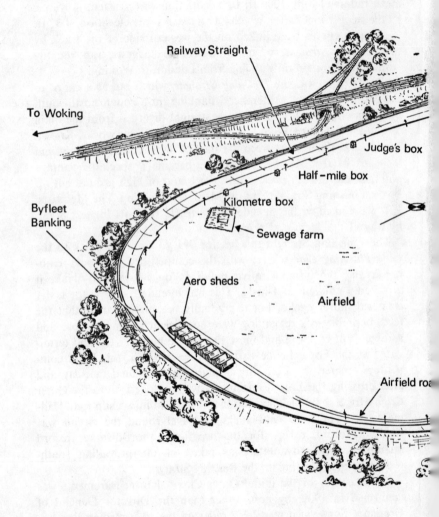

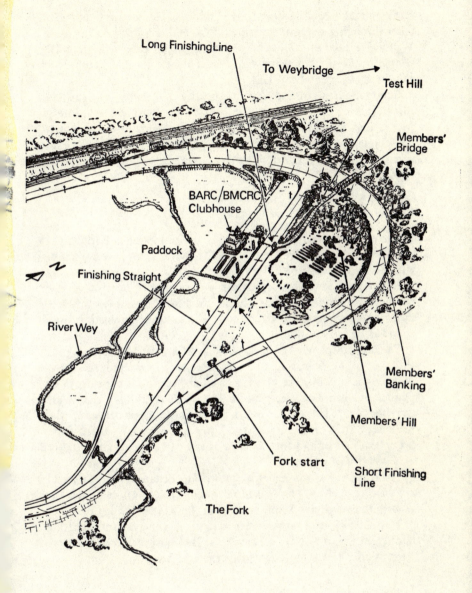

Banking and a road leading to the paddock. Pedestrians could also enter through a series of turnstiles at the end of a private road near Weybridge railway station. Good seating was provided for 5000 people, while tiers of seats were available for some 30,000 others—mostly on the Members' Hill.

Beside the first entrance road were some 28 garages, and shelters for 75 cars or motor cycles were provided in the paddock. Safety precautions included a double line of railings spaced 15 ft apart. Telephone boxes were located at 300-yd intervals around the track in case of accident, and there were several pull-in bays in case of breakdown.

Electrical timing

A most important innovation was the adoption of electrical timing from the outset. Designed by Colonel Holden in conjunction with Mr Elphinstone of Elliott Bros, the timing gear used inflatable pneumatic rubber strips separating a duplicated system of copper contacts. Each time a vehicle wheel passed over these strips an electrical circuit was completed and the recording mechanism was actuated.

The equipment worked as follows: a Morse feeder led tape past three recording pens, and three ink-line traces were produced; the middle trace, which received two-second interval blips from a pendulum-controlled electrical timer, acted as a time base; the top trace recorded a blip each time a vehicle wheel traversed the pneumatic strip on the track; the lower one merely operated from a duplicate set of contacts, in case of failure of the first set. Power was supplied by dry batteries.

From these records and the known lap distances, speeds could be measured. A similar electrical circuit had been laid out for recording flying-start $\frac{1}{2}$-mile speeds on the Railway Straight.

The chronograph proved very reliable in practice and accurate enough in the early days of the track. But as speeds rose after the First World War a more advanced system was installed.

The track is opened

Racing at the new track was to be administered by the *Brooklands*

Automobile Racing Club or *BARC*, with Mr E. de Rodakowski as the Clerk of the Course.

The official opening took place on Monday, June 17th, 1907 and fourteen days later S. F. Edge had completed his memorable record by averaging 65.905 mph. The first official car race meeting took place on July 6th, and by the end of the year motor car racing was well established at the track.

Meanwhile, racing motorcyclists were watching the situation with extreme interest and were clamouring for a chance to try their machines at the new track.

Motor cycle racing before Brooklands

British motor cycles of 1907 were a primitive bunch compared with modern machines. Most makes had belt drive, no clutch, and were single-geared. Lacking modern materials, they were distinctly restricted in design. Overhead valve machines were a comparative rarity, the vast majority having mechanically operated side exhaust valves with inlet valves either overhead and atmospherically operated (a.i.v.) or side mechanically operated (s.v.) Mechanical breakdowns were frequent.

Because of their early start in racing, French engines tended to be the best designed and the most powerful. But J. A. Prestwich & Company with a.i.v. and o.h.v., and the Triumph concern with s.v. engines, were beginning to make something of a dent in the motor cycle market in England.

It was in 1895 that the French first started to organise their series of inter-city marathon races for cars, motor tricycles and motor cycles. Gradually one man and one make in particular—the Monsieur Bucquet and his Werner—established themselves as firm favourites in racing. Bucquet won the Paris-Vienna race of 1902 and was the favourite for the Paris-Madrid event of the following year. This race unfortunately ended as a fiasco, with many riders colliding with each other *en route* and spectators being killed by the racing cars. Such races were rapidly becoming too dangerous to run so in 1904, it was decided to organise in France, a new type of motor cycle race over a closed circuit—for the International Motor Cycle Cup. In this event, teams of riders from the different competing countries rode under their national colours: the French in blue, the Germans in white, the British in green, and so on. The regulations stipulated a maximum weight limit of 50 kg (110 lb). Much sharp practice such as the scattering of tin tacks on the course, ensued. Another fiasco resulted and the race results were annulled.

The Second International Cup Race, held in 1905, was better organised and can be considered the first true international road race in the sense that we recognise racing today. The event was won by C. V. Wondrick (Laurin et Klement) of Austria, at an average speed of 54.5 mph for the 270-km race.

These races were intensely disliked by British riders and entrants alike, who found the race rules being used against them in less than an impartial manner. They also felt that they were developing a type of machine quite unlike that which could be used on the road. With big engines and the 110 lb weight limit, tyres were necessarily undershod and engineering progress was being restricted. Freakish machines were tending to evolve.

In 1906 the Third—and what proved to be the final—International Cup Race took place. This was also held in Austria. The first and second men past the winning post were Ed Nikodem and Louis Ortuba on Puchs, with Harry Collier (Matchless-JAP) third for Britain. Again squabbles broke out.

A protest was made against the Austrian riders, that they had received unfair assistance with spare parts during the race. This protest was in fact never formally heard, as the race meeting broke up in disorder and the international series was finally abandoned.

Because of their general disgust at these events and at what seemed to them like malpractices on the part of the continentals, the Collier brothers (Harry and Charlie) returned to England and, together with their father H. H. Collier (founder of the Matchless concern) and the Auto Cycle Club (later the Auto Cycle Union), they approached the Manx Government, with a view to organising a race for 1907 in the Isle of Man. The Manx Government not only readily agreed to the suggestion, but also offered to subsidise the event: the first Isle of Man TT Race, in June 1907.

To that date the major course in the British Isles was the third-of-a-mile-to-the-lap cycle track at Canning Town, London, where Charlie Collier held the lap record at over 60 mph. The motor cycle speed record at that time was that established by the Frenchman Henri Cissac on the Blackpool front, on July 27th, 1905. Riding his

16 hp Peugeot* he averaged 87.32 mph for the one-way flying-start kilometre. This monstrous machine weighed a little over 110 lb and, ridden at the Parc des Princes circuit near Paris the same year, by J. Giuppone, it had set up a new unlimited hour record at an average speed of 63.61 mph.

Clearly if British riders, with only basically standard machines at their disposal, were to compete with such performances, the Isle of Man circuit would not be enough. It was too far away for regular testing and the roads would only be closed once a year during race week. Hence the enormous interest evoked by Mr Locke-King's new Surrey track. Such was the situation at the start of 1908.

---

* In the early days of motor cycle engine design, swept cylinder volume was not considered so important a criterion of performance as the calculated theoretical horsepower development. Thus an arbitrary series of categories was evolved, which roughly corresponded to engine capacity as follows: $1\frac{1}{2}$ hp=250 cc, $2\frac{3}{4}$ hp=350 cc, $3\frac{1}{2}$ hp=500 cc, 5-6 hp=750 cc, 7-9 hp=1000 cc, and 12-20 hp=2500 cc.

It became apparent in the years that followed that the rated horsepower bore no relation whatsoever to the actual power developed by an engine. So it was that the more rational and helpful system of classification by cubic capacity came about.

2
1908—THE ADVENTURE STARTS

It is difficult to prove who was the first motorcyclist to travel round the new Brooklands motor course. Some would confer this honour on one of a group of naval officers who, it was rumoured, came down to the track late in 1907 and circulated it until their engines became red hot. Others would have it that the eleven-year-old Dougal Marchant, who became famous at Brooklands in the twenties as a successful rider/tuner, went round the course on his mother's tricycle early in 1907, before it was officially opened even to cars. At all events, the first authenticated motor cycle race took place the following year.

It was on Tuesday, February 25th, 1908, that two undergraduates from Magdalen College, Oxford—W. Gordon McMinnies and his friend Oscar L. Bickford—brought their machines down by rail from Oxford and arrived at the track for a private match race.

After some initial tuning, with McMinnies on his $3\frac{1}{2}$ hp TT Triumph—nicknamed "Puffing Billy"—and Bickford on his 5 hp Light TT Vindec-Special, they lined up for the start at the Members' entrance to the track at 12.30 p.m. It was a cold day and the two warmly-clad riders were eager to start.

The race was over one lap from a standing start and McMinnies won by 150 yd at an unofficially timed average speed of 53.55 mph on the 50-ft line. During the race he had his first experience of a speed wobble, due to the "flip-flop" fork action of his Triumph causing alterations in fork rake. After the race he was electrically timed to cover the flying start $\frac{1}{2}$-mile at a mean speed of 58.92 mph, with a fastest one-way speed of 59.80 mph, for which he was awarded the first BARC certificate to be presented to a motorcyclist—No. 37.

Both machines were single-geared at $3\frac{1}{4}$-to-1, with belt-drive transmission and magneto ignition. The Triumph had a 476 cc

(84 x 86 mm) s.v. engine, whereas Bickford's machine was fitted with a 670 cc V-twin Peugeot engine with atmospherically operated inlet valves (a.i.v.).

The race between McMinnies and Bickford so interested Mr E. de Rodakowski, the BARC secretary, that he decided to invite some prominent racing motorcyclists of the day down to the track, to investigate the possibility of holding motor cycle races on a regular basis at Brooklands. It was then made known that the first official motor cycle race (a scratch event) would take place at the BARC's Easter Monday Race Meeting.

The first official race at the track

Twenty-one riders appeared on the starting line on Easter Monday, April 20th, 1908. They included Will Cook on his a.i.v. 7-9 hp NLG-Peugeot, who was reported to have covered more than 30 miles at over 68 mph, during practice the preceding Tuesday. Also present were the two Collier brothers—Charlie on the 6 hp International Cup Race Matchless and Harry on his $3\frac{1}{2}$ hp 1907 TT machine of the same make. Other marques represented were: Leader-Peugeot, Triumph, Vindec-Special, NSU, Rex, DOT-Peugeot, Chater-Lea, Minerva, Laurin et Klement, and a solitary four-cylinder shaft-driven FN. All the other machines were belt-driven.

It was a fine day and Will Cook raced away from the field to an easy win by over five-eighths-of-a-mile, without once being challenged. But the strong wind and his relatively high gear of $2\frac{5}{8}$-to-1 kept his average speed down to 5 mph below his practice performance. Gordon McMinnies was fourth on his Triumph and Billy Wells (670 Vindec-Special) fifth. Cook was awarded 20 sovereigns for his win—quite a fortune in those days. The full result was:

MOTOR CYCLE SCRATCH RACE (over 2 laps/$5\frac{1}{4}$ miles) for machines not exceeding 80×98 mm per cylinder. Long start and finish.

1. W. Cook (984 NLG-Peugeot)   63 mph
2. E. Kickham (984 Leader-Peugeot)
3. C. R. Collier (861 Matchless-JAP)

The clear verdict on the race, by both riders and spectators, was that successful as it was, there was a distinct need for some form of handicapping in future events of the kind, if motor cycle racing was ever to become popular at Brooklands.

The first motor cycle handicap

Encouraged by the large entry for their first Brooklands motor cycle race, the BARC decided to hold another similar event as part of their May 9th race meeting, but this time it was to be a handicap as had been suggested. The cylinder size limit was raised to 85 × 95 mm for this Handicap Plate of 25 sovereigns. It was to be a two-lap affair (5.48 miles) starting and finishing at the Long Finishing Line, as in the previous motor cycle race. Riders passed the Fork once and then re-entered the straight to finish on their last laps. Handicap times were based on the Easter Monday scratch event.

Thirty-one machines lined up and nearly all made a good start. The limit man was A. C. Wright (1¾ hp KD), while at scratch were Will Cook (7 hp NLG-Peugeot) and J. Merfait (7 hp Laurin et Klement) whose machine had competed so successfully in the 1905 International Cup Race.

The result was a win for a relatively unknown rider, H. Shanks (2¾ hp Chater-Lea). The first three were as follows:

MOTOR CYCLE HANDICAP PLATE (over 2 laps/5.48 miles) for engines up to 85 × 95 mm per cylinder. Long start and finish.

	H'cap start	
1. H. Shanks (2¾ hp Chater-Lea)	2 min 45 sec	42.3 mph
2. H. G. Partridge (6 hp NSU)	1 min 45 sec	
3. W. H. Bashall (3½ hp Triumph)	1 min 40 sec	

S. F. Edge's twenty-four hour record attempt in 1907 had upset local residents and later they had sued Mr Locke-King in the High Court on the grounds of the "noise nuisance" at the track. He lost the case and was ordered to pay £7000 in costs, as well as build a new entrance road to appease the plaintiffs. Albeit without proof, motor cycles were made the scapegoats and the BARC decided to discontinue motor cycle racing and not allow any motor cycles on the track until further notice. This move was considered very harsh, in view of the "open" exhausts then in use on racing cars and the extra "phons" they produced over and above anything then possible from a motor cycle engine.

Anyway, there the situation was, and it was not until the Autumn of 1908 that the Brooklands authorities were to relent and stop making the racing motorcyclists the "whipping boys". Nevertheless, the threat of injunction on noise grounds was to bedevil the track scene many times in later years.

A return to the track

Much to the motorcycling fraternity's relief, the bar on two-wheeler racing was lifted in September 1908, when the BARC announced that a handicap race for motor cyclists would be included in their Brooklands race meeting scheduled for Saturday, October 3rd.

Regulations and capacity limits were as for the May event, except that the start was at the Fork and out of view of the spectators, who were confined to the paddock by the clubhouse at the northern end of the Finishing Straight. This fact was bemoaned by *The Motor Cycle* magazine's reporter at the track, at the time.

There were twenty-eight starters and the race proved a win for Gordon Gibson (3½ hp s.v. Triumph) from the 2-min 20-sec mark, long-start men filling the other places as well—a fact causing much criticism of the BARC handicapping. The official result was:

MOTOR CYCLE HANDICAP RACE (over 2 laps/5½ miles) for up to 85 × 95 mm per cylinder. Fork stark and Long finish.

		H'cap start	
1.	G. Gibson (3½ hp Triumph)	2 min 20 sec	53 mph
2.	R. O. Clark (5 hp FN)	2 min 20 sec	
3.	R. J. Bell (2¾ hp NSU)	2 min 15 sec	

World's hour record broken

During the following Thursday afternoon, October 8th, Charlie Collier, riding Bert (H. V.) Colver's 1908 TT 7-10 hp Matchless-JAP, set about an attempt on the world's one-hour record. The engine was an 85 × 85 mm (964 cc) o.h.v. parallel-valved JAP V-twin. Ignition was by CAV coil and accumulators, while Pratts Motor Spirit fed the two cylinders via a single Longuemare carburetter. No throttle was fitted, control being by air lever and valve lifter.

The incredibly spindly wheels were shod with Dunlop beaded-edge tyres, 26 × 2½ in on the back and 26 × 2¼ in on the front: sizes that today would be regarded with grave suspicion even for a 125 cc racer! Drive was by Shamrock-Gloria belt on a single fixed-gear of 2⅔-to-1.

Charlie made a push start at 2.49 pm using the valve lifter, the engine firing almost as soon as the exhaust valves were dropped. He soon got into his stride with a standing lap at 63.24 mph, and completed the hour without incident, raising the distance covered to 70 miles 105 yd. His fastest lap was his fourth at 72.89 mph.

All these speeds were calculated on a line 50 ft from the inside of the track. It was noted, however, that Charlie Collier had stayed within 11 ft of this perimeter for most of his hour's run. This led to the decision that this and all subsequent motor cycle events and records should be timed on the 10-ft line and not the 50-ft line as used for car records. After re-calculation, this gave Charlie and his Matchless a total official mileage of 68 miles 1380 yd for the hour, which, although lower than as originally calculated, substantially beat J. Giuppone's 1905 record on the Peugeot.

The record-breaking Matchless, none the worse for its remarkable achievement, was put on display as the centrepiece of the Matchless Motors stand at the Stanley Motor Cycle Show the following month.

Undergraduates get the speed bug

The 1908 season, the first for motor cycles at Brooklands, was rounded off by a small private race meeting held on Saturday, November 7th, by and for members of the Cambridge University MCC. It was an informal affair, five races being run. Among the winners were E. D. Dickson (5 hp Vindec-Special) and E. H. Lees (5 hp Peugeot), who became well-known in small club events at Brooklands before the First World War.

3
1909—THE BIRTH OF BEMSEE

AT the beginning of the year the colourful, but erratic, Mr E. de Rodakowski was succeeded as the Clerk of the Course at Brooklands, by Major F. Lindsay Lloyd.

His first encounter with racing motorcyclists in his new capacity, was when Harry Collier applied in January to be allowed to set up a 24-hour record. Unfortunately Major Lloyd was obliged to report that the BARC committee could not countenance such a long period of flat-out running on the track, in view of the recent court case lost by Mr Locke-King.

Oxfordians go racing

The first race meeting of 1909 was a private affair for Oxford undergraduates, held on Monday, February 22nd. The majority of the machines were standard s.v. Triumphs. There was also a s.v. TT Triumph and a solitary 7 hp Vindec-Special.

Flying-lap and ½-mile distances were timed. During these time trials the fastest speed attained was that of M. K. Mackenzie (3½ hp TT Triumph) who achieved 54 mph over the flying-start ½-mile.

The Test Hill is inaugurated

Major Lloyd's first important project for enlivening Brooklands was the construction of the Test Hill. This was 352 ft 3 in long and built up the side of the Members' Hill from just opposite the paddock at the top of the Finishing Straight. It had three electrically-timed sections: an initial 105 ft 10 in of 1-in-8, then 91 ft 9¼ in of 1-in-5, and finally 154 ft 7¾ in of 1-in-4 at the top. The average gradient was 1-in-5.027.

The first motorcyclist to attempt the climb on the day of the hill's formal opening, Thursday, March 25th, 1909, was George Reynolds (6 hp single-geared Matchless-JAP). With a 30-yd run-in and a leap into the saddle, he took 6.173 sec averaging 38.9 mph.

Bemsee is born

It was George Reynolds who was the prime mover in the formation of the first national club in the world to be devoted solely to the interests of racing motorcyclists.

A meeting was held at the BARC headquarters in London at Carlton House, where by general assent the new club—the *British Motor Cycle Racing Club* or *BMCRC*—was formed. With Reynolds as secretary and an elected committee consisting of Major Lloyd, Messrs. H. H. Collier senior, Harry (W. H.) Bashall, O. L. Summers, the American—Billy (W. H.) Wells, W. Pratt, R. M. Brice, R. O. Clark, A. G. Forster (of NLG Motors) and A. V. Ebblewhite, a programme was drawn up for a season's racing at Brooklands.

A new Test Hill record

On March 29th, the Monday following the Test Hill's formal opening, Freddie (F. W.) Barnes—whose Zenith Motor Works lay close to the track—wheeled out one of his production $3\frac{1}{2}$ hp Zenette-JAPs and set up the first standing-start record for the climb from the start of the initial gradient.

Fitted with Barnes' patented "Gradua" variable gear the machine took 18.633 sec averaging 12.899 mph.

The Zenette had a specially sprung sub-frame for rider comfort. Its Gradua gear was later used on the Zenith-Gradua which superseded it and which gained the reputation of near-invincibility in hill-climbs. Hence the later adoption of the "barred gate" motif for Zenith-Gradua petrol tanks, when the machines were banned from certain hill climb events, as being unfair competition for single-geared motor cycles.

The Gradua gear was operated by a "coffee mill" type of hand wheel mounted on the side of the tank. The belt drive was always direct and a range of gear ratios from $3\frac{1}{2}$-to-1 down to 9-to-1 was obtainable. A system of rods and levers moved the rear wheel backwards or forwards in slotted lugs and simultaneously expanded or contracted the engine pulley. One of its flanges was keyed to the engine shaft and the other was free to slide, actuated by a quick thread.

Although the system worked well enough in practice, it did give undesirable changes in wheelbase and increased belt wear due to belt misalignment. These were minor points, however, at 1909 racing speeds.

In Spring a young man's fancy . . .

Spring time had arrived and the BARC had arranged to include two motor cycle races on each of the two days of its Easter motor race meeting at Brooklands.

On the Saturday, April 10th, forty-one starters assembled for the first motor cycle race—The Spring Handicap (for machines up to 1000 cc)—over some 5½ miles. Among the starters was Frank (F. A.) McNab, designer and builder of the Trump-JAP motor cycle, riding one of his 3½ hp s.v.-engined machines. Harold Bowen and J. Stewart Geddes were on similar models. Bowen's machine used Hellesen-Hunt/Nilmelior coil ignition and a single-geared fixed belt drive at 3-to-1.

Eddie Kickham rode one of the new Bristol-built 2¾ hp Douglas machines with horizontally-opposed fore-and-aft disposed s.v. twin engines. R. O. Clark rode a four-cylinder FN and J. T. ("Bizzy") Bashall was 3½-hp-Triumph mounted. Also present was the official Matchless-JAP team of Charlie and Harry Collier, and Bert Colver who was riding a small 2¾ hp model. Harry Martin, having recently severed his connection with the Matchless Company, rode a JAP-engined special of his own manufacture.

Amongst the riders of 3½ hp TT Rexs were: Frank Applebee, Oliver Godfrey (a cousin of "H. R." of Frazer-Nash car fame), W. A. Jacobs and J. P. Le Grand, two riders who were to become known later as the "inseparables", and Walter O. Bentley—a young newcomer to Brooklands who was to achieve fame with his Bentley cars during the thirties.

Moreover, the first Norton was to make its first appearance at the track in the hands of F. A. Hardy. It was an 83 × 90 mm single-cylinder s.v. model, complete with pedalling gear.

The race itself proved an easy win for Harold Bowen (3½ hp Trump-JAP) with J. F. Crundall (on G. A. Phillips's 3½ hp Humber) second. Result:

SPRING MOTOR CYCLE HANDICAP (up to 1000 cc) over 5½ miles with a Long start and finish.

		H'cap start	
1.	H. H. Bowen (3½ hp Trump-JAP)	1 min 20 sec	55½ mph
2.	J. F. Crundall (3½ hp Humber)	1 min 25 sec	
3.	J. C. Smyth (3½ hp Rex)	1 min 30 sec	

The second motor cycle race of the afternoon—the Easter Motor Cycle Plate—was a two-lap scratch race for single-cylinder machines up to 500 cc.

Twenty-one starters came to the line and the event was won in convincing style by Harry Bashall (3½ hp Triumph). Close behind in second place was the Guildford rider Archie (A. G.) Fenn (3½ hp Triumph), while the winner of the first event had to be content with third position. Harry Bashall's brother "Bizzy" was fourth, W. Gordon McMinnies (3½ hp Triumph) fifth and J. F. Crundall (3½ hp Humber) sixth. The official result was:

EASTER MOTOR CYCLE PLATE (up to 500 cc), a scratch race over 5½ miles with a Long start and finish.

1. W. H. Bashall (3½ hp Triumph) 58¼ mph
2. A. G. Fenn (3½ hp Triumph)
3. H. H. Bowen (3½ hp Trump-JAP)

The winner was the same Harry Bashall who had finished second on a BAT-JAP in the Multi-Cylinder Class of the 1908 Isle of Man TT Race, when he set up the fastest lap at 42.25 mph.

The bright sunny weather of the Saturday gave way to a cold and showery Monday. Despite this, spectators turned out in force and only six out of forty-five entries failed to start in the first motor cycle race of the day—The Surrey Handicap for up to 1000 cc machines, over two laps. A strong wind blew directly up the Railway Straight towards the Members' Stand, to the disadvantage of the higher-geared machines.

At the start of the race, Will Cook (7 hp NLG-Peugeot), on the 10-sec mark, made a "scarifying" run up the Members' Banking. just after the bend leading from the Finishing Straight. He looked at first as though he would go over the top of the track into the woods beyond, but he quickly recovered control and rejoined the race. Both Bert Colver (8 hp Matchless-JAP) and J. Slaughter (3½ hp Triumph) vetoed their chances of places by bad getaways. A. Baker White (4¼ hp JAP special) was thrown rather badly, but escaped with minor injuries.

The result was a fine win for Archie Fenn on his Triumph:

SURREY MOTOR CYCLE HANDICAP PLATE (up to 1000 cc) over 2 laps/5½ miles. Long start and finish.

H'cap start
1. A. G. Fenn (3½ hp Triumph)   1 min 10 sec speed unknown
2. H. H. Bowen (3½ hp Trump-JAP) 1 min 20 sec
3. F. W. Barnes (3½ hp Zenette) 1 min 45 sec

Crundall, McNab and scratch man Charlie Collier were next to finish in that order.

An hour-and-a-half later, after some car events, came the final motor cycle race of the weekend—the Byfleet Plate. This was a scratch event, over 2 laps or 5½ miles, for machines up to 1000 cc. There were only twelve starters for this race, which provided an easy win by almost a kilometre for Charlie Collier. His brother Harry, beat Harry Bashall for second place by only a few yards, after an exciting tussle up the Finishing Straight. Result:

BYFLEET MOTOR CYCLE PLATE (up to 1000 cc).
A scratch race over 2 laps/5½ miles with a long start and finish.

1. C. R. Collier (8 hp Matchless-JAP)   62¾ mph
2. H. A. Collier (8 hp Matchless-JAP)
3. W. H. Bashall (8 hp BAT-JAP)

All three placemen were using 85 × 85 mm (964 cc) o.h.v. JAP engines to power their machines.

The very first BMCRC race meeting

The morning of Thursday, April 22nd, 1909, was brilliantly sunny despite a south-westerly gale and a falling glass, as competitors and spectators arrived at Brooklands for the first-ever race meeting organised by the newly-formed British Motor Cycle Racing Club.

Riders entered included: V. Olsson (5 hp Vindec-Special); W.

Smith and Gordon Fletcher on little Swiss-made 2 hp Moto Rêves; Harry Bashall, A. W. Whittet, H. D. Teague and J. Slaughter—who had replaced the horizontal fork springs on their $3\frac{1}{2}$ hp Triumphs with felt pads in an attempt to obviate speed wobble; R. T. Exshaw and Freddie Barnes on their new $3\frac{1}{2}$ hp Zenith-Graduas; Will Cook (7 hp NLG-Peugeot); and Martin Geiger, on a special racing 7 hp NSU V-twin with overhead inlet and side exhaust valves (o.i.v.). Harry Martin, Harry Collier and T. A. Carter were mounted on 7 hp Matchless-JAPs, and Tommy Loughborough was on a solitary four-cylinder $3\frac{1}{2}$ hp FN.

Some fifty to sixty spectators witnessed the first race, a scratch event over 2 laps, organised to assess handicaps. All but Teague and Whittet appeared on the line and all got their engines to fire except for Harry Bashall, who was forced to retire. Martin Geiger made a fine start and kept his lead to the end, finishing half-a-mile ahead of Will Cook. Fletcher finished with a broken sparking plug; while Loughborough, after much misfiring, seized his engine. Result:

SCRATCH RACE OVER TWO LAPS (up to 1000 cc) with Long start and finish.

1. M. Geiger (7 hp NSU)   64.11 mph
2. W. E. Cook (7 hp NLG-Peugeot)
3. H. H. Bowen ($3\frac{1}{2}$ hp Trump-JAP)

While the handicap start times were being calculated, riders moved over to the base of the Test Hill for the Preliminary Hill Test. In this, individual competitors' times were taken for runs up the hill starting some 70 yd on the level from its base. This provided the necessary information for starts to be allotted in the Hill-Climb Handicap event.

There were ten runners in the two-lap handicap race, with Martin Geiger (7 hp NSU) scratch and Gordon Fletcher (2 hp Moto Rêve) as the limit man. At the start the wind still blew hard, and it began to rain. This proved Geiger's undoing, his wide flat driving belt being allergic to moisture. All got away well, however, except Will Cook who failed to start at all.

The handicap times were so well calculated that all finished within seconds of each other, Fletcher only being caught up by the back-markers just before the finish. Geiger's slipping belt handed the

First man reported to have won a motor cycle race at Brooklands: W. Gordon McMinnies, seen here on his 476 cc racing Triumph. In 1909 he became editor of the re-launched *Motor Cycling* journal.

Charlie Collier (964 Matchless-JAP) congratulated by his father after covering 68 miles 1380 yd in the hour, at Brooklands on Thursday, October 8th, 1908. This was a new world's record for motor cycles.

Harry Bashall (8 hp BAT-JAP), *left*, and Frank McNab (3½ hp Trump-JAP), *right:* winners of the first-ever 1000 cc and 500 cc hour races at the track, Wednesday, May 19th, 1909.

Will Cook (16-20 hp NLG-JAP). After repeated attempts in 1909 and 1910 on Frenchman Henri Cissac's world records, he finally gave up and disposed of his unwieldy machine.

race to Harry Collier, who won after a hard fight, by two or three lengths from Olsson:

HANDICAP RACE OVER TWO LAPS (up to 1000 cc) with a Long start and finish.

H'cap start
1. H. A. Collier (7 hp Matchless-JAP) 1 min 46 sec   48.6 mph
2. V. Olsson (5 hp Vindec-Special)   2 min 47 sec
3. F. A. McNab (3½ hp Trump-JAP)   1 min 42 sec

J. Slaughter (3½ hp Triumph), who broke an exhaust valve, failed to finish.

Finally came the Hill Climb Handicap, with riders going up the Test Hill in pairs. Olsson and Bowen had a close struggle, the latter's 3½ hp Trump-JAP winning the heat by a wheel. Harry Collier and Freddie Barnes (3½ hp Zenith-Gradua) both made fine climbs, with Barnes gaining by virtue of his variable gear, but too late to beat Harry.

The result was a win for Harry Collier, who averaged 23 mph. As it had now begun to rain quite heavily, the last event—a scratch race—was postponed to the next Bemsee race meeting.

Oxford versus Cambridge

The first of many "Intervarsity" motor cycle race meetings took place on Friday, April 30th, 1909. Oxford was represented by A. H. Wilkie, A. K. Mackenzie, R. Legh and Aitken (all on 3½ hp Triumphs) and Gordon McMinnies (3½ hp Zenith-Gradua-JAP). All wore white numbers on a dark-blue background. Their Cambridge opponents, with white numbers on a light-blue background, were: C. L. Mere, H. E. Ashtead, E. H. Lees (on 3½ hp Triumphs); C. E. Torrey (2¾ hp JAP special) and J. Ashworth (3½ hp Humber).

There were three Intervarsity team races; a flying-start ½-mile speed test, and a 2-mile and a 5-mile scratch race. These resulted in an aggregate win for Oxford on points, by 17-to-13.

The ½-mile speed test was won by Mackenzie at 54¾ mph. McMinnies won the 2-mile scratch race, and, at 53 mph he also won the 5-mile scratch. After the Intervarsity events, three final events were held for Cambridge MCC members only. The first, a 2-lap handicap, was split into classes and provided wins for J. H. Whitlark (3hp

Triumph) in Class B (500 cc), E. D. Dickson (5 hp Vindec-Special) in Class C (500-750 cc) and F. P. Dickson (7 hp Vindec-Special) in Class D (up to 1000 cc).

Then followed a flying-start ½-mile speed test for Cambridge members. E. H. Lees (3½ hp TT Triumph) won Class B (500 cc) at 55.7 mph and Class D (up to 1000 cc) at 58.06 mph. Class C (500-750 cc) was won by E. D. Dickson (5 hp Vindec-Special) at 52.3 mph. The last event was a 7½-mile scratch race in two classes—again for Cambridge members only. Class I (up to 500 cc) was won by C. L. Mere (3½ hp Triumph) at 53.75 mph while Class II (over 500 cc) provided a win for V. F. M. Oliver (7 hp Vindec-Special) at 51.75 mph.

Measuring the lap distance

During May 1909, the Director General of Ordnance Surveys confirmed earlier measurements of the Brooklands lap distances. Using a No. 31 Invar tape, at a steady tension of 20 lb, he obtained a value of 2.7668774 miles measured on a line 50 ft from the inside perimeter of the track. On the 10-ft. line used for motor cycle races and records at that time, the lap came to 2.717676 miles. He apologised for being unable to give the actual error, as he only took one measurement, but he guaranteed this to within ±0.002%! The RAC also formally recognised the new world-record attempt distances laid out by the Director General over the ½ mile and mile, and kilometre. Previously only ½-mile and lap distances had been available for record attempts.

As it was difficult for members to attend Thursday racing at Brooklands, the BMCRC changed the weekday of its monthly race meetings to a Wednesday; a move that was appreciated.

The first one-hour race

An interesting innovation at the Second BMCRC Members' Meeting held on Wednesday, May 19th, was the first event—a one-hour race. It was split into two classes: Class A (up to 500 cc) and Class B (500-1000 cc); a silver cup was offered as first prize in each category. Furthermore, a club gold medal was offered to the rider who beat the existing hour record of 68 miles 1380 yd by the greatest margin. H. H. Collier senior, head of Matchless Motors, offered an additional 2-guinea award for the same achievement.

The hour race attracted a large entry and the sunny weather promised keen racing. The starters were as follows: *Class A*—J. H. Slaughter ($3\frac{1}{2}$ hp Triumph), H. Shanks ($3\frac{1}{2}$ hp MMC-Chater-Lea), W. Smith (2 hp Moto Rêve), E. C. W. FitzHerbert ($4\frac{1}{2}$ hp 4-cyl. FN), E. Gwynne ($3\frac{1}{2}$ hp Triumph) and Frank McNab ($3\frac{1}{2}$ hp Trump-JAP); in *Class B*—Harry Bashall and Harold Bowen (8 hp BAT-JAPs), F. C. Dee, G. G. Mead and V. Olsson (7 hp Vindec-Specials), and M. Krause (5 hp Vindec-Special). All the machines in Class B, other than the FN, were twin-cylinder models.

Both classes started together at 3.30 pm. By the end of lap one Harry Bashall led easily, covering it at $55\frac{1}{2}$ mph. Mead, McNab, and Slaughter followed in a bunch with FitzHerbert trailing in the rear. Harry steadily increased his lead but developed a misfire and on his eighth lap he was passed by Mead.

Krause stopped to screw up a loose exhaust pipe nut on his ninth lap; meanwhile Harry Bashall had cured his misfire and regained the lead on lap twelve, holding it to the end of the race. Slaughter, who led Class A at half distance, stopped to replace an exhaust valve and thereby allowed Frank McNab to win.

ONE-HOUR SCRATCH RACE

CLASS A (up to 500 cc)
1. F. A. McNab ($3\frac{1}{2}$ hp Trump-JAP)   48 miles 400 yd
2. J. H. Slaughter ($3\frac{1}{2}$ hp Triumph)
3. H. Shanks ($3\frac{1}{2}$ hp MMC-Chater-Lea)

CLASS B (up to 1000 cc)
1. W. H. Bashall (8 hp BAT-JAP)   55 miles 1576 yd
2. G. G. Mead (7 hp Vindec-Special)
3. F. C. Dee (7 hp Vindec-Special)

Although capacity class records were not officially recognised yet, Frank McNab's distance represented a new 500 cc hour record. It exceeded that set up by Bert Colver ($2\frac{3}{4}$ hp Matchless-JAP) at Canning Town track on June 4th, 1907, when he covered 47 miles 770 yd.

After an interval for tea in the clubhouse, came a 2-lap $5\frac{1}{2}$-mile handicap for machines up to 1000 cc. This event saw the first appearance at Brooklands, of the American-made Indian machines—a 5 hp model in the hands of Billy Wells and one of 2½ hp ridden by Guy Lee Evans, the ex-Rex rider.

Wells had difficulty getting away due to a flooding carburetter. Gordon Fletcher (2 hp Moto Rêve), one of the two limit men, was never overtaken and finished an easy winner.

The official result was:

UP TO 1000 cc HANDICAP (over 2 laps)
with a Long start and finish.

		H'cap start	
1.	G. L. Fletcher (2 hp Moto Rêve)	3 min 24 sec	39.4 mph
2.	G. Lee Evans (2½ hp Indian)	1 min 56 sec	
3.	H. H. Bowen (8 hp BAT-JAP)		

Billy Wells finished fourth.

The final event of the day was an up to 500 cc ½-mile rolling-start sprint. All the competitors were taken to a point some 300 yd along the Members' Banking from where the Finishing Straight joined the Outer Circuit, going west along the track. At a given signal they all aligned themselves with the Brooklands' official Sizaire-Naudin car, driven by Major Lloyd. Then as soon as they had been "dressed" into position, "Ebbie" Ebblewhite the starter—standing in the back of the car—blew his whistle and they were off. It was a good start, avoiding the undue handicapping of machines which did not fire immediately from cold. The result was a win for Slaughter, by about a length:

SCRATCH HALF-MILE ROLLING-START SPRINT
(up to 500 cc)

1.	J. H. Slaughter (3½ hp Triumph)	43.9 mph
2.	F. W. Barnes (3½ hp Zenith-Gradua-JAP)	
3.	F. A. McNab (3½ hp Trump-JAP)	

Great interest was aroused at this meeting by the overhead inlet valve (o.h.i.v.) chain-driven Indians, for which Billy Wells was the first UK concessionaire after relinquishing his ties with the Vindec-Special agency. He rode a 60° V-twin of 638 cc (70 × 83 mm bore and stroke) with detachable cylinder heads and valve pockets. Lee Evans' 319 cc machine had an engine that represented the rear cylinder of this twin, the crankcase opening for the front cylinder being blanked off. On both machines the inlet valves were operated by long adjustable pushrods. Two camshafts were employed—one for the inlet and the other for the exhaust—and the Splitdorf magneto was driven by enclosed gears. A novel idea was the imposition of a perforated spool between the top of the exhaust valve spring and its seating, to help reduce loss of spring temper by heat feed back from the cylinder. Lubrication was by splash from a cast-in sump fitted with a sight glass. The Hedström carburetter resembled, in principle, the early De Dion spray carburetters.

The chief departure from British practice lay in the use of metal linkages rather than control cables, in the use of a shock-absorber-cum-clutch fitted to the countershaft sprocket in conjunction with a final chain drive, and twist grip throttle control.

No suspension was used on either front or rear and the brakes, as with most other machines of the day, were of the largely ineffectual "stirrup" type.

The Whitsun weekend

Despite Bemsee taking over the organisation of most of the Brooklands motor cycle fixtures, the BARC continued to include motor cycle races in its meetings and had four in its two-day Whitsun weekend meeting.

Two such events were scheduled for Saturday, May 29th: these were the May Handicap (over 8 miles for under 1000 cc machines), and the Roadster Handicap (under similar conditions for touring models). For the first time, waist sashes in various identifying colours were to be worn by riders, in a similar fashion to horse racing on the turf.

Fine weather, little wind, and no dearth of entries, despite the running of the MCC's London to Edinburgh run that weekend, promised a good two-days' sport.

Twenty-seven starters arrived on the line for the May Handicap. Charlie Collier (8 hp Matchless-JAP) was on the scratch mark and J. Kennedy (2 hp Kennedy) was sent off first with a 4 min start. Harry Bashall (3½ hp Zenith-Gradua-JAP) and A. H. Wilkie (3½ hp Triumph), were both sent off after 2 min, and collided at the first corner into the Members' Banking whilst avoiding a large puddle there. They continued without damage, however, to finish third and second respectively. Gordon McMinnies (3½ hp Zenith-Gradua-JAP) retired with sparking plug trouble and H. G. Partridge (6 hp NSU) with a broken oil pipe. The result was a win for Will Cook on the big Peugeot-engined NLG, by half-a-mile:

MAY MOTOR CYCLE HANDICAP (up to 1000 cc) over 8½ miles with a Long start and finish.

		H'cap start	
1.	W. E. Cook (7 hp NLG-Peugeot)	40 sec	68 mph
2.	A. H. Wilkie (3½ hp Triumph)	2 min	
3.	W. H. Bashall (3½ hp Zenith-Gradua-JAP)	2 min	

Charlie Collier finished fifth.

There were seventeen starters in the Roadster Handicap, Harry Collier (8 hp Matchless-JAP) being at scratch. The limit man this time was W. Pollard (3½ hp Quadrant) with a start of 2 min 15 sec. R. C. Griesbach (3½ hp Triumph) was not allowed to start because he had no front mudguard or throttle.

The result was a win for D. Thomas (5 hp DOT) by a 100 yd. A. Schmutz (4½ hp 4-cyl. FN) and P. W. Bischoff (5 hp 4-cyl. FN) both suffered from engine overheating, and A. R. Hunter (3½ hp Triumph) was forced to retire with a broken petrol pipe.

ROADSTER MOTOR CYCLE HANDICAP (up to 1000 cc touring machines) run over 8½ miles with a Long start and finish.

		H'cap start	
1.	D. Thomas (5 hp DOT)	unknown	55½ mph
2.	G. Lee Evans (5 hp Indian)	unknown	
3.	H. A. Collier (8 hp Matchless-JAP)	scratch	

On Whit-Monday, May 31st, the weather was just as brilliant as on the Saturday and even larger crowds were in attendance. Two motor cycle events were on the programme—the Championship Plate and the Metropolitan Handicap—both for up to 1000 cc machines.

At the start of the Championship Plate, which was a scratch race, all kept close company except Harry Martin and Frank Dayrell (8 hp Matchless-JAPs) who had made bad getaways.

Passing the Fork towards the end of the first lap, Will Cook

(7 hp NLG-Peugeot) and Bert Colver (8 hp Matchless-JAP) struggled for the lead, passing and re-passing each other for almost half the following circuit. Cook gradually moved ahead, steadily increasing his lead to win by half the length of the Finishing Straight:

CHAMPIONSHIP MOTOR CYCLE PLATE (up to 1000 cc) a scratch race over 8½ miles, Long start and finish.

1. W. E. Cook (7 hp NLG-Peugeot)   68¾ mph
2. H. V. Colver (8 hp Matchless-JAP)
3. C. R. Collier (8 hp Matchless-JAP)

Harry Collier, the third member of the Matchless team, finished fourth.

The Metropolitan Handicap, fifth event on the race card, brought twenty-three starters to the line. Scratch man Charlie Collier (8 hp Matchless-JAP), was set a real task to catch the limit man in only three laps, for several riders had completed a whole lap before all had been dispatched by the starter.

Half way through the race, R. J. Shanks (2½ hp Peugeot) turned off down the Finishing Straight and reported news of a collision between W. Smith (2 hp Moto Rêve) and Charlie Collier. Smith, who was well ahead of the field on his second lap, was being overtaken by Charlie, who was on his first at the time. Both were brought down heavily but not seriously injured, although badly scratched and cut about the arms and head. This accident further accentuated comment about the need for some form of head protection for riders in future events.

The race resulted in a win for Guy Lee Evans, this time mounted on a larger (5 hp) Indian. Less than a quarter-of-a-mile separated the first four men home:

METROPOLITAN MOTOR CYCLE HANDICAP (up to 1000 cc) run over 8½ miles with a Long start and finish.

		H'cap start	
1.	G. Lee Evans (5 hp Indian)	1 min 45 sec	61¼ mph
2.	W. E. Cook (7 hp NLG-Peugeot)	40 sec	
3.	L. C. Munro (3 hp NSU)		

The ninth and last event of the day was the Whitsun Winners' Handicap over 8½ miles, in which both car and motor cycle race winners competed.

The result was in doubt until the end of the second lap, when it was noticed that Blunt (Sizaire-Naudin car) and Lee Evans (5 hp Indian) had established a good lead over the field. Blunt won by 150 yd from Lee Evans. Cars filled the next five places and Will Cook (7 hp NLG-Peugeot) came in eighth.

The handicapping was generally criticised, it being suggested that it should be based on practice times and not nominal horsepower ratings—meaningless anyway—of the vehicles taking part. It was further proposed that the actual cubic capacity of engines should be made known in the race programmes.

A new track record

On the Monday after Whitsun, Will Cook arrived at the track with a special 20 hp 90° V-twin o.h.v. JAP-engined NLG, of 120 × 120 mm bore and stroke, with the object of attacking Henri Cissac's long-standing flying-start kilometre and flying-start mile records. The engine was one of three specially built by the JAP concern. Of the two others, one was sold to the Matchless firm and the other to Harry Bashall the well-known rider of BAT-JAPs. Cook's machine had non-detachable cylinder heads and drilled auxiliary exhaust ports. A single large Longuemare carburetter fed the cylinders, final drive being by belt at 1½-to-1. The front forks were rigid.

He achieved a time of 26.553 sec (84.247 mph) for the flying kilometre, which although not a British or World's record, was an unlimited track record.

During 1909 Charlie Collier tried the 20 hp Matchless at Brooklands, but found it unmanageable at speed. Later the engine was built into a special Matchless monoplane intended to compete for the *Daily Mail* newspaper's prize of £10,000 for the first successful circuit of Britain by a flying machine. A crash, during secret tests on the old Arsenal football ground at Woolwich marshes in south-east London, put paid to the project.

The Third BMCRC Members' Race Meeting

Held on Wednesday, June 16th, this meeting included two scratch races, one handicap, and an innovation—Record Time Trials from a flying start over the measured half-mile, kilometre and mile distances on the Railway Straight.

After a dull morning, the sun came through the clouds in time for the first event—the Tourist Trophy Scratch Race over 8¼ miles, for machines up to 750 cc generally conforming with the 1909 Isle of Man TT Race regulations. Another innovation was the use of a Fork start and finish.

The first time they went under the Members' Bridge after the start, it was clear that only three riders were really in the running: Guy Lee Evans and Billy Wells (638 Indians), and Archie Fenn (499 Triumph). At the end of lap one Lee Evans led Fenn by a few yards, with Wells lying a useful third a long way ahead of the field. Fenn gained on the leader, until by lap two hardly a machine's length separated them. Lee Evans held his lead, however, beating Fenn to the finish by a mere ten yards, with Billy Wells third some 80 yd to the rear. Then came J. H. Slaughter and "Bizzy" Bashall (476 Triumphs), and Freddie Barnes (482 Zenith-Gradua-JAP), in that order. Frank McNab (482 Trump-JAP) retired with an unscrewed throttle control. Result:

TOURIST TROPHY SCRATCH RACE (up to 750 cc) 1909 IoM TT regulations. Over 8¼ miles with a Fork start and finish.

1. G. Lee Evans (638 Indian)　　　　　　59 mph
2. A. G. Fenn (499 Triumph)
3. W. H. Wells (638 Indian)

A similar pattern, of a pair of riders struggling for the lead, was set up in the All-Comers' Scratch Race for machines of 450-1000 cc. In this case the combatants were Will Cook (944 NLG-Peugeot) and Harold Bowen (964 BAT-JAP), Cook eventually obtaining a useful lead to win with comparative ease:

ALL-COMERS' SCRATCH RACE (450-1000 cc) over 8¼ miles. Fork start and finish.

1. W. E. Cook (944 NLG-Peugeot)　　　　59 mph
2. H. H. Bowen (964 BAT-JAP)
3. A. G. Fenn (499 Triumph)

For once, much praise was bestowed on the handicappers of the next event, run over 8¼ miles: the Afternoon Handicap for machines up to 500 cc. A reversion was made to the Long Finishing Line for the start and finish. The limit men, Gordon Fletcher and

W. Smith (332 Moto Rêves), had 3-min 30-sec starts over Archie Fenn (499 Triumph), the scratch man.

Fletcher immediately took the lead and all the starters got away well, especially Fenn, who was clearly out to win despite his heavy handicap. Smith caught Fletcher, and the field had rapidly closed up by the start of the last lap. A mass of riders entered the Finishing Straight together and Fenn came up to the front to win in fine style. The handicappers had done a good job as only 26 sec separated first and last men at the finish:

AFTERNOON HANDICAP (up to 500 cc) over $8\frac{1}{4}$ miles. Long start and finish.

		H'cap start	
1.	A. G. Fenn (499 Triumph)	scratch	$56\frac{1}{2}$ mph
2.	H. H. Bowen (482 BAT-JAP)	24 sec	
3.	F. A. McNab (482 Trump-JAP)	33 sec	

After tea in the clubhouse, spectators were conveyed by lorry to the Railway Straight for the Record Time Trials. There were five classes down for decision: A (up to 275 cc), B (up to 350 cc), C (up to 500 cc), D (up to 750 cc) and E (up to 1000 cc). These were to form the basis of the classes recognised for record purposes, hitherto un-defined. No entries materialised in A, the smallest class, so it was scratched.

The fastest speeds achieved in each class were as follows:

RECORD TIME TRIALS

Class		Speed (mph) over:		
		fs $\frac{1}{2}$ ml	fs km	fs ml
B	G. L. Fletcher (332 Moto Rêve)	40.228	40.351	40.25
C	A. G. Fenn (499 Triumph)	61.486	61.772	61.846
D	W. H. Wells (638 Indian)	65.158	64.854	64.356
E	W. E. Cook (944 NLG-Peugeot)	75.898	75.921	75.678

As can be seen Cook made the fastest time of the day.

The BARC June meeting

For its June meeting, the BARC abandoned the usual practice of having Saturday as race day, and staged one on Wednesday, June 30th instead. The one-and-only motor cycle race on the programme was the City Handicap, for machines up to 1000 cc and run over 8¼ miles, and it was particularly well-supported with an entry of thirty-three. A Fork start and a Long-Finishing-Line finish were again the order of the day, in common with the car events.

The large entry was doubtless due in no small measure to the very excellent prize money offered: twenty sovereigns for a first place, ten for a second and five for a third.

Will Cook (7 hp NLG-Peugeot) was once again at scratch, while at the other end of the scale was the limit man, W. Pollard (2 hp Minerva) with 5 min start. At the end of lap one Pollard still led, but Frank Applebee (5 hp Rex) was catching up fast. Soon Harry Collier (5 hp Matchless-JAP) had established himself in the lead, and he settled down to win eventually by almost a mile, at the fastest motor cycle race average yet. Result:

CITY MOTOR CYCLE HANDICAP (up to 1000 cc) over 8¼ miles. Fork start and Long finish.

		H'cap start	
1.	H. A. Collier (8 hp Matchless-JAP)	25 sec	69¾ mph
2.	H. G. Partridge (6 hp NSU)	1 min 55 sec	
3.	H. V. Colver (8 hp Matchless-JAP)	12 sec	

The bookies, who were now firmly established at the track, appeared to be equally as fooled by the handicapping as the riders, and they gave odds of 5-to-1 on the field.

After the meeting several riders indulged in some practice laps. One of these, Will Cook, hit a bump at something over 60 mph on his 7 hp NLG-Peugeot and was thrown from his machine. Fortunately he was wearing a leather helmet which saved him from serious injury.

A fast five-hundred

On Wednesday, July 14th, Bemsee held their Fourth Members' Race Meet at Brooklands, during which some very much improved 500 cc performances were seen. The first event was for novices on machines up to 1000 cc, a novice being defined as: "anyone who had not won a first place in any motor cycle race on a closed track". Furthermore their machines had to be the *bona fide* property of the rider concerned. The event was to be a handicap.

Before this event, however, a preliminary novices' scratch race was run off to assess their handicaps. Should a competitor in the handicap improve on his preliminary time by more than $2\frac{1}{2}\%$, he would be disqualified. This initial scratch race was won by G. G. Mead on his Vindec Special.

Whilst the novices' handicaps were being determined, the ten starters for the All-Comers' Handicap (up to 1000 cc) came to the starting line at the Fork. The race resulted in a fine win for Harold Bowen ($3\frac{1}{2}$ hp BAT-JAP) at the fastest speed yet for an under 500 cc machine:

ALL-COMERS' HANDICAP (up to 1000 cc)
over $8\frac{1}{4}$ miles. Fork start and Long finish.

		H'cap start	
1.	H. H. Bowen ($3\frac{1}{2}$ hp BAT-JAP)	1 min 12 sec	$62\frac{3}{4}$ mph
2.	G. Lee Evans (5 hp Indian)	52 sec	
3.	H. E. Parker (7hp NLG-Peugeot)	scratch	

Then came the Novices' Handicap, over $8\frac{1}{4}$ miles. At the end of the first lap, viewed from the Fork, A. Pennington ($3\frac{1}{2}$ hp Triumph) was leading, followed by A. E. Morgan (5 hp Rex) and W. H. S. Sharpe ($3\frac{1}{2}$ hp Triumph). Next after a short interval came M. Krause (5 hp Vindec-Special), Billy Wells (5 hp Indian) and G. G. Mead (7 hp Vindec-Special). Pennington still led on the second lap, followed by Morgan, Sharpe, Wells and Krause, in that order. The result was a win for Morgan. Pennington and Krause, who finished second and third, were disqualified for exceeding their time allowance. The official result was:

NOVICES' HANDICAP (up to 1000 cc)
over $8\frac{1}{4}$ miles. Fork start and Long finish.

		H'cap start	
1.	A. E. Morgan (5 hp Rex)	2 min $30\frac{2}{5}$ sec	$53\frac{3}{4}$ mph
2.	G. G. Mead (7 hp Vindec-Special)	scratch	
3.	H. W. Wells (5 hp Indian)		

The TT Handicap race (for machines up to 750 cc) followed. Again a Fork start was used and the race was run over three laps. It provided yet another win for Harold Bowen, who certainly seemed to have found some extra speed in his $3\frac{1}{2}$ hp s.v. BAT-JAP Result:

1909—THE BIRTH OF BEMSEE

TT HANDICAP (up to 750 cc) over 8¼ miles, with a Fork start and Long finish.

		H'cap start	
1.	H. H. Bowen (3½ hp BAT-JAP)	52 sec	speed unknown
2.	G. G. Mead (5 hp Vindec-Special)	35 sec	
3.	G. Lee Evans (5 hp Indian)	12 sec	

After the tea interval, there followed the Record Time Trials. The event was again split up into classes, the competitors running the reverse way, clockwise, from the Fork to the Railway Straight, to take advantage of the prevailing wind. The class winners were as follows:

RECORD TIME TRIALS

Class	Speed (mph) over:	
	fs km	fs ml
A (275 cc) G. L. Fletcher (274 Moto Rêve)	45.990	45.447
C (500 cc) H. H. Bowen (482 BAT-JAP)	65.023	64.283
D (750 cc) G. Lee Evans (638 Indian)	64.711	64.702

Another fast five hundred was Archie Fenn's 499 cc s.v. Triumph, which did 62.743 mph and 62.539 mph over the flying-start kilometre and mile respectively.

Indian on the warpath

A foretaste of the future came with a series of wins for Guy Lee Evans (638 Indian) at the two-day BARC August holiday weekend race meeting. Held on Saturday, July 31st and Bank Holiday Monday, August 2nd, the combined meeting included no fewer than six motor cycle races in its programme.

The first of these was the opening event on the Saturday—an up to 500 cc two-lap handicap. This resulted in a close race between L. C. Munro (499 NSU) and W. W. Genn (340 Eland), who came first and second, with J. C. Smyth (499 Rex) 300 yd behind in third place. Result:

JUNIOR MOTOR CYCLE HANDICAP (up to 500 cc) over 5½ miles, Fork start and Long finish.

		H'cap start	
1.	L. C. Munro (499 NSU)	65 sec	50 mph
2.	W. W. Genn (340 Eland)	80 sec	
3.	J. C. Smyth (499 Rex)	40 sec	

Fourth was Walter O. Bentley (499 Rex).

There then followed the August Handicap and Sprint Race for cars, before the next motor cycle event—the August Motor Cycle Handicap over two laps, for machines from 350 to 750 cc. It was in this race that Lee Evans first showed his form, albeit aided by the poor handicapping, which had now become associated with BARC-organised events.

It proved an easy win for Lee Evans' Indian, which was pulling a single gear of $3\frac{1}{2}$-to-1 and was fitted with a Bosch magneto and 28×2 in R.O.M. tyres.

AUGUST MOTOR CYCLE HANDICAP (350-750 cc) over $5\frac{1}{2}$ miles, with a Fork start and Long finish.

		H'cap start	
1.	G. Lee Evans (638 Indian)	scratch	$60\frac{1}{4}$ mph
2.	A. R. Abbott jun. (476 Triumph)	45 sec	
3.	J. C. Smyth (499 Rex)	40 sec	

Charlie Bennett (616 Indian), Harry Bashall (482 Zenith-Gradua-JAP) and L. C. Munro (743 NSU) followed.

The last event on the Saturday was the Senior Handicap over $8\frac{1}{2}$ miles, a motor cycle race for 500 to 1000 cc machines. This event was an easy victory for Lee Evans by almost three times the length of the Finishing Straight. One hundred yards separated the second and third finishers:

SENIOR MOTOR CYCLE HANDICAP (500-1000 cc) over $8\frac{1}{2}$ miles, with Fork start and Long finish.

		H'cap start	
1.	G. Lee Evans (638 Indian)	1 min 5 sec	$60\frac{1}{4}$ mph
2.	H. G. Partridge (796 NSU)	1 min 20 sec	
3.	H. V. Colver (964 Matchless-JAP)	25 sec	

On the Monday, the first motor cycle race was a special event for standard touring machines up to 1000 cc. They were required to be fully equipped for the road and fitted with tyres of not less than $2\frac{1}{4}$-in section, two brakes, metal mudguards, a tool bag with contents weighing not less than three pounds, a stand and a touring saddle. The petrol tank had to hold not less than a gallon of petrol. All machines had to have efficient silencers, without cut-outs. The Second Roadster Handicap, as the race was called, was a three-lap affair with a Fork start and again a Finishing Straight finish. For the third time Lee Evans won!

SECOND ROADSTER HANDICAP (up to 1000 cc) over 8½ miles, with a Fork start and Long finish.

		H'cap start	
1.	G. Lee Evans (638 Indian)	35 sec	57½ mph
2.	H. A. Collier (964 Matchless-JAP)	scratch	
3.	W. H. Bashall (482 Zenith-Gradua-JAP)	1 min 45 sec	

Harry Collier, the second man home, was lapping at around 63 mph on his two flying laps.

The Second Championship Plate, the only motor cycle scratch race for up to 1000 cc machines on the weekend's programme, was also one of the few events not to be won by Guy Lee Evans. It provided an exciting duel between Charlie Collier and Bert Colver, the issue being in doubt right up to the last twenty yards before the finish. The third man was the length of the Finishing Straight behind at the end of the race:

SECOND CHAMPIONSHIP PLATE SCRATCH RACE (up to 1000 cc) over 8½ miles, from a Fork start with a Long finish.

1.	C. R. Collier (964 Matchless-JAP)	69¼ mph
2.	H. V. Colver (964 Matchless-JAP)	
3.	L. C. Munro (995 NSU)	

Final event of the day was the August Winner's Handicap in which Lee Evans was pitted against three cars, which included: H. J. D. Astley's 59.2 hp Napier (at scratch), and Sir George W. Abercromby's 39.5 hp Napier (18 sec start). The result was yet another win for the irrepressible Lee Evans at 60¾ mph, this time with a start over scratch of 1 min 46 sec.

Almost sixty miles in the hour on a five-hundred

Bad weather almost ruined the Fifth BMCRC Members' Meeting of the year, held on Wednesday, August 18th. George Reynolds, the club's secretary, was almost for postponing the meeting because of the rain. At all events, the first of the two competitions scheduled, the Record Time Trials, was eventually started at 4.30 p.m. Though the rain had stopped by then, it was cold and a strong north-westerly wind made it more like April than August.

The riders started at the Fork, and gathered speed round the Byfleet Banking before entering the timed strips on the Railway Straight. As before, the event was split up into classes and the fastest speeds, on a wet track, were as follows:

RECORD TIME TRIALS

Class		Speed (mph) over:	
		fs km	fs ml
B	(350 cc) F. W. Dayrell (340 Martin-JAP)	46.706	47.345
C	(500 cc) W. O. Bentley (472 Rex)	53.308	54.428
D	(750 cc) G. Lee Evans (638 Indian)	63.742	64.024
E	(1000 cc) W. H. Bashall (964 BAT-JAP)	68.364	68.581

The other event on the programme was a Multi-Class One-Hour Race. The start took place at 5.48 pm at the Fork. From the outset the struggle for first place lay between Harold Bowen (482 BAT-JAP) and Harry Bashall (964 BAT-JAP), and for four laps Harry led on his larger machine. Then Bowen shot ahead and maintained his lead to the finish, while Harry stopped and started a number of times, with various troubles. Although in different classes, Lee Evans and R. O. Clark (FN) had a keen fight for overall second place. Result:

ONE-HOUR RACE WINNERS

Class		Distance covered
B	(350 cc) F. W. Dayrell (340 Martin-JAP)	47 miles 1260 yd
C	(500 cc) H. H. Bowen (482 BAT-JAP)	59 miles 485 yd
D	(750 cc) G. Lee Evans (638 Indian)	56 miles 880 yd
E	(1000 cc) W. H. Bashall (964 BAT-JAP)	43 miles 1300 yd

Bowen's fine performance substantially beat Frank McNab's for the same period earlier in the year. Under better weather conditions, so observers considered, he might well have become the first man to accomplish sixty miles in the hour on a 500 cc machine.

For many riders, the hour race was a tale of woe. Griesbach broke a petrol pipe on his Triumph, R. O. Clark broke an oil pump

The winner of the Autumn Handicap on Wednesday, October 6th, 1909—W. D. Chitty (340 Frays-JAP)—who averaged 50½ mph for this, his first-ever race at the track. In 1910, he became the first to do 60 mph on a "350".

The official Matchless-JAP racing team. *Left to right:* Harry Collier, Charlie Collier and Bert Colver. They finished 1, 2, 3, in that order, in the October Handicap on Wednesday, October 6th, 1909.

American Billy Wells (wearing cap) and his team of Indian-riders, who filled the first three places in the Brooklands' One-Hour TT Race on Wednesday, March 16th, 1910. *Left to right:* Walter Bentley, of Bentley-car fame, Guy Lee Evans and Charlie Bennett.

The start of the June Handicap at the BARC meeting on Saturday, June 18th, 1910. No. 6, Harry Collier, and No. 5, Bert Colver (666 Matchless-JAPs) and No. 7, D. R. Clarke (662 Indian), push their machines off from the 18-sec mark. Waiting to go is scratch man Guy Lee Evans (994 Indian).

on his FN, and Walter Bentley on his 472 cc Rex ran out of oil altogether. This last rider had a pipe connecting the induction pipe and crankcase, which served to pass oil to the cylinder as an upper-cylinder lubricant. Rex adopted this system as standard on their 1912 models.

Class records

Early in August the Auto Cycle Union (the ACU) Competitions Sub-Committee agreed to recognise class records at Brooklands based on engines' swept volumes. This represented a further move towards rationalising capacity limits in motor cycle racing.

The Sixth BMCRC Members' Monthly Meeting at Brooklands, was originally scheduled for Wednesday, September 15th, but it was postponed until the 29th of the month because many riders would be over in the Isle of Man preparing for the TT Races of the 23rd.

Bad weather on the 29th led to a further postponement of the meeting until October, with a rearranged programme.

Last BARC meeting of the year

Bright sunny weather greeted competitors in the last BARC meeting of the year, when they arrived at Brooklands on Wednesday, October 6th. Two motor cycle races were featured in the programme, The first, the October Handicap, was for machines of from 450 to 1000 cc. The second, the Autumn Handicap, was for those up to 500 cc. Both events were run over three laps (8½ miles) from a Fork start to a Long-Finishing-Line finish.

There were only three non-starters in the October Handicap. Harry Collier (964 Matchless-JAP) was at scratch and the result was a one-two three win for the Matchless Motors team:

OCTOBER MOTOR CYCLE HANDICAP (450-1000 cc) over 8½ miles, Fork start and Long finish.

		H'cap start	
1.	H. A. Collier (964 Matchless-JAP)	scratch	70 mph
2.	C. R. Collier (738 Matchless-JAP)	10 sec	
3.	H. V. Colver (964 Matchless-JAP)	20 sec	

Harry's winning speed was a new motor cycle race record.

The eighth race—the Autumn Handicap—had seventeen starters. Lee Evans, as usual, got away well. The result was an unexpected win by a newcomer to Brooklands: W. D. Chitty (340 Frays-JAP) at the very respectable speed, for a three-fifty, of just over 50 mph. Result:

AUTUMN MOTOR CYCLE HANDICAP (up to 500 cc) over 8½ miles, from Fork start to Long finish.

		H'cap start	
1.	W. Chitty (340 Frays-JAP)	1 min	50½ mph
2.	W. Pollard (453 Quadrant)	1 min	
3.	G. Lee Evans (497 Indian)	scratch	

Bert Colver (482 Matchless-JAP) joint scratch man with Evans, finished sixth.

Two-Hours Race

The final BMCRC race meeting of 1909 was the postponed Sixth Members' Meeting, held on Saturday, October 9th. Two events were run: a Multi-Class Two-Hour Race and a Three-Lap Handicap. The start of the meeting was somewhat delayed. This combined with a long interval between the races and the onset of dusk, put paid to the running of the last scheduled event. This was to have been a 25-mile scratch race run under 1909 IoM TT Race Regulations, for 500 cc singles and 750 cc twins.

In the Two-Hour Race, the competitors got away well, but of the fourteen starters, four retired: three with engine trouble and one, Harry Martin (964 BAT-JAP) with a broken driving belt. Another BAT-JAP rider, Harry Bashall, had not only the partition of his combined oil and fuel tank split, but also the tank itself. Despite being smothered in petrol and oil, he gamely completed the distance. The winners were as follows:

TWO-HOUR SCRATCH RACE (Fork start and finish)

Class			distance covered
B	(350 cc)	F. W. Dayrell (340 Martin-JAP)	78 miles 132 yd
C	(500cc)	G. Lee Evans (497 Indian)	105 miles 60 yd*
D	(750 cc)	L. W. Bellinger (714 Indian)	100 miles 1189 yd
E	(1000 cc)	H. V. Colver (964 Matchless-JAP)	118 miles 14 yd**

(*Class C record. Evans also set a new 100-mile record.

**Class E record. Colver also set up new 50-mile and 100-mile records).

The second event proved an easy win for Frank McNab, by half-a-mile over W. D. Chitty. Result:

AFTERNOON HANDICAP over 8½ miles.
Fork start and finish.

		H'cap start
1.	F. A. McNab (482 Trump-JAP)	15 sec
2.	W. D. Chitty (340 Martin-JAP)	50 sec
3.	F. W. Dayrell (340 Martin-JAP)	50 sec

The very last meeting of the year was staged by the Motor Cycling Club (the MCC) and held the following Saturday, October 16th. The weather was bad but the entry large, with many future well-known names featured. They included George Brough (later famous for his Brough Superiors), Captain Sir Robert (R. K.) Arbuthnot and young Malcolm Campbell, on a 4 hp JAP-engined special. All events had a Fork start and finish.

The results gave wins for T. F. Maw (4 hp Rex) at 29.8 mph in the 500 cc Tourist Handicap, and Tony Sale at 32.13 mph in the 344-1000 cc Handicap. Both races were over two laps. The three-lap 1000 cc scratch event provided a win for A. V. Deacock (3 hp Wanderer) at 37.70 mph, with Malcolm Campbell second. These low speeds were due to the slipping of driving belts under the appallingly wet track conditions.

Finale to the year

The Brooklands' racing season for 1909 ended with a number of record attempts, some more successful than others.

At about midday on Thursday, November 11th, Frank McNab (482 Trump-JAP), in company with Frank Dayrell (482 BAT-JAP), set out after Class-C (500-cc solo) records. Dayrell soon retired with a puncture, but McNab successfully took the 100-mile and 2-hour records, averaging 53.80 mph and 53.89 mph respectively.

Now Will Cook (16-20 hp NLG-JAP) took to the track for another crack at Henri Cissac's old flying-start kilometre record speed. According to unofficial hand-timing Cook averaged over 90 mph, but the exact truth will never be known, as the electrical timing equipment unfortunately failed at the crucial moment.

He had another attempt, this time offically hand-timed, but this run was not fast enough. At the end of it his valve-timing pinion sheared and he could not carry on.

Frank McNab's records did not last long, for on the Saturday November 15th, Guy Lee Evans was out on the track on his single-cylinder i.o.e. 497 cc Indian, which was now fitted with mechanical oil pump, and of course was chain driven.

The machine ran well and he successfully gained the 50-mile, 100-mile and 2-hour records at averages of 55.58 mph, 54.34 mph and 54.38 mph. Billy Wells and E. Frasetti did the pit work.

Monday, November 22nd, saw Harry Martin assisted by Frank Dayrell successfully breaking the Class E (1000 cc) 3-hour record, at an average speed of 55.17 mph. He could not continue, however, because his 964 cc BAT-JAP was plagued with valve trouble.

Two days later Oliver Godfrey (481 Rex), despite having his front wheel hit by—of all things—a partridge, managed to break Harold Bowen's Class C (500 cc solo) hour record, with a new distance of 59 miles 1350 yd.

He also became the first man to average more than 60 mph for 50 miles on a 500 cc machine—60.01 mph to be exact. But for the partridge incident, he might have become the first on a five-hundred to cover more than sixty miles in the hour.

4

1910—THE TUNER FINDS HIS FEET

If the previous year had been one of experiment and innovation for the race organisers at Brooklands, nineteen-ten was to be the same for the motor cycle engine tuners—particularly those of the small single-cylinder engined machines.

Track activity started early in the year when on Wednesday, January 3rd, Freddie Barnes (3½ hp Zenith-Gradua-JAP) clipped 3.02 sec off the standing-start record for the Test Hill, by averaging 15.386 mph for the climb.

On Thursday, January 27th, the BMCRC—at its first ever AGM—voted in Tommy Loughborough as secretary in place of George Reynolds, who had to relinquish the post through ill health. Eight prospective monthly Brooklands' race meetings were announced and scheduled for the 1910 racing season, to take place on Wednesdays, as in the latter half of 1909.

The BARC announced a ban on auxiliary exhaust ports, which they felt gave an undue advantage to professional riders. This ruling they quickly rescinded though, when it was realised that most of the amateurs were using them as well!

Thursday, March 10th saw a number of well-known racing men testing their machines at the track. Jack Marshall and Billy Newsome were out on their 3½ hp Triumphs testing new exhaust valves. Harry Martin (750 ASL-JAP) attempted to set up new long-distance records, but was prevented by mechanical troubles.

On Wednesday, March 16th, in brilliant Spring weather, was held the first Bemsee motor cycle race meeting of 1910, which was also the first motor cycle race meeting ever to be attended by Royalty. Two races were on the programme: the All-Comers' Handicap (up to 1000 cc) over two laps, and a One-Hour Race for machines conforming to the 1910 Isle of Man TT Race regulations. Both started at the Fork.

The first "Royal" meeting

Shortly after the start of the second event, the One-Hour Race, Prince Francis of Teck, the father-in-law to the Prince of Wales (later George V), arrived to present the awards at the prize-giving ceremony at the close of the meeting. Knowledge that he was due to be present, accounted in no small measure for the vast crowds of spectators at this race meeting.

The All-Comers' Handicap attracted thirteen starters. Bert Colver (964 Matchless-JAP) was scratch man, while Cyril Patteson (334 Moto Rêve) was on the limit mark with a start of 4 min. Harry Martin, mounted on a very much "over-square", 85 × 60 mm, 340 cc Martin-JAP o.h.v. single, came in an easy winner far ahead of the field. Just as he crossed the Finishing Line, the trembler blade from his ignition came adrift and he was lucky to finish the race when he did. Result:

ALL-COMERS' HANDICAP (up to 1000 cc) over 8½ miles, Fork start and Long finish.

		H'cap start	
1.	H. Martin (340 Martin-JAP)	2 min 20 sec	49.54 mph
2.	W. O. Bentley (638 Indian)	36 sec	
3.	H. H. Bowen (482 BAT-JAP)	1 min 9 sec	

Tourist Trophy regulations were not rigidly enforced in the One-Hour Race, so that, for example, mudguards could be dispensed with. Billy Wells had put up a silver cup for the winner, with the BMCRC's gold and silver medals as second and third place prizes. A Fork start and finish helped spectators more closely to follow the race, which was a scratch affair with ten starters. Among these was a strong Indian contingent comprising Guy Lee Evans, Walter Bentley and Charlie Bennett, all on 638 cc twins now fitted with mechanical oil pumps*. Charlie Collier rode a 658 cc Matchless-JAP, while Archie Fenn was on his 499 cc "Imperial" Triumph—a much-modified s.v. TT Triumph whose re-naming had brought down on his head the wrath of no less a figure than M. J. Schulte, the head of the Triumph Company.

---

* There is no doubt that the use of mechanical oil pumps meant that the hand could be kept on the handlebars the whole time: a very important factor over the "tricky" Brooklands' bumps.

All but A. Oberländer (499 NSU) made a good start and by the end of the first lap the Indians, headed by Bennett, easily held the first three places, followed by Harold Bowen (482 BAT-JAP), Charlie Collier, Frank McNab (482 Trump-JAP) and Oberländer. On lap two, the first three were Bennett, Bentley, and Lee Evans—an order which was maintained to the end of the race.

The winner, Charlie Bennett, covered the first fifty miles at an average speed of 60.01 mph, a new Class D (up to 750 cc) record.

ONE-HOUR TT RACE with a Fork start and finish.

		Distance covered	
1.	C. E. Bennett (638 Indian)	59 miles	870 yd
2.	W. O. Bentley (638 Indian)	58 miles	1040 yd
3.	G. Lee Evans (638 Indian)	55 miles	690 yd

The fastest five-hundred was that of Frank McNab (482 Trump-JAP), who completed 54 miles 1715 yd, to finish fourth.

As a whole the meeting was an interesting one, in that it was the first at which starters were allowed—that is, people to assist riders in the push-starting of their machines. The need for such assistance was becoming increasingly apparent with the faster high-geared machines and an initial start on an upgrade. The distance over which such assistance was allowed, however, was strictly limited to a few yards—on pain of disqualification.

Brooklands' Easter races

Held under the auspices of the BARC, the Easter Monday, March 28th, race meeting consisted of seven events, five for cars and two for motor cycles. Both of the two-wheeler races received a good entry, twenty-three runners turning out for the Easter Handicap (up to 500 cc) and nineteen for the Spring Handicap (500-1000 cc). Each race was run over three laps and the BARC retained its ban on the use of starters.

A new single-cylinder Humber in the hands of J. F. Crundall, was tried out in the Easter Handicap, but the scratch mark proved too much of a handicap for it. In fact the handicapping in general left much to be desired.

The race provided a runaway win at an outstandingly good speed for the redoubtable Harry Martin, on his short-stroke three-fifty:

EASTER MOTOR CYCLE HANDICAP (up to 500 cc) over 8½ miles, with a Long start and finish.

		H'cap start	
1.	H. Martin (340 Martin-JAP)	1 min 15 sec	53¼ mph
2.	E. C. W. FitzHerbert (448 FN)	2 min 15 sec	
3.	F. A. McNab (482 Trump-JAP)	27 sec	

J. P. Le Grand appeared on the starting line for the Spring Handicap with a new pattern 670 cc o.h.i.v. Rex. It finished eleventh and was clearly only in the development stage. The race itself was closely fought and provided a win for Harry Collier (658 Matchless-JAP) who had just managed to beat Charlie Bennett (639 Indian). Close behind was another Indian rider, Arthur Moorhouse, the secretary of the Manchester and District Motor Cycle Club. Result:

SPRING MOTOR CYCLE HANDICAP (500-1000 cc) over 8½ miles, with Long start and finish.

		H'cap start	
1.	H. A. Collier (658 Matchless-JAP)	1 min 6 sec	63 mph
2.	C. E. Bennett (639 Indian)	57 sec	
3.	A. J. Moorhouse (639 Indian)		

Ten days later, during the afternoon of Friday "April Fools' Day"—perhaps an unfortunate day to choose—Harry Martin set out once again on his 750 cc ASL-JAP to attempt Class D (750 cc solo) records. He again had to give up due to engine troubles.

The machine was an interesting one. Made by Air Springs Ltd of Stafford, the ASL represented one of the first serious attempts to design a machine to combat road shocks and vibration. The standard models used pneumatic front and rear suspension. Although he did not use the spring frame, Harry Martin clearly realised the advantage of the ASL leading-link parallel-ruler-type front forks, which acted against a pneumatic shock absorber unit, and he was using a pair on this 750 cc machine. Air pressure was built up to the required value in the shock absorber, through a conventional valve, using a hand pump.

High speeds from small machines

Brooklands habitués, amazed at the recent performances by

Harry Martin's 340 cc model, were to be fairly staggered by the performances of this machine and an even smaller one in the Record Trials at the Second BMCRC Monthly Meeting, held on Wednesday, April 13th, 1910. Harry was rapidly acquiring a reputation, if there had ever been any previous doubt, as a "Wizard of Tune".

The other event held on the 13th included a relay race, a somewhat light-hearted affair over four laps for two-man teams of riders, and a One-Hour TT Race run on similar lines to that of the previous Bemsee meeting.

The day's weather proved mild if spasmodically showery, while a gusty wind blew from the south-east. Because of the wet track the first event, the Record Time Trials, could not start until after 3.0 pm. But once underway all ran smoothly enough. The speeds of W. D. Chitty (270 Givaudan), Harry Martin (340 Martin-JAP), and Harold Bowen (658 BAT-JAP) in this event, all constituted world's records in their respective classes.

Harry Martin had fitted a pair of ASL forks to his 340 cc machine, and it was rumoured that he was using a fuel containing ethyl alcohol. If this was the case, it must have been the first time that alcohol had been used in a motor cycle at the track.

The fastest times in the sprint event were as follows:

RECORD TIME TRIALS

Class		Speed (mph) over fs ml	
A	(up to 275 cc)	W. D. Chitty (270 Givaudan)	50.5
B	(350 cc)	H. Martin (340 Martin-JAP)	58.5
C	(500 cc)	F. A. Applebee (482 Rex)	60.7
D	(750 cc)	H. H. Bowen (658 BAT-JAP)	68.2
E	(1000 cc)	G. Lee Evans (994 Indian)	71.7

Frank Applebee's machine was fitted with Oliver Godfrey's hour-record-breaking engine.

The next event to be run off, the Relay over four miles, provided a win for Harry Collier (658 Matchless-JAP) and Archie Fenn (499 Triumph), with Frank McNab (482 Trump-JAP) and Harold Bowen (658 BAT-JAP) the second team home, and Frank Applebee (482 Rex) and Martin Geiger (666 Vindec-Special) the third.

Up until the end of the Relay, the weather had stayed fine, but during the TT One-Hour Race there were several heavy showers. A good getaway was made by all except J. T. ("Bizzy") Bashall, whose machine packed up within 200 yd of the start at the Fork. By the end of lap one Harold Bowen (658 BAT-JAP) led, with Charlie Bennett (639 Indian) second followed by Charlie Collier on the first of the 658 cc TT Matchless-JAPs, all in close order. Then, in procession, came D. R. Clarke (639 Indian), Harry Collier on the second TT Matchless, Guy Lee Evans (639 Indian), Martin Geiger (666 Vindec-Special), Walter Bentley (639 Indian), Bert Colver on the other TT Matchless, Archie Fenn (499 Triumph), Bert Yates (499 Humber), Frank McNab and John Gibson (482 Trump-JAPs) and S. A. M. ("Sam") Witham on his 499 cc Triumph.

In the second lap Bowen retained his lead, Charlie Collier moved into second place with Bennett third. In lap three, Bennett took second place which he kept until lap eight, when he caught up Bowen. Harry Collier had by then moved into third spot. On lap ten Bowen stopped for petrol, leaving Bennett in the lead on the Indian until the thirteenth round, when he overtook Bennett, whose machine had gone a little off colour.

The Collier brothers then moved into second and third positions and with Bowen well in the lead, that was the order at the finish:

ONE-HOUR TT RACE

	Distance covered
1. H. H. Bowen (658 BAT-JAP)	56 miles 1038 yd
2. C. R. Collier (658 Matchless-JAP)	53 miles 326 yd
3. H. A. Collier (658 Matchless-JAP)	51 miles 740 yd

Lee Evans was early in trouble in the One-Hour Race through losing his filler cap on the track. The Matchlesses, which were prospective Isle of Man TT machines, had very large filler caps enabling rapid refuelling. Bowen's machine used a Watawata belt for final drive, that was relatively unaffected by the wet conditions.

Between this race meeting and the next at Brooklands, Archie Fenn—ever an experimentalist—tried the effect on engine power of picric acid dissolved in his petrol. It would seem that disaster struck, the engine "blowing up". Fortunately he managed to acquire an Indian machine to ride in future meetings.

The Second BARC Meeting of 1910 received rather a sparse entry of cars, so that what was originally intended to be a two-day meeting had to be reduced to a single-day's sport,

The Scott makes its Brooklands debût

Held on Wednesday, April 27th, this second car meeting included, as usual, two motor cycle handicaps in its programme. Several newcomers to Brooklands appeared on the starting lines for these races. They included: Bob Dicker (372 Chater-Lea), later to achieve fame on Nortons and Rudges, Eric Myers on one of 636 cc twin-cylinder two-stroke Scotts which he had helped build, and E. B. Ware, who was later to become a great three-wheeler exponent, and who was riding a 964 cc V-twin JAP-engined King's Own fitted with chain drive and a P. &. M. two-speed gear.

Fine weather, but a strong south-westerly breeze, greeted the large crowds who turned up to watch the racing. Amongst the throng was Oscar Hedström, the designer of the Indian motor cycle, who had just arrived from the States on a visit.

The first race, the April Handicap (up to 670 cc) over three laps, had a Fork start and a Long finish. Just as he left the paddock to make his way to the Fork for the start of this race, Bert Yates who was riding a 499 cc Humber broke the fastener of his machine's driving belt, and had to effect a hurried repair. Despite this he managed to finish fourth to his team-mate Crundall. Result:

APRIL MOTOR CYCLE HANDICAP (up to 670 cc) over $8\frac{1}{4}$ miles, with a Fork start and Long finish.

		H'cap start	
1.	A. Oberländer (314 NSU)	3 min 54 sec	$46\frac{1}{2}$ mph
2.	A. E. Woodman (639 Indian)	42 sec	
3.	J. F. Crundall (499 Humber)	1 min 9 sec	

Both Harold Bowen (658 BAT-JAP) and Guy Lee Evans (639 Indian) suffered plug troubles, and at the end of the race Walter Bentley (639 Indian) found that he had burst his rear tyre. The two Colliers again rode their TT machines, but were beaten by the handicapping.

This race must have severely "caned" the bookmaker's pockets since the starting prices quoted on the first two men to finish were at odds of 10-to-1!

The other motor cycle event—the Weybridge Handicap—also had a Fork start and Long-Finishing-Line finish. It covered the same distance as the first race, but this time was for machines of from

500 to 1000 cc. It resulted in yet another win for an Indian motor cycle, with young New Zealander Alan Woodman romping in first, ahead of Arthur Moorhouse, who was also on an Indian. Frank Dayrell (964 JAP Special) just pipped Harold Bowen (658 BAT-JAP) on the line for third place, while Charlie Bennett and Lee Evans (639 Indians) dead-heated for fifth.

This time odds of 2-to-1 on Woodman saved the bookies' financial bacon. Results:

WEYBRIDGE MOTOR CYCLE HANDICAP (500-1000 cc) over 8¼ miles, with a Fork start and Long finish.

		H'cap start	
1.	A. E. Woodman (639 Indian)	1 min 3 sec	61¾ mph
2.	A. J. Moorhouse (994 Indian)	12 sec	
3.	F. W. Dayrell (964 JAP Special)	45 sec	

During the following week the makers of the Gradua gear, Zenith Motors, announced that they would issue certificates signed by Major Lindsay Lloyd, to any owner whose motor cycle had been converted to the Gradua gear and had successfully negotiated the Brooklands' Test Hill.

Things hot-up for the TT

Several of the entrants for the BMCRC Third Members' Meeting, held on Wednesday, May 4th, were using the racing that day as a final test before the Isle of Man TT Races. The One- and Two-Hour Races incorporated in previous race meetings had proved particularly useful for sorting out the mechanical bugs in preparation for the big Island event. Such a race was included in May 4th's race programme and was of one-hour's duration.

In the first race: the All-Comers' Handicap (over three laps, starting and finishing at the Fork), Charlie Collier and Bert Colver (666 Matchless-JAPs) and Guy Lee Evans (994 Indian) were all three at scratch together. The limit man was Gordon Fletcher (340 Douglas), who at the end of the first lap lost his lead to John Gibson (488 Trump-JAP), with Frank McNab second to John on a similar machine. Approaching the finish Harold Bowen (666 BAT-JAP) led until his rear tyre blew off the rim, bending his mudguard in the process. This put Charlie Collier in the lead. Forgetting that the finish was at the starting line on the Outer Circuit, just beyond the Fork, Charlie turned off down the Finishing Straight—so losing the race. Result:

ALL-COMERS' HANDICAP (up to 1000 cc)
over 8 miles 269 yd. Fork start and finish.

		H'cap start	
1.	J. Gibson (488 Trump-JAP)	1 min 33 sec	57.62 mph
2.	F. A. McNab (488 Trump-JAP)	1 min 33 sec	
3.	G. Lee Evans (994 Indian)	scratch	

The next event was a rolling-start one-mile sprint race on the lines of that held at the second BMCRC race meeting the previous year. The riders rode for some distance until caught up by the official car, in the back of which stood Ebbie waiting to give the "go" signal as soon as the machines were dressed in-line with him. It resulted in wins for Harry Martin (340 Martin-ASL-JAP), in Class B (350 cc); John Gibson (488 Trump-JAP), in Class C (500 cc); Charlie Bennett (663 Indian), in Class D (750 cc); and for Guy Lee Evans (994 Indian), in Class E (1000 cc).

Only seven starters were on the line for the event for which all the spectators had been waiting, the One-Hour TT Race, which was held under the 1910 IoM TT Race regulations (with the exception that there was no restriction as in previous such events, regarding the minimum weight of tools to be carried in the machine's tool kit). Several well-known riders failed to make an appearance on the starting line despite being entered in the programme, and it was not until the race was about to commence that it was announced that Lee Evans would also not be running. Up to that moment the betting on Evans had been heavy. This was despite the fact that Tom Tyler the bookmaker, by now quite a regular attender at Bemsee race meetings, would only give odds of 2-to-1 on him to win. Much to everyone's amusement, right up until the news of Evans' withdrawal from the race, Tom continued to shout Evans' starting price with the added rider: "Certain to win! Beat a motor car once he did!", as if ashamed of giving such short odds. Other starting prices offered were Bert Colver's at 4-to-1 and Frank McNab's at 6-to-1.

Tom Tyler was one of the real characters of Brooklands and was present at most of the meetings held at the track during its long history. He later became better known under the nickname "Long Tom", which he adopted as his trade name.

These early meetings were reminiscent in many ways of modern horse racing, not only because of the betting and bookmakers, but also because the riders wore coloured sashes for identification purposes during a race. This practice did not survive long at the track, however, the sashes proving more of a hindrance than a help.

After several showers of rain, the weather eventually cleared and the big event got underway at 4.15 pm, a quarter of an hour later than planned. The field consisted of: Bert Colver (666 Matchless-JAP), Charlie Bennett (663 Indian), Martin Geiger (663 Vindec-Special), J. F. Crundall (499 Humber), A. Oberländer (499 NSU), Frank NcNab and John Gibson (488 Trump-JAPs) and E. Gwynne (476 Triumph).

Colver had a long lead by the end of the first lap, with Bennett second and Gibson third. On lap three Colver passed with his stand trailing, while Gwynne retired with a broken valve. Valve trouble also struck Gibson's machine on lap four and he did not restart until the leader was on his seventh lap, and then only to retire eight l aps later.

On the sixth lap Colver stopped and fixed his stand, restarting in hot pursuit of Bennett. In the ninth round Bennett stopped, giving the lead back to Colver with McNab second and Geiger third. This order was maintained until Colver's fourteenth lap, when he stopped for oil, giving McNab the lead. The rain was now coming down like stair-rods and Colver, who had restarted, rode with his hand shielding his face to prevent it from being cut by the falling torrent, in hot pursuit of Frank McNab. Geiger retired on the leader's fifteenth lap, with a broken petrol pipe.

The excitement amongst the crowds of spectators now became intense as McNab was soon being hard-pressed. At the beginning of the twentieth lap a mere second separated the two men, and on the next circuit Bert Colver passed his rival and went on to win amongst clouds of spray:

ONE-HOUR TT RACE (for 500 cc singles and 670 cc twins)

		Distance covered
1.	H. V. Colver (666 Matchless-JAP)	55 miles 720 yd
2.	F. A. McNab (488 Trump-JAP)	55 miles 550 yd
3.	A. Oberländer (499 NSU)	50 miles 45 yd

Distances in these early hour races were measured by assuming constancy of pace in the lap in which the hour terminated, and back calculating. In later years direct observation of the race leaders at the time of completion of the hour, was used to determine the place men.

The May meeting

With the death of King Edward VII on May 6th, the BARC did not consider it appropriate to hold their race meeting on the Whit-Monday as originally scheduled, and postponed it for what they held to be a decent interval, until Saturday, May 28th.

Contrary to expectations, the holding of the Isle of Man TT Races only two days before and of a major hill-climb race meeting the day after, did not materially reduce the entry received. Some well-known riders were non-starters, however. Amongst these were the Collier brothers, and Alan Woodman, who had suffered a nasty crash in practice for the IoM TT on his Indian machine. One of his legs had to be amputated above the knee in consequence, and it looked as though that popular rider might never race again. Yet only a year later he was to be back in the saddle again competing at Brooklands.

Eight starters turned out for the May Handicap, over $8\frac{1}{2}$ miles, Will Cook (995 Peugeot), the scratch man, stopped shortly after passing under the Members' Bridge on his second lap. H. G. Partridge (808 NSU), the limit man, made full use of his generous start and was never caught:

MAY HANDICAP (500-1000 cc) over $8\frac{1}{2}$ miles,
with a Fork start and Long finish

		H'cap start	
1.	H. G. Partridge (808 NSU)	1 min 33 sec	$55\frac{3}{4}$ mph
2.	J. T. Bashall (666 BAT-JAP)	30 sec	
3.	A. Oberländer (955 NSU)	9 sec	

In the other motor cycle race of the otherwise all-car programme, the Whitsun Handicap, there were twenty-two starters. The limit man, F. E. Broom (413 FN)—with a start of 1 min 48 sec—got away badly, but once again the short-start men were handicapped out of the running. Angus Maitland (488 Trump-JAP) proved the eventual winner by two-to-three-hundred yards. The scratch man, Bert Colver (666 Matchless-JAP), finished eighth. Result:

WHITSUN HANDICAP (up to 670 cc). Over 8½ miles, from Fork start to Long finish.

		H'cap start	
1.	A. C. Maitland (488 Trump-JAP)	1 min 12 sec	55¾ mph
2.	W. Dewar (476 Triumph)	1 min 20 sec	
3.	G. F. Hunter (499 Triumph)	1 min 12 sec	

The handicapping by A. V. Ebblewhite ("Ebbie") and T. D. Dutton was somewhat below par at this particular meeting.

The MCC goes racing

The first of the June meetings to incorporate motor cycle races at Brooklands during 1910, was organised by the Motor Cycling Club. Held under rather dull weather conditions, on Saturday the 4th, it featured no less than five track races and a hill-climb event on the Test Hill.

F. H. Mullett and Dr C. B. Moss-Blundell, founder only a few months before the of Leicestershire and District MCC, were the stars of the meeting on their 3½ hp Triumphs—winning two events each. The two well-known Indian riders E. D. Dickson and Guy Lee Evans, were respective winners of the two remaining races. Lee Evans' 994 cc machine lapped at 70.8 mph—the fastest circuit of the day's racing.

Fine win for small machine

The outstanding performance of the two motor cycle races, held as part of the BARC meeting on Saturday, June 18th, was the fine win in the second by A. Oberländer at 54 mph on his 314 cc twin-cylinder German NSU.

The first of these races—the June Handicap—had fifteen starters, all of them on twin-cylinder machines of from 500 to 1000 cc. BARC prize money had diminished during the three years since motor racing had started at the track and a win in this event brought only £5. Of course this was not a small amount in 1910 terms and certainly it was a small fortune compared with Bemsee awards,

1910—THE TUNER FINDS HIS FEET

which were generally measured in shillings rather than pounds, or consisted of club medals instead of cash. The BMCRC was well-nigh impecunious compared with the BARC.

Of the two scratch men Guy Lee Evans (994 Indian) was off form, but Charlie Collier (976 Matchless-JAP) was very definitely on and out to win! This he did at a new race-record speed. He also set up a new flying-lap record of 75.6 mph. Results:

JUNE HANDICAP (500-1000 cc). Over 8½ miles,
Fork start and Long finish.

		H'cap start	
1.	C. R. Collier (976 Matchless-JAP)	scratch	72¾ mph
2.	H. V. Colver (666 Matchless-JAP)	18 sec	
3.	F. W. Dayrell (964 Martin-JAP)	24 sec	

The rewards for the second motor cycle race, the Summer Handicap for machines up to 670 cc, were more encouraging: namely £10 for a win, £5 for a second and £3 for a third place. The good prize money reflected itself in the large field of twenty-nine starters.

Among the first away was A. Brunton (344 New Century-Givaudan), who soon got going well and rapidly overhauled C. E. Peach, the limit man, on a similar-sized Minerva. By the start of lap two, A. Oberländer (314 NSU) had gained the lead and was soon a long way ahead. He went on to win completely unchallenged. Joint scratch man Charlie Collier finished fourth on his 666 cc Matchless-JAP. Result:

SUMMER HANDICAP (up to 670 cc). Over 8½ miles,
Fork start and Long finish.

		H'cap start	
1.	A. Oberländer (314 NSU)	1 min 30 sec	54 mph
2.	E. D. Colrick-Herne (499 Triumph)	52 sec	
3.	H. V. Colver (666 Matchless-JAP)	scratch	

There were several interesting machines running in this race. W. D. Chitty had a single-cylinder engined 482 cc Frays-JAP, fitted with what in effect was a twin-port cylinder head. Twin exhaust ports that is, with two separate exhaust pipes. The 499 cc Calthorpe ridden by A. G. Tapley, which was making its Brooklands debut had a single-cylinder side-valve engine, a front-mounted chain-driven magneto, and a petrol tank that sloped away at the rear like that of the Rex.

Brunton's machine had auxiliary exhaust ports fitted with radially disposed short "pepper pot" silencers. Most riders rode in shirt sleeves—it was too hot for jerseys, the usual racing attire.

Mid-Summer marathon

For a long time it had been evident that the multi-cylinder machine was nowhere near as reliable in long-distance racing, as the single-cylinder. Thus in the Isle of Man races the multi-cylinder class had always been given a higher capacity limit to make up for this deficiency. Moreover it was to help engine tuners working on multis, that the One-Hour TT events had been organised at Brooklands. Such events, however, proved inadequate as tests for the lengthier Island races.

So it was, that a sixty-lap marathon was organised for the Fourth BMCRC Brooklands' meeting on Wednesday, June 22nd, 1910. A total distance of 163 miles 103 yd was involved.

The event, which was run under 1910 IoM TT Race Regulations, had two classes: one for singles up to 500 cc, the other for multis up to 670 cc. The start and finish were at the Fork, where pit facilities had been set up for refuelling and repairs during the race.

Although a heavy thunderstorm spoilt the morning, improving weather enabled the race to start on time at 4.00 pm. By then a considerable crowd of spectators had gathered at the Fork. In view of the historic nature of this, the first really long long-distance race to be staged at Brooklands, it is worth considering its entry list in detail. There were thirty-seven entrants, who were as follows:

SINGLE-CYLINDER CLASS (up to 500 cc). Will Cook and H. E. Parker (482 NLG-JAPs); Sam Wright and Bert Yates (499 Humbers); Lieut. Spencer Grey RN, Ray Abbott, E. Colrick-Herne, Jack Marshall, Billy Newsome, Billy Creyton, E. Gwynne, W. Dewar, Rex Mundy and F. Lister Goodacre (all on 499 Triumphs); Frank McNab, John Gibson and Angus Maitland (488 Trump-JAPs); G. E. Stanley (499 Premier); and J. H. Slaughter (498 Ariel).

MULTI-CYLINDER CLASS (up to 670 cc). Guy Lee Evans, Arthur Moorhouse, Charlie Franklin and Archie Fenn (639 Indians); D. R. Clarke (662 Indian); Harry and Bizzy Bashall, Sam Witham, and Harold Bowen (all on 666 BAT-JAPs); Martin Geiger and F. H. Arnott (662 Vindec-Specials); Vickers Jones and F. Savory (665 Premiers); E. C. W. FitzHerbert and R. O. Clark (448 FNs); Noel E. Drury (665 Chater-Lea-JAP); A. V. Deacock (666 Wanderer); and Harry Reed (658 DOT-JAP). All of the multis were twins, except for the FNs which had four cylinder engines.

The only non-starters were Geiger, Arnott and Colrick-Herne, whose front wheel had buckled in practice.

Both classes were started simultaneously and within a quarter of a mile, the tailing out process had begun, with Sam Witham in the lead. For the first few laps the BAT-JAP riders were dominating the leading positions. Midfield struggles were developing between Moorhouse and Marshall, and between the two FN riders.

Bowen was the first to come into the pits, changing a defective sparking plug and getting away quickly. Harry Bashall had plenty of plug trouble in this race as well, due to central electrode breakages. In fact one piece the size of a pea, remained trapped inside a cylinder of his engine for the whole of the race, without being blown out of the exhaust or causing damage!

Four or five laps at the pace set by the leading BAT-JAPs were beginning to weed out the field, and a number of riders had disappeared from the scene on the Railway Straight, the fastest part of the circuit. One of the first to go was Stanley, drenched with fuel due to his large and heavy filler cap having been shaken loose from his petrol tank and lost somewhere on the track.

Lee Evans was early in trouble. His engine was off form and needed excessive lubrication, so he was forced to stop for oil after only eight laps. Plug trouble caused him another pit stop a lap later. In contrast, the other Indians were going well as was also Sam Wright, on his new single cylinder o.h.v. chain driven Humber. But his team mate Bert Yates had to retire after only two laps.

Of the Trump-JAPs, Angus Maitland's (pulling a 4-to-1 gear and revving higher than most) was amongst the fastest single-cylinder machines. He soon had valve-lengthening troubles, but after a short spell in the pits and the use of a file he was soon away again.

Only one pit helper per rider was officially allowed, and the race officials at the Fork had their work cut out preventing extra unauthorised assistance from causing the disqualification of some competitors.

Many riders suffered from valve-lengthening and had to come in to the pits to remedy it.

The Triumphs as a team had been going very rapidly and consistently, but unfortunately two of the best Triumph riders dropped out of the race early on. Billy Creyton like Colrick-Herne came to grief badly with a buckled wheel, in his case just beyond the Members' Bridge. A few laps later Billy Newsome was unlucky enough to run over Stanley's lost filler cap. His back wheel ended up in a similar condition.

Archie Fenn came in to his pit, changed his engine sprocket and was quickly away again. Then both Jack Marshall and Arthur Moorhouse came in to refuel. Their partnership of some fifteen laps was about to be dissolved, for Moorhouse seemed to have acquired a lot more "steam". He soon left the restarted and pursuing Marshall far behind.

At fifty miles Sam Witham (666 BAT-JAP) still led, having broken Bert Colver's Class D (750 cc) record for the distance by averaging 65.56 mph. Scarcely had he accomplished this than he was put out of the race: on the Byfleet Banking his front mudguard came adrift, locking the wheel, bringing him off his machine at something in the region of 70 mph. Fortunately he escaped with but a few bruises. Bizzy Bashall then took over the lead with his brother, Harry, and Bowen close behind, so that BAT-JAPs still held the first three places.

Casualties now seemed to increase, valve troubles being the dominant cause. Harry Bashall stopped to clean oil off his driving belt, while his brother still led after fifty two laps with Moorhouse now in second place—having completed forty eight laps. Fate now caught up with Bizzy, when on the Byfleet Banking, a valve broke and its head dropped into the cylinder. This misfortune let Moorhouse (49 laps) and Franklin (46 laps) into first and second spots on their Indians. At this juncture Gwynne's front tyre burst and almost caused a mass pile up of riders and machines, but with great skill he managed to save the situation and pulled up safely. The race finished shortly after 7. 05 pm with Harold Bowen just scraping into second place despite his engine failure. Arthur Moorhouse rode in an easy winner 24 min 54 sec ahead of Bowen, to a highly popular victory. The single cylinder race resulted in yet another win for Frank McNab: Result:

BROOKLANDS 60-LAP TT RACE (1910 IoM TT Regulations) over 163 miles 103 yd. Fork start and finish.

Class		Speed (mph)
Multis (up to 670 cc) 1.	A. J. Moorhouse (639 Indian)	56.72
2.	H. H. Bowen (666 BAT-JAP)	49.56
3.	C. B. Franklin (639 Indian)	49.01
Singles (up to 500 cc) 1.	F. A. McNab (488 Trump-JAP)	53.71
2.	J. Marshall (499 Triumph)	52.66
3.	A. R. Abbott (499 Rex)	completed 54 laps

The fourth finisher in the Multi-Cylinder Race, was E. C. W. FitzHerbert (448 FN four-cylinder) who averaged 43.34 mph.

In the course of the racing a number of long-distance records were set up, including a new Class D (750 cc) one-hour record by J. T. (Bizzy) Bashall at 62.74 mph.

Clearly many lessons had been learnt from this event by competitors and officials alike. Snags to be avoided in the organisation of similar events, and the tuning requirements for high-speed reliability, were becoming clearer. Taken over all the event was judged a great success.

Oxford versus Cambridge

On the Saturday following the sixty-lap Bemsee marathon an Intervarsity Meeting was held, between teams of riders from Oxford and Cambridge Universities. Usually interesting, this particular intervarsity affair was afflicted by an incessant downpour. Three events were run, two two-lap elimination handicaps for Oxford MCC and Cambridge MCC members respectively, and then an Intervarsity Scratch Race. This last event was between teams representing the two universities and selected from the place men in the first two events. The result was an easy points-win for the Cambridge team.

The Oxford Elimination Handicap was won by E. D. Tate (499 Triumph) at $49\frac{1}{2}$ mph and that for Cambridge by E. D. Dickson (639 Indian) at 58 mph.

More world's records and the first sidecar race

Many regular track habitués had not yet returned after competing in the Scottish Six Days' Trial, which led to a somewhat meagre field at the BMCRC's Fifth 1910 Meeting on Saturday, July 20th. The programme was an interesting one, however, including as it did the Record Time Trials and, as an innovation, two sidecar races. An end-of-racing-season aggregate award was to be given for the Record Time Trial series, which stimulated much greater interest in these events than during 1909.

The Record Time Trials was the first event. Considerable delay was caused by incorrect working of the electrical timing equipment, and several competitors made fruitless attempts on this account before matters were rectified. Eventually all short circuits were located and remedied, and matters proceeded smoothly. A number of records were broken, Charlie Collier becoming the first officially to exceed 80 mph in the 1000 cc category. Billy Wells recorded 54.23 mph and 52.72 mph respectively for the flying-start kilometre and mile on his 994 cc Indian sidecar outfit. The fastest speeds were as follows:

RECORD TIME TRIAL

Class			Speed (mph) over:	
			fs km	fs ml
A	(275 cc)	W. D. Chitty (270 Givaudan)	52.05*	51.89
B	(350 cc)	W. D. Chitty (345 Frays-JAP)	61.38*	59.20
C	(500 cc)	A. C. Maitland (488 Trump-JAP)	63.78	62.48
D	(750 cc)	S. A. M. Witham (666 BAT-JAP)	71.72*	70.35
		H. V. Colver (666 Matchless-JAP)	71.51	70.61*
E	(1000 cc)	C. R. Collier (976 Matchless-JAP)	80.18*	78.45*

(*New class records).

Chitty became the first rider officially to exceed 60 mph at Brooklands on a three-fifty. Charlie Collier's machine had sprung forks, coil ignition and silenced auxiliary exhaust ports. As with all early Brooklands' record attempts they were one-way, and wind assisted using the Byfleet Banking to pick up speed.

Two runners took part in the first-ever sidecar races at the track: Billy Wells on his Six Days' Trial 994 cc Indian sidecar outfit and Martin Geiger on a 955 cc Vindec-Special sidecar combination. Both machines used two-speed gears, were in touring trim and had combined passenger-rider weights in excess of 18 stone.

The first race was from scratch and acted as a basis for a subsequent one—a handicap. Both races were over one lap. In the scratch event Geiger got away first, but was soon passed by Wells who won at 43.8 mph by 53⅕ sec. This time served as Geiger's handicap start in the second race.

He had obviously held back in the scratch race, for Wells could not catch him in the handicap. He won at 35.4 mph.

Next followed the July Junior Handicap (up to 500 cc) over three laps. In the first lap W. D. Chitty (345 Frays-JAP) was well ahead, followed by Harry Martin (340 ASL-JAP), Frank McNab (488 Trump-JAP) and scratch man Angus Maitland (488 Trump-JAP). At the end of lap two McNab led with Chitty second, Maitland third and Harry Martin last. It proved an easy win for McNab, immediately after which his back tyre collapsed because of an inner tube being nipped between cover and rim. Results:

JULY JUNIOR HANDICAP (up to 500 cc)
over 3 laps. Fork start and finish.

		H'cap start	
1.	F. A. McNab (488 Trump-JAP)	15 sec	55.9 mph
2.	A. C. Maitland (488 Trump-JAP)	scratch	
3.	W. D. Chitty (345 Frays-JAP)	30 sec	

The last event on the programme—the July Senior Handicap (up to 1000 cc) was also a three-lap event.

At the end of the first lap the limit man B. Roberts (976 BAT-JAP), who had a 66-sec start, still maintained his lead. Next came Charlie Bennett (634 Indian), A. E. Morgan and Bert Colver (666 Matchless-JAPs), and Charlie Collier (976 Matchless-JAP) from scratch. Meanwhile D. R. Clarke (662 Indian) had retired.

At the end of lap two Colver had a good lead but the novice, Roberts, who like Morgan was hugging the inside of the track, still kept up in second place. Then engine trouble struck Roberts who had to retire. Results:

JULY SENIOR HANDICAP (up to 1000 cc)
over 3 laps, Fork start and finish.

		H'cap start	
1.	H. V. Colver (666 Matchless-JAP)	18 sec	67.4 mph
2.	C. R. Collier (976 Matchless-JAP)	scratch	
3.	C. E. Bennett (634 Indian)	48 sec	

With the increase in the number of long-distance events being held at Brooklands the ACU announced, during July, that it would bring its hour records into line with American practice by recognising flying-start attempts. Hitherto only standing-start period record attempts had been recognised by that body.

New style handicaps

At their car race meetings the BARC had been running a few races in which cars of roughly equivalent observed performance were invited to run. Following on from this they devised a method of handicapping which lasted the active life of the track. This system was further extended by them to motor cycle races, so that for their race meeting on Bank Holiday Monday, August 1st, 1910, the BARC introduced the so-called 60- and 70-mph Handicaps.

Both events started at the Fork and ended in the straight at the Long Finishing Line. The 60-mph Handicap, over two laps, was for machines whose observed lap speeds *had not* exceeded 60 mph, and whereas the 70-mph Handicap, over three laps, catered for machines whose observed lap speeds *had* exceeded 55 mph. The overlap of 5 mph in qualifying speeds enabled the most popular class—the 500 cc machines—to have a double bite of the racing cake.

Scratch man in the 60-mph Handicap was H. G. Partridge (795 NSU), while C. E. Peach (344 Minerva) was on the limit mark with 1 min 4 sec start. The betting was: F. H. Arnott (663 Vindec-Special), 10-to-1; Partridge, 10-to-1; and W. Dewar (499 Triumph), evens. This was in fact the exact order in which they finished:

60-MPH HANDICAP over 5¾ miles,
Fork start and Long finish.

	H'cap start	
1. F. H. Arnott (663 Vindec-Special)	10 sec	60¾ mph
2. H. G. Partridge (795 NSU)	scratch	
3. W. Dewar (499 Triumph)	34 sec	

The 70-mph Handicap also provided a win for Arnott, who gained the lead on the second of his three laps. At the start of the third he made a mistake similar to that made by Charlie Collier at the Third BMCRC Race Meeting back in May. In apparently misjudging the length of the race he made as if to turn off down the Finishing

Straight. Fortunately he realised his mistake in time, recovered, and losing only one place in the race soon caught up the new leader—passing him to finish in front by some three-hundred yards.

70-MPH HANDICAP over 8½ miles,
Fork start and Long finish.

		H'cap start	
1.	F. F. Arnott (663 Vindec-Special)	1 min 27 sec	57 mph
2.	E. D. Colrick-Herne (499 Triumph)	1 min 15 sec	
3.	W. E. Cook (995 NLG-Peugeot)	scratch	

The second, third and fourth men all finished in close order.

A three-fifty breaks the five-hundred record

Harry "Wizard" Martin shook everybody rigid on Wednesday, August 17th, at the BMCRC's Sixth Monthly Race Meeting of 1910. He demolished the 500 cc flying-start kilometre and mile records, on his 340 cc Martin-ASL-JAP, with speeds of 68.28 mph and 65.97 mph! These were absolutely unheard of performances for a three-fifty at that time.

It was in the Record Time Trials that he achieved this and he was not alone in breaking records, W. Chitty, F. H. Arnott, and Charlie Collier also being successful. But Harry's speeds were by far the most outstanding of the meeting. The fastest in these record attempts were as follows:

RECORD TIME TRIALS

Class			Speed (mph) over:	
			fs km	fs ml
A	(275 cc)	W. D. Chitty (270 Givaudan)	52.67*	51.78*
B	(350 cc)	H. Martin (345 Martin-ASL-JAP)	68.28*	65.97*
C	(500 cc)	F. A. McNab (488 Trump-JAP)	64.13	64.31
D	(750 cc)	F. H. Arnott (663 Vindec-Special)	75.11*	73.08*
E	(1000 cc)	C. R. Collier (996 Matchless-JAP)	84.89*	82.63*

(*New class records).

F. H. Arnott's Vindec-Special, which he had christened the "Humming Bird" because of its peculiar exhaust note, had specially modified carburetter and sparking plugs. These plugs, which were of Bosch manufacture, were made with variable gap electrodes—Arnott's own patented idea. The threaded ends of these plugs were in inclined planes, while their central electrodes could be turned by means of fibre levers, thereby altering their spark gaps. He claimed that he was able to give small gaps for starting and increase them for flat-out work, whilst running.

The next event was the All-Comers' Unlimited Handicap, over $5\frac{1}{2}$ miles, and starters (that is pushers) were allowed. The handicapping was based on a trial scratch race over the same distance. Any rider in the handicap whose race time was more than 5% under that in the trial would be automatically disqualified. The idea was to penalise those who tried to deceive the handicappers and so obtain too generous a start over the scratch man.

In the trial scratch race, all made a good start with the exception of Harry Martin. This led, unfortunately, to his disqualification in the handicap in which he finished first. Result:

ALL-COMERS' PRELIMINARY SCRATCH RACE
TRIAL over $5\frac{1}{2}$ miles, Fork start and finish.

		Speed (mph):
1.	C. R. Collier (996 Matchless-JAP)	69.84
2.	J. T. Bashall (666 BAT-JAP)	64.97
3.	H. V. Colver (666 Matchless-JAP)	63.45

In the actual handicap, Cyril Patteson was awarded first prize as a result of the disqualification.

ALL-COMERS' UNLIMITED HANDICAP over $5\frac{1}{2}$ miles Fork start and finish.

		H'cap start	Speed (mph):
1.	C. Patterson (240 Moto Rêve)	4 min $58\frac{4}{5}$ sec	35.53
2.	F. H. Arnott (663 Vindec-Special)	$58\frac{2}{5}$ sec	60.03
3.	C. R. Collier (996 Matchless-JAP)	scratch	71.27

Both Barry Brown (666 Chater-Lea-JAP) and W. D. Chitty (340 Frays-JAP) stopped, the latter with a broken valve. Harry Martin averaged 55.28 mph.

The final event of the day was a relay race, open to two-man teams of riders whose total engine capacity did not exceed 1170 cc. Each team had to include one single-cylinder and one multi-cylinder machine. The race was run over four laps and five competing teams had entered. As in previous such events, the riders in each team rode alternate laps.

The result was a win for Harry Martin and Bert Colver.

The Auto Cycle Union's Annual Race Meet

The ACU Annual Race Meeting was generally accepted as the unofficial track-racing championship meeting. Since its inception in 1902 it had usually been held on small, one third-of-a-mile to the lap, tracks such as Canning Town. For a change, in 1910, it was decided to hold the meeting at Brooklands where the speed potential was greater.

It was held on Saturday, September 24th, under a cloudless sky and in brilliant sunshine, scarcely a breath of wind stirring the leaves of the trees beside the track.

The first event due to be staged was the Open Scratch Race over one lap, for the *Automotor Journal* Challenge Cup, for machines of up to 76 × 76 mm bore and stroke, or 345 cc maximum cylinder capacity. As with all other races that day, a Fork start and finish were used. The result was a narrow win for Harry Martin from the previous holder of the trophy, Charlie Collier:

OPEN SCRATCH RACE FOR THE "AUTOMOTOR JOURNAL" CHALLENGE CUP over one lap, with a Fork start and finish.

1. H. Martin (344 Martin-ASL-JAP)　　　　　　　57.21 mph
2. C. R. Collier (340 Matchless-JAP)
3. F. E. Barker (340 Dart-JAP)

For the Open Touring Handicap (up to 1000 cc), a two-lap scratch race was run to assess handicap starts. There were three non-starters, of whom Chitty (488 Frays-JAP) was disqualified before the race, the judges not considering his machine to be a touring model as defined by the competition regulations. Harry Collier (770 Matchless-JAP) had a full touring model fitted with a two-speed gear and twin driving belts. There were two adjustable pulleys on the engine shaft.

At the finish Angus Maitland (482 Trump-JAP) won by three-quarters of a mile from Charlie Bennett (634 Indian), while Guy Lee Evans on the big Indian came in third.

While the start times were being calculated for the Open Touring

Handicap, the four-lap Open Scratch Race for machines up to 1000 cc was run off for the *Motor Car Journal* Challenge Cup, previously held by Harry Martin.

In the first lap the order was Guy Lee Evans (994 Indian), Bert Colver (964 Matchless-JAP) and Charlie Collier (976 Matchless-JAP), together in a bunch, followed by H. E. Parker (995 NLG-Peugeot), F. H. Arnott (663 Vindec-Special) and F. P. Johnson (930 Matchless-JAP).

In the second round Colver and Collier led the field, with Bert ahead by half-a-wheel. Lee Evans and Johnson followed.

In the third Charlie Collier took the lead, and Lee Evans moved into second place. The result was an easy victory for Charlie:

OPEN SCRATCH RACE FOR THE "MOTOR CAR JOURNAL" CHALLENGE CUP over 4 laps. Fork start and finish.

1. C. R. Collier (976 Matchless-JAP) 71.62 mph
2. G. Lee Evans (994 Indian)
3. F. P. Johnson (930 Matchless-JAP)

The handicaps now having been worked out, the Open Touring Handicap over two laps was run. This resulted in a win for F. A. Hardy on his 663 cc Vindec-Special. F. P. Johnson (930 Matchless-JAP), who actually finished first, was disqualified for having finished in a time more than 5% faster than his time in the trial run. Result:

OPEN TOURING HANDICAP (up to 1000 cc) over two laps. Fork start and finish.

H'cap start
1. F. A. Hardy (663 Vindec-Special)   1 min 17 sec   48.80 mph
2. H. A. Collier (770 Matchless-JAP) 27⅘ sec
3. G. Lee Evans (994 Indian)   28 sec

The last event before the tea interval was the Open Passenger Handicap (for sidecar outfits up to 1000 cc) run over one lap, with a trial run to decide the start times. Among the starters, E. Frasetti (952 Vindec-Special s/car) and Charlie Collier (770 Matchless-JAP s/car) both had single-geared outfits. The trial scratch race resulted in a curious grouping of competitors in pairs. F. H. Arnott was not ready to go at the start of the trial run, but was allowed to carry out a lap on his own afterwards so that the handicappers could assess his performance and allocate him a start time in the handicap.

Martin Geiger (who had returned to riding his old love, NSU) finished first in the actual handicap, but was disqualified for beating his trial time by more than 5%. This gave the race to Harry Collier.

OPEN PASSENGER HANDICAP (up to 1000 cc)
over one lap. Fork start and finish.

1. H. A. Collier (770 Matchless-JAP
   s/car)   1 min 4$\frac{2}{5}$ sec   31.77 mph
2. E. Frasetti (952 Vindec-Special
   s/car)   39$\frac{2}{5}$ sec
3. C. R. Collier (770 Matchless-JAP
   s/car)   scratch

After the welcome rest afforded for tea, aeroplanes started to appear on the Flying Ground in the centre of the track. A special event had been organised at the suggestion of George Reynolds: a handicap race between an aircraft and a racing motor cycle. The participants were to be the French aviator Monsieur Blondeau with his Farman biplane, and Frank McNab on his 482 cc Trump-JAP.

Blondeau had to keep to a course around the track pylons and cover four laps. McNab started as the plane topped the pylon nearest the southern end of the track and began very soon to lap the Frenchman; he ended up by passing the finish 36 sec ahead of him. In later years, when asked about this race, McNab recalled how before the race Fred Straight—then ACU secretary—had asked him not to go too fast, but make a race of it. Such was the performance of aircraft at the start of the century!

The final event of the day was the big race on the programme: an hour race for *The Motor Cycle* journal's Challenge Cup, held by Charlie Collier, for machines up to 500 cc and conforming to 1910 Isle of Man TT Race regulations. This was the first time that it had been held for 500 cc machines only. There were two non-starters: Charlie Collier and Harry Martin.

Angus Maitland (482 Trump-JAP) led at the end of the first lap with Charlie Bennett (497 Indian) second and J. Harrison Watson (499 Triumph) third. Then on lap five Bennett stopped to tighten his carburetter which had worked loose, Norman Gray (499 Triumph) moving up to third place in the process. On lap seven, Frank McNab moved into third place, while W. Chitty (488 Frays-JAP) gradually moved up through the field. This order was kept until half-time and Maitland looked a certain winner; but in the ninth lap he fell out with a broken inlet valve.

Harrison Watson now led with McNab second and F. P. Johnson (465 Matchless-JAP) third. Then Harrison Watson dropped out and Chitty moved into third place. From lap 19 onwards Chitty led and the finishing order was reached. Towards the end of the hour it was almost dark and the usual red flag could not be used to stop the competitors, so a red lamp was used instead. Meanwhile the timekeepers got busy and worked out the distances by lamp light. The final result was:

ONE-HOUR SCRATCH RACE FOR "THE MOTOR CYCLE" JOURNAL'S CHALLENGE CUP (up to 500 cc) Fork start.

		Distance covered
1.	W. D. Chitty (488 Frays-JAP)	53 miles 3 yd
2.	F. P. Johnson (465 Matchless-JAP)	52 miles 1170 yd
3.	F. A. McNab (482 Trump-JAP)	52 miles 1160 yd

Fourth was Charlie Bennett (497 Indian) who completed a total of 52 miles 1145 yd in the hour.

The general opinion was that the meeting had been the best yet run by the ACU, and that Brooklands had been an excellent choice of venue.

Last BARC meet of the year

Both motor cycle races at the last BARC meeting of 1910 on Wednesday, October 5th, were new-style handicaps. The first of these was the Second 60-mph Handicap, which started at 3.15 pm in fine conditions. It was for all classes of machine not observed officially to have lapped in excess of 60 mph. The race was over two laps from a Fork start.

H. Shanks jun. (340 Kingfisher-JAP) broke his transmission belt on the line and had to retire. Of the other machines, several were fitted with drip-lubricators, in addition to their ordinary hand pumps.

At the end of the first lap Harry Martin (340 Martin-ASL-JAP) led, Capt. Sir Robert Arbuthnot (476 Triumph) was second and Guy

Lee Evans (497 Indian) lay third. At the finish Martin won and Lee Evans had managed to nose ahead of Arbuthnot to finish second:

60-MPH HANDICAP over 5½ miles, Fork start and Long finish.

		H'cap start	
1.	H. Martin (340 Martin-ASL-JAP)	34 sec	53½ mph
2.	G. Lee Evans (497 Indian)	10 sec	
3.	Capt Sir R. K. Arbuthnot (476 Triumph)	24 sec	

The other motor cycle event was the Second 70-mph Handicap over three laps, for machines whose lap speed had been observed to exceed 55 mph. Again a Fork start and Long finish were used.

By the end of lap one the scratch men had already moved into the first three places and these they held to the end of the race, Lee Evans winning by five yards:

70-MPH HANDICAP over 8½ miles, Fork start and Long finish.

		H'cap start	
1.	G. Lee Evans (994 Indian)	scratch	73¾ mph
2.	C. R. Collier (976 Matchless-JAP)	scratch	
3.	H. A. Collier (976 Matchless-JAP)	scratch	

The race speed was a new Brooklands' three-lap motor cycle record.

Two interesting machines appeared on the starting line at this meeting: Cyril Patteson rode a single-cylinder 82 × 94 mm, 496 cc Norton, and Charlie Bennett had a new drop-frame 3½ hp Kerry Abingdon.

High-Speed Reliability Trial

The BMCRC decided to postpone their final race meeting of the year until Saturday, October 8th: on that day they proposed to run a 100-mile High-Speed Reliability Trial for all classes of machine.

It was in fact to be a test of more or less standard touring machines. There were no restrictions on equipment, but the combined weight of the competitors on each of the passenger-carrying machines, had to exceed 19 stones. These were various classes, according to type and capacity (up to 1000 cc), scheduled to maintain set minimum average speeds. Each class had its own identifying coloured number plates, as outlined in the following table:

Class	Colour of number plate	Max. capacity (cc) Solos	s/cars	Min. av. speed (mph)
A	Yellow	275	500	25
B	Red	350	750	30
C	White	500	1000	35
D	Green	750	—	40
E	White (with red numbers)	1000	—	45

A silver cup was to be awarded regardless of class, to the competitor whose fastest and slowest laps differed by the least amount. Gold medals for similar performances within each class were also to be awarded. All other riders who completed the scheduled 37 laps (100.55 miles) of the Brooklands' Outer Circuit non-stop would receive silver medals, and those who did so despite stopping *en route*, bronze medals.

The afternoon of the meeting proved gloriously fine and warm for October, while there was practically no wind. A record entry for a Bemsee event of fifty-eight had been received and there were only five non-starters. Although it lacked the spectacular interest of a true race, the event certainly tested the reliability of the machines and a lot of lessons were learnt from the troubles that ensued. One of the most interesting entries turned out to be the eventual winner overall. This was the Reverend P. W. Bischoff's 499 cc Triumph-sidecar combination driven by his fiancée—Miss Beatrice Langston—the first woman to take part in a Brooklands' motor cycle event.

At the start Bischoff pushed off and leapt into the wicker-work Shapland sidecar just as the engine started to fire. The machine ran well and consistently. Bischoff in the sidecar timing the laps and jotting them down on a writing pad strapped to his knee, was able to advise Miss Langston when to slow down or speed up so as to adhere to their strict pre-arranged schedule.

Note the modern-looking leading-link air-sprung front forks of Harry Martin's 344 cc Martin-ASL-JAP. It is Saturday, September 24th, 1910 and he has just won the *Automotor Journal* Challenge Cup.

At the BARC's opening race meeting of 1911, Oliver Godfrey (cousin to Ron Godfrey of GN-car fame) appeared on this 994 cc Indian and won the 70-mph Handicap, running from the scratch mark.

Riding one of the new 499 cc Rudge Whitworths, 21-year-old Victor Surridge, in May 1911, became the first rider of a "500" officially to cover more than sixty miles in the hour.

The American track-racing champion, Jake de Rosier (994 Indian), who won two of his three match races against Charlie Collier (998 Matchless-JAP), at the BMCRC's Fifth Monthly Race Meeting of 1911.

The principal results were as follows:
HIGH-SPEED RELIABILITY TRIAL for touring machines over 37 laps or 100.55 miles.

Class	Winner	Av. speed (mph)	Lap time diff. (sec)	Award
A	Miss B. Langston (499 Triumph s/car)	25.94	12.4	Silver cup
B	L. A. Baddeley (314 Indian)	32.60	21.0	Gold medal
C	S. Wright (499 Humber)	38.06	24.6	Gold medal
D	V. Wilberforce (639 Indian)	48.65	14.6	Gold medal

All three runners in Class E were afflicted with troubles and none of them made a non-stop run. The only finisher in that class was J. J. Cookson (976 Matchless-JAP), who was awarded a bronze medal. He had several stops with a broken petrol pipe, and eventually turned the end of the broken pipe direct into the carburetter intake, controlling flow by means of the petrol tap.

Many competitors, afraid that their petrol would run short, rode with spare cans of it slung round their necks. Several Class C machines had obviously been tuned for economy and several completed the distance on less than a gallon of petrol, despite averaging more than 40 mph.

Three world's records were set up during the course of the day: Bert Yates (198 Humber) averaged 29.60 mph for 50 miles and 30.17 mph for 100 miles, both Class A (275 cc) records; A. Webster (340 Hobart) in Class B (350 cc) averaged 32.85 mph for 100 miles— also a new record.

At the conclusion of the 100-mile Reliability Trial there was a break for tea in the paddock and then with the track clear of machines Will Cook (16-20 NLG-JAP) prepared his machine for an attempt on Cissac's long-standing records. Unfortunately there was a lot of delay and it became so dark that the attempt had to be abandoned. Cook got started twice, but the fastener on his driving belt snapped on his first attempt. Poor visibility prevented the second.

Thoroughly disappointed with his cumbersome machine, Cook

sold it. Harry Bashall similarly disappointed with his 16-20 hp JAP engine, which he had mounted in a BAT frame, disposed of it to a budding aviator who needed the engine. He in turn lost interest in it and the engine made a re-appearance at Brooklands in 1912, powering W. Ward's cyclecar. It proved too much for the flimsy chassis, however, and was soon replaced with a less powerful engine.

End of the season record attempts and testing

Partly because of the forthcoming Motor Cycle Show in London and its accompanying publicity value, and partly because of the effect of cooler weather improving engine power, the Autumn of each year was proving more and more popular a time for attempts on records.

On Monday, October 24th, Bert Colver started out on the 666 cc Matchless-JAP which he had ridden in the 1910 Isle of Man TT Race, in an attempt on the Class D (750 cc) six-hour world's record. Despite two stops due to sparking plug trouble, he covered just over 55 miles in his first hour. Then after a further half-hour a valve stem broke, the valve head being forced by the piston clean through the top of the cylinder head. He had to retire.

Friday, November 4th, despite a wet track, saw Freddie Barnes out on his Six-Days'-Trial 488 cc Zenith-Gradua. He had set his sights on the Class C (500 cc) two- and three-hour records but contented himself that day with a new record ascent of the Brooklands' Test Hill, in $12\frac{1}{5}$ sec. He then co-operated with track officials in testing a new electrical acceleration-measuring device.

Meanwhile F. Wright, C. S. Burney and the young 21-year-old rider Victor Surridge, were busy testing the new 499 cc Rudge-Whitworths. Guy Lee Evans and Billy Wells were putting the finishing touches to a 497 cc Indian single, prior to an attempt on the Class C two-hour record. Loss of compression and the bitter cold put paid to this though.

Frank McNab and Angus Maitland (488 Trump-JAPs) both made attempts on records on Thursday, November 17th. McNab tried for the 100-mile and 2-hour records, and Maitland for the 50 miles and one hour. They had troubles, however, both retiring with broken valves.

J. Harrison Watson, the Nottinghamshire rider, had been practising for some weeks for an attempt on Oliver Godfrey's Class C (500 cc) hour record, but found difficulty in maintaining the necessary performance. In announcing his intention, Watson had stimulated other riders to announce their intention of attacking the same record. These included Godfrey, this time riding a Bradbury, and J. H. Slaughter on an LMC.

On Tuesday, November 22nd, Sam Witham came out with a new racey-looking Zenith-Gradua fitted with a 666 cc o.h.v. twin JAP engine. His attempts on his own Class D (750 cc) records were not quite fast enough and it seemed as though he was over-revving due either to belt slip or under-gearing. He decided to attempt standing-start records for the mile and kilometre in the same class, and in this he at last achieved success. His records were:

Standing start 1 km 50.10 mph
Standing start 1 ml 56.67 mph

These figures were quite good considering that Witham was a newcomer to the idiosyncracies of the Gradua gear, and that the weather was both extremely cold and foggy.

Thus the sport for the year 1910 ended at Brooklands, and the track closed down for its Winter repairs.

The "Blue Bird" café

In 1909 a shed had been put up on what was to become the Flying Ground, to accommodate Louis Paulhan's Farman biplane "La Gypaète" which he intended to use for his demonstration flights that Autumn. It was occupied at the beginning of 1910 by the pioneer British aviators H. P. Martin and G. H. Handasyde who were awaiting the erection of proper aeroplane sheds by the track authorities. They took over shed No. 12 and by the end of 1910 their original shed had been converted into a place of refreshment for spectators. The manageress was a Mrs. Billings. So the famous "Blue Bird" café came into being.

This establishment became a favourite meeting place for competitors after race meetings, right up to 1914, when war clamped down. There was sleeping accommodation for up to ten at the Blue Bird, and people who were staying over for a race meeting after pre-race practising, record-attempt men or just people carrying out routine track testing, would frequently take advantage of this facility.

Unfortunately, this famous Brooklands institution was accidentally burnt to the ground during 1917, when the Flying Ground was under the control of the Royal Flying Corps.

5
1911—AN INDIAN SUMMER

TOWARDS the end of 1910 news began to filter through of some exceptional speed records set up in the United States. When early in February, 1911, the motorcycling press announced that a certain Jake de Rosier had covered 84 miles 135 yd in the hour on his 994 cc Indian—the response was rank disbelief. Most of the Brooklands' coterie considered that this was yet another example of "fast" American stop-watch work. They were in for a shock later in the season, however, when the great Jake first rode at Brooklands prior to competing in the Isle of Man TT Races, on the new "Mountain" circuit.

After the finish of the Winter track repairs, the ACU staged its "Lamp Trials" on Thursday, February 9th, 1911. Long dissatisfied with the quality of the light fittings on standard motor cycles, that body decided to organise a competition which would encourage improvements in such equipment. The event involved two-hours' riding on Brooklands Track with lamps continuously in operation and photometric tests of their lighting efficiency. Marks were awarded on the basis of lighting efficiency *versus* lamp weight, cost, ease of cleaning, facility of generator re-charging if acetylene operated (and most were), absence of rattle, and general quality of the fitting.

Saturday, February 11th, saw Frank McNab make an attempt on the Class C (500 cc) two-hour record riding a 488 cc o.h.v. Trump-JAP. Starting at 12.30 pm he lapped consistently for $1\frac{1}{2}$ hours inside record, until his power began to fall away. A stop to investigate was made. After restarting on a second attempt, he was put out by broken piston rings.

In the meantime Freddie Barnes, the de la Ferte brothers and P. Weatherilt were carrying out speed tests on the Test Hill with their Zenith-Graduas.

First meeting of the year

As with the previous season Bemsee opened the racing ball. For this first 1911 BMCRC meeting, held on Saturday, March 18th, the weather was cold and showery but, surprisingly, the attendance was much greater than at an average club race meeting.

Several interesting new machines were competing, including: the 499 cc o.h.i.v. Rudges of Victor Surridge and C. S. Burney; and the 295 cc Martin-Zedel, of Harry Martin, which was fitted with a small tubular steel seat shaped like a horizontal pram wheel—more light than comfortable.

The first event was the All-Comers' Penalty Handicap. To decide the handicap start times, a trial scratch race was first run off over the same distance, namely three laps. This gave Oliver Godfrey an easy win on his new 994 cc Indian. This machine was one of the latest pattern and fitted with an engine-driven oil pump. In the handicap Godfrey was, naturally, enough, at scratch.

Victor Surridge finished first on his Rudge, followed by Angus Maitland and A. Baker White (488 Trump-JAPs). All three riders were disqualified for beating their trial performances by more than 5 sec per lap and the declared official result was as follows:

ALL-COMERS' PENALTY HANDICAP (up to 1000 cc) over 3 laps. Fork start and finish.

		H'cap start	
1.	S. T. Tessier (580 BAT-JAP)	1 min 45 sec	51.49 mph
2.	J. H. Slaughter (499 LMC)	2 min 51 sec	
3.	O. C. Godfrey (994 Indian)	scratch	

The use of an engine-driven oil pump on the Indian removed the necessity for continually taking a hand off the handlebars to operate a tank-mounted hand pump, as was the case with most British machines. Some Indian machines did retain a hand pump, however, in case of mechanical pump failure or the need of additional lubricant.

Incidentally two interesting entries in the last race were those of E. B. Ware (490 Norton) and Jack Holroyd (241 Motosacoche).

The 1911 Isle of Man TT Races had been switched to the longer and more arduous Snaefell Mountain Course, which has been used ever since. The old classes were scrapped and it was decided to run

Junior and Senior Races instead. In the Junior Races single-cylinder machines of up to 300 cc were to compete with twins up to 340 cc (twins were still considered unreliable compared with the single-cylinders). In the Senior Race singles were to have a maximum capacity of 500 cc and twins 585 cc.

With this in mind, at this meeting the BMCRC had decided to stage the first of a series of similarly capacitied Junior and Senior One-Hour Races. The Junior One-Hour Brooklands' TT Race was the next on the programme. In this Bert Colver (290 Matchless-JAP single) moved into the lead on the first lap, but was soon displaced by Harry Martin (295 Martin-Zedel single) who stayed ahead for the next two laps. Driving-belt slip eventually pushed Martin back to third place, behind Freddie Barnes (299 Zenith-Gradua-JAP single), until on the ninth round Barnes stopped with a broken oil pipe. He restarted but retired on the thirteenth lap with bad misfiring.

Bert Colver came in an easy winner at the end of the hour, a lap ahead of Harry Martin, who had a sick engine. Third was Cyril Patteson, who lapped consistently throughout on his o.h.i.v. V-twin 340 cc Moto Rêve. Results:

JUNIOR ONE-HOUR BROOKLANDS' TT RACE (up to 300 cc singles and up to 340 cc twins) from a Fork start.

		Distance covered
1.	H. V. Colver (290 Matchless-JAP)	48 miles 1568 yd
2.	H. Martin (295 Martin-Zedel)	46 miles 1336 yd
3.	C. Patteson (340 Moto Rêve)	39 miles 1143 yd

In the Senior One-Hour Brooklands' TT Race all made a good start, Charlie Collier (580 Matchless-JAP twin) establishing a lead from the outset. Sidney Tessier (580 BAT-JAP twin), Lieut. R. N. Stewart and the burly Frank McNab (488 Trump-JAPs), Jack Haswell (499 Triumph)—an amateur rider from Crick near Rugby, Oliver Godfrey (this time on his 497 cc Indian) and Victor Surridge (499 Rudge), followed in that order.

Charlie kept first place until the seventeenth lap. Then, tyre trouble put him out, giving the race to Tessier. McNab kept well to the fore, but in the last few seconds of the hour his new engine seized and he was forced to retire.

The final result was:

SENIOR ONE-HOUR BROOKLANDS' TT RACE (up to 500 cc singles and up to 585 cc twins) from a Fork start.

		Distance covered
1.	S. T. Tessier (580 BAT-JAP)	55 miles 874 yd
2.	V. J. Surridge (499 Rudge)	55 miles 496 yd
3.	J. R. Haswell (499 Triumph)	54 miles 587 yd

This meeting was the first at which the new Rudges had appeared, and most successfully too. Surridge's machine, which retained the standard pattern Rudge spring forks showed much better handling characteristics than that of C. S. Burney, which had been converted to rigid forks. It was rumoured that the Triumph Company had perfected a new exhaust valve which did not stretch. Certainly, Haswell's Triumph performed well despite suffering driving-belt slip in the the later laps. Most of the Triumph riders had given up the practice of using felt pads instead of fork springs. It was found that they threw too severe a strain on to the steering heads of their machines over the worst of the bumps around the track. Instead, they used fork springs which were much stronger than the standard ones and wide dropped handlebars, to compensate for any loss of steering control with the flip-flop action of the Triumph front fork.

The BARC opening meeting

Attendance was good despite intermittent snow and hail, during the afternoon of the BARC's opening race meeting at Brooklands on Saturday, March 24th.

The first of the motor cycle events, the Third 70-mph Handicap, had Oliver Godfrey (994 Indian) and Charlie Collier (976 Matchless-JAP) as joint scratch men. They finished in that order well ahead of the field.

70-MPH HANDICAP over 8½ miles.
Fork start and Long finish.

		H'cap start	
1.	O. C. Godfrey (994 Indian)	scratch	70 mph
2.	C. R. Collier (976 Matchless-JAP)	scratch	
3.	H. D. Shaw (994 Indian)	30 sec	

The seventh event on the race card was also a motor cycle affair, the First 65-mph Handicap, for all classes of machine which had not been observed to exceed 65 mph for a flying-start lap of Brooklands' Track. A two-lapper, it attracted twenty-seven entries. Again the start was at the Fork.

All but two got away well. The order of the leading men as they passed the Fork at the end of their first lap was: Freddie Barnes (488 Zenith-Gradua-JAP), D. C. Bolton (499 Triumph), and E. B. Ware (490 Norton). Ware dropped out with unspecified machine trouble and Barnes won by about thirty yards.

65-MPH HANDICAP over $5\frac{3}{4}$ miles.
Fork start and Long finish.

		H'cap start	
1.	F. W. Barnes (488 Zenith-Gradua-JAP)	50 sec	$55\frac{1}{2}$ mph
2.	D. C. Bolton (499 Triumph)	50 sec	
3.	H. Shanks jun. (340 Kingfisher-JAP)	1 min 4 sec	

Surridge finished fourth, Godfrey fifth and V. Wadham (482 Zenith-Gradua-JAP) sixth.

Freddie Barnes' win, made in a hailstorm, certainly proved the worth of his variable gear: the ability to lower it when battling against the northerly gale and raise it when it blew in his favour, accounted in no small measure for his win.

This BARC meeting also saw a BSA entered for the first time, but the rider, Kenneth Holden, did not turn up to ride.

Track testing

During the first two weeks of April Billy Newsome, the Triumph TT rider, was busy circulating the track testing the new Triumph exhaust valve. He was joined early in the second week by G. E. Stanley, who was due to make an attempt on the Class C (500 cc) hour record. Stanley, formerly a Premier rider, had joined the Singer Motor Company and was riding a 499 cc s.v. model of that make.

The evening of Thursday, April 13th, saw Stanley make his bid. Starting at 4.30 pm he began reeling off laps at over 61mph, but disaster in the shape of a broken valve stopped him on the tenth lap.

He restarted an hour later, but valve lengthening and a petrol pipe breakage forced an abandonment of the attempt.

Racing at Easter

Something of a cloud was cast over the BARC Easter meeting on Bank Holiday Monday, April 17th. During one of the car events G. Williamson (27.3 hp Benz) failed to stop at the Long Finishing Line, and ran straight up over the top of the Members' Banking. His car was smashed to pieces and he was seriously hurt.

This was the first of many similar incidents which eventually led, albeit many years later, to the abandonment of the Long Finish as being too dangerous.

The first of the two motor cycle races was run over $5\frac{3}{4}$ miles and was limited to machines whose observed lap speeds were under 65 mph. Dr Gaskell, who finished first by the length of the Finishing Straight, was disqualified for starting too early. Result:

65-MPH HANDICAP over $5\frac{3}{4}$ miles.
Fork start and Long finish.

		H'cap start	
1.	V. Wilberforce (297 NLG-JAP)	1 min 50 sec	$53\frac{1}{2}$ mph
2.	H. A. Collier (580 Matchless-JAP)	16 sec	
3.	F. A. McNab (488 Trump-JAP)	48 sec	

McNab, who came in third, had returned to using a side-valve engine.

The 70-mph Handicap over three laps provided an exciting tussle between Charlie Collier (976 Matchless-JAP), with a 3-sec start, and Oliver Godfrey (994 Indian) the scratch man. The winner, however, proved to be Harry Collier (580 Matchless-JAP), Charlie's brother, who was closely followed in by Frank McNab. Charlie Collier narrowly beat Godfrey for third place:

70-MPH HANDICAP over $8\frac{1}{2}$ miles.
Fork start and Long finish.

		H'cap start	
1.	H. A. Collier (580 Matchless-JAP)	1 min 15 sec	65.5 mph
2.	F. A. McNab (488 Trump-JAP)	2 min 3 sec	
3.	C. R. Collier (976 Matchless-JAP)	3 sec	

After the racing the crowds of spectators were entertained by a display of flying.

1911—AN INDIAN SUMMER

The 500 cc hour record goes

At its Second Monthly Meeting of the year on Wednesday, April 26th, the BMCRC again staged Junior and Senior One-Hour Races. In the Senior Race, Billy Newsome (499 Triumph) was successful in gaining Class C (500 cc) one-hour record despite finishing only second.

The first event, the Second Junior One-Hour Brooklands' TT Race, was, as before, for single-cylinder machines up to 300 cc and twins up to 340 cc. The regulations were those relating, as with the Senior, to the Isle of Man races to be held in June. Also all machines had to be efficiently silenced, as complaints were increasing from local residents on the score of noise.

There were only four entries—all single-cylinders—and of these Harry Martin (295 Martin-Zedel) was a non-starter, having injured a hand in a spill during practice the previous day.

At the end of the first lap Victor Wilberforce (297 NLG-JAP) and Freddie Barnes (297 Zenith-Gradua-JAP) ran almost neck-and-neck, while F. P. Johnson (297 Matchless-JAP), who appeared to be pulling too high a gear, lay third. The lead changed continually, until on lap 55 Wilberforce dropped out with a valve rocker pin adrift. The two remaining runners kept their order to the end.

JUNIOR ONE-HOUR BROOKLANDS' TT RACE
(up to 300 cc singles and up to 340 cc twins). Fork start.

		Distance covered
1.	F. W. Barnes (297 Zenith-Gradua-JAP)	48 miles 746 yd
2.	F. P. Johnson (297 Matchless-JAP)	46 miles 1317 yd

After the second event of the afternoon, a series of four-lap relay races for two-man teams, won by Frank McNab (488 Trump-JAP) and Harry Collier (976 Matchless-JAP), came the second of the One-Hour Brooklands' TT Races. This was the Senior Race for singles up to 500 cc and twins up to 585 cc. There were nineteen starters.

In this race the new "90-bore" JAP engine was seen for the first time. This was the $90 \times 77\frac{1}{2}$ mm bore and stroke power unit of Harry Collier's single-cylinder Matchless entry. His brother Charlie was mounted on a twin-cylinder 580 cc (76×76 mm) model, which, running very consistently, gave him victory by over a lap.

Victor Surridge (499 Rudge) made a strong fight of it for second place on his single-geared machine, the newly-designed Multi-Gear being reserved for the Isle of Man race. He lost too much time after a stop for petrol, however, to be able to get back amongst the leaders before the end of the race. G. E. Stanley (499 Singer) who was second at one stage, stopped with valve trouble, but restarted to finish fourth.

SENIOR ONE-HOUR BROOKLANDS' TT RACE
(up to 500 cc singles and up to 585 cc twins). Fork start.

		Distance covered
1.	C. R. Collier (580 Matchless-JAP)	63 miles 735 yd*
2.	W. F. Newsome (499 Triumph)	59 miles 1478 yd*
3.	C. S. Burney (499 Rudge)	57 miles 869 yd*

(*New class records).

An interesting finisher was C. Gordon Bell (490 Norton), who was eighth with a distance of 49 miles 771 yd in the hour. Charlie Collier's distance was a new Class D (750 cc solo) record. Harry's new 90-bore engine ran consistently, but was clearly too new yet for sustained high-speed work.

Six-hour record broken

The following Saturday morning saw an attempt by Lieut. R. N. Stewart (488 Trump-JAP) on the Class C (500 cc) six-hour record. The weather was appalling, the wind blowing strongly from the south-west acompanied by heavy rain and hail squalls. This rendered the track almost a sheet of water at times.

At the start Stewart managed to average 50 to 52 mph until the rain fell, when he had to shorten his driving belt. A puncture and stops for petrol, and further belt adjustments, followed at intervals, the rider suffering increasingly from wet and the bitter cold. He kept going, though, despite all. Apart from a stop on lap 76 of eight minutes to repair a broken petrol pipe, Stewart's engine functioned reliably and at the end of the sixth hour he was relieved to learn that he had covered some 254 miles 37 yd—a new record. This with a side-valve motor and a single-geared belt drive, which did not help matters.

Although racing and records were attracting most of the attention, routine testing was still going on at Brooklands. On Tuesday, May 9th, for example, Roy Walker (292 New Hudson), his machine fitted with a three-speed gear and clutch, became the first rider of a touring lightweight of under 350 cc to climb successfully the Test Hill from a standing start.

High speeds from lightweights

Two motor cycle events figured on the BARC race card at the club's mid-week meeting on May 10th, and both were won by small capacity machines.

Twenty-six starters turned out for the first motor cycle race, the second event on the programme. This was a Short Handicap over two laps with a Fork start and Long Finish, as in previous such events. Charlie Collier was mounted on a smart red-enamelled 976 cc Matchless-JAP at scratch, with Oliver Godfrey on his red 994 cc Indian. The limit men were D. C. Bolton (344 Forward) and Harry Martin (270 Martin-JAP). Several machines were slow in picking up speed at the start.

Godfrey got away well on the Indian, but Charlie Collier's machine proved a bit sluggish off the line on the high gear it was pulling. At the end of the first lap, Harry Martin was half-a-mile ahead of the field, which was led by Dr Gaskell (499 Triumph).

The finish was something of a procession, Harry winning by over a quarter-of-a-mile.

SHORT MOTOR CYCLE HANDICAP (up to 1000 cc) over 5¾ miles. Fork start and Long finish.

		H'cap start	
1.	H. Martin (270 Martin-JAP)	2 min 14 sec	53 mph
2.	Dr Gaskell (499 Triumph)	1 min 42 sec	
3.	V. J. Surridge (499 Rudge)	58 sec	

The next three finishers were H. D. Shaw (994 Indian), A. Baker White (488 Trump-JAP) and P. Y. Harkness (499 Triumph). Harry's flying lap was covered at 56.53 mph.

Ray Abbott (Bradbury) had driving-belt trouble and E. B. Ware (490 Norton) retired with a broken petrol pipe. Freddie Barnes, who had been unable to compete due to a recent road accident, was limping disconsolately around the paddock at this meeting.

The other race for motor cycles, the Long Handicap, over three laps, saw G. E. Stanley (499 Singer) make a good getaway, as did also scratch man Charlie Collier (976 Matchless-JAP). The other scratch man, Oliver Godfrey (994 Indian), rode the first two-hundred yards with only one cylinder firing before getting going in earnest.

At the end of the first lap, D. C. Bolton (344 Forward) was well ahead of the bunch, which was headed by Jack Haswell (499 Triumph), Gordon Bell (490 Norton) and Dr Gaskell (499 Triumph). Gaskell led at the end of the second round, with W. Chitty (340 Frays-JAP) second and Haswell third. It was a hopeless task for the scratch men though, and the result was an eventual win for Chitty at the fine speed of 57 mph. Results:

LONG MOTOR CYCLE HANDICAP (up to 1000cc) over 8½ miles. Fork start and Long finish.

		H'cap start	
1.	W. D. Chitty (340 Frays-JAP)	2 min 24 sec	57 mph
2.	H. Martin (345 Martin-JAP)	2 min 15 sec	
3.	J. R. Haswell (499 Triumph)	2 min 24 sec	

H. D. Shaw (994 Indian) and A. Baker White (488 Trump-JAP) were once again fourth and fifth respectively, as in the Short Handicap, while the sixth home was Harry Collier (580 Matchless-JAP).

More record attempts

The following Friday, May 12th, saw Victor Surridge out on the track early in the afternoon on his 499 cc Rudge, with Class C (500 cc) records in view. It was an ideal Spring day, with the sun shining and a gentle breeze blowing from the north-west—just the weather, in fact, for record breaking.

The first attempt was on the flying-start kilometre. The Rudge was in good fettle and averaged 65.79 mph to beat Harold Bowen's previous record of 65.027 mph on a BAT-JAP. Through a misunderstanding with the timekeepers Surridge made a second and unnecessary attempt on the kilometre, easing up before reaching the mile post, during what was ostensibly a flying-start mile record attempt. Realising his error, he again attempted the mile, but unwisely returned the wrong way round the track to do so, and collided with a motor car which suddenly appeared from behind the aeroplane sheds.

Fortunately he was not injured, but the front forks of his machine were badly damaged. This led to an hour's delay whilst they were being replaced.

He covered the mile at 66.18 mph to beat by almost 2 mph John Gibson's record on the Triumph. The next thing was an attempt on the hour record, and, armed with a spare Lyso driving belt and a spare petrol pipe wired to his front forks, he started at 5.50 pm. A broken exhaust valve put him out after two laps. He kept circulating the track consistently after a fresh start, at 6.20 pm, with a new valve in place, and was well inside the record up until the twentieth lap, when, with only six minutes to go, his inlet valve cotter disappeared and the spring broke. Nevertheless, Surridge gained the 50-mile record—averaging 58.83 mph.

The engine of his machine, a stripped standard model, was said to produce some 8.5 bhp at a peak engine speed of 2400 rpm.

The following day saw another contender in the "Class C One-Hour Record Stakes" out on the track chasing glory: G. E. Stanley and his 499 cc Singer. The prospect of being the first to accomplish the sixty miles in the hour on a 500 cc machine, proving an ever-increasing attraction to Class C record men.

Valve trouble was also the "Achilles' Heel" in Stanley's attempt. He covered ten laps at an average of 61.05 mph before being forced to give up the attempt. His fastest lap was his fifth at 62.66 mph.

The Third Bemsee Meeting

It had been a habit on the part of some competitors to hide their true speed capabilities, by going deliberately slowly during the preliminary scratch races for deciding handicap starts. To overcome this, at its Third 1911 Monthly Race Meeting on Wednesday, May 17th, the BMCRC decided to run its first event—a handicap—on a knockout basis. First, however, a preliminary scratch race over one lap was held. This gave the following result:

PRELIMINARY SCRATCH RACE over a standing-start one lap. Fork start and finish.

		Speed (mph)
1.	A. J. Luce (580 BAT-JAP)	58.44
2.	V. J. Surridge (499 Rudge)	56.64
3.	S. T. Tessier (580 BAT-JAP)	54.90

In the handicap, pairs of competitors were run off in one-lap heats, with the exception of Victor Surridge and Sidney Tessier who had "byes" to the one-lap semi-finals. These were competed for by pairs of winners from the heats, and were also one-lap races. Then there came the one-lap final between W. L. T. Rhys (499 Triumph) and A. Baker White (488 Trump-JAP), which the former won. Third and fourth places were decided by a one-lap race between the fastest losers: Sidney Tessier and Billy Elce (499 Rudge). The final result was:

KNOCKOUT HANDICAP FINAL over a standing-start one lap. Fork start and finish.

1. W. L. T. Rhys (499 Triumph)　　　　　　　50.13 mph
2. A. B. White (488 Trump-JAP)
3. S. T. Tessier (580 BAT-JAP)

Both White and Rhys suffered broken driving belts in the final.

Next on the programme was the first in the 1911 series of Record Time Trials, over the flying-start kilometre, mile and five miles. Harry Martin (345 Martin-JAP) was unable to go for the five-miles' distance in Class B (350 cc), because his engine cylinder had cracked around the auxiliary exhaust ports shortly after he had covered the flying-start mile.

New records were set in all but Class B. The fastest speeds in each class were as follows:

RECORD TIME TRIALS

Class			Speed (mph) over:		
			fs km	fs ml	fs 5 ml
A	(275 cc)	H. Martin (270 Martin-JAP)	62.54*	62.14*	59.80*
B	(350 cc)	H. Martin (345 Martin-JAP)	63.99	63.07	—
C	(500 cc)	W. F. Newsome (499 Triumph)	66.38*	65.43	63.83
		V. J. Surridge (499 Rudge)	65.46	65.38	65.22*
D	(750 cc)	S. T. Tessier (580 BAT-JAP)	74.74	73.05	69.77*
E	(1000 cc)	O. C. Godfrey (994 Indian)	80.29	80.20	76.65*

(* New class records).

Jack Haswell (499 s.v. Triumph) fitted his machine with dual silencers to comply with the new noise regulations and set up new long-distance records on Tuesday, November 21st, 1911.

Harry Martin (998 Morgan-Martin-JAP) on the line for the start of the first-ever Cyclecar Scratch Race, at the BMCRC's first Brooklands meeting of 1912. He won the event at 57.31 mph.

The ill-fated Arthur Moorhouse (994 Indian), seen after winning Class E of the Hundred-Mile All-Comers' Scratch Race at the BMCRC's first 1912 race meeting. The following month, in the course of an hour race, he became the first motor cyclist to be killed at the track.

Charlie Collier (998 Matchless-JAP), after winning the 1000 cc "Car Challenge" Scratch Race on Saturday, May 11th, 1912, at the BMCRC's Second Monthly Meeting.

The Class E five-mile record had stood since July 14th, 1906, to George Barnes, on an 8 hp Buchet.

At this time a machine was not allowed to hold records in any class other than its own. Thus the 350 cc flying-start record of 68.28 mph by Harry Martin, was some 4 mph higher than Newsome's new 500-cc record over the same distance.

The racing had no great interest for spectators up to this point, but now came the big event of the afternoon: a three-lap scratch race for the Palmer Tyre Company's Silver Cup. It was for machines up to 500-cc and was expected to be keenly contested.

At the end of the first lap, Victor Surridge and Billy Newsome were practically level, and both were credited with a new 500 cc standing-start lap record at 60.62 mph, with W. L. T. Rhys (499 Triumph) third. It was a close tussle and the end of lap two saw Surridge slightly ahead. Rhys still kept third place.

In the last lap Surridge and Newsome had a tremendous struggle; Newsome briefly held the lead, but Surridge soon re-established himself and eventually won. The final result was:

THE PALMER TROPHY SCRATCH RACE (up to 500 cc) over three laps. Fork start and finish.
1. V. J. Surridge (499 Rudge)   63.60 mph
2. W. F. Newsome (499 Triumph)   63.24 mph
3. W. L. T. Rhys (499 Triumph)

Surridge won by only $2\frac{2}{5}$ sec, his second lap being covered at 65.93 mph. The remainder finished in this order: A. Baker White (488 Trump-JAP), A. J. Sproston (499 Rudge), Billy Elce (499 Rudge), T. G. Meeten (488 Meeten-JAP) and B. Roberts (488 BAT-JAP).

Sixty miles in the hour on a five-hundred

The following Saturday, May 20th, saw Bert Yates out on the track breaking Class A (up to 275 cc) records on a 198 cc Humber. He accomplished 39 miles 1615 yd in the hour at the first attempt, on what was reported to be a standard machine.

Victor Surridge was so close to breaking the 500 cc hour record earlier in the month, that ultimate success seemed inevitable if he persisted. On Thursday, May 25th, he decided to have another attempt at 3 pm but then postponed matters for an hour, because of the glare of reflected sunlight from the concrete of the track which he had experienced during a practice lap. Then, when conditions had considerably improved, he got under way.

An experimental exhaust valve had been fitted in his 499 cc Rudge and the breakage of this forced a stop after only five laps. A new valve fitted Victor made a second attempt, but with a standing-start lap at 55 mph and his second at only 58½ mph, the pace was much too slow. Wisely he stopped and the record attempt was restarted.

Victor's third and successful attempt to beat Newsome's record began well. He tried to maintain a record-breaking average but found it difficult to keep his lap speeds consistent.

Between the twentieth and the twenty-first laps a stop was made for oil, and he made up for his slowing-down lap by breaking the Brooklands' 500 cc flying-lap record on his twenty-second circuit, at 66.47 mph. Victor Surridge carried on without incident to cover a record distance of 60 miles 783 yd. Thus he became the first rider of an under 500 cc machine to cover more than sixty miles in the hour.

The machine was a standard 499 cc (85 × 88 mm) single-cylinder o.h.i.v. Rudge-Whitworth, with single-geared direct belt drive, fitted with a Brown and Barlow (B & B) carburetter, Dunlop tyres and magneto ignition. Only the large capacity petrol tank was non-standard as far as external appearances were concerned.

Whit-Monday Racing

At the BARC Whitsun race meeting on Monday, June 5th, the usual two motor cycle races were contested.

In the Short Handicap, over two laps, P. Weatherilt (297 Zenith-Gradua-JAP) led at the end of the first lap, with G. E. Stanley (499 Singer) second and Dr. H. S. Gaskell (499 Triumph) third. Last was a newcomer, Cyril Pullin (964 JAP-Special), whose engine was misfiring badly.

Weatherilt eventually won by a quarter-of-a-mile from the scratch man Oliver Godfrey (994 Indian), who did well to get second place.

SHORT MOTOR CYCLE HANDICAP (up to 1000 cc).

Over two laps. Fork start and Long finish.

		H'cap start	
1.	P. Weatherilt (297 Zenith-Gradua-JAP)	1 min 46 sec	55.90 mph
2.	O. C. Godfrey (994 Indian)	scratch	
3.	F. P. Johnson (658 Matchless-JAP)	38 sec	

Fourth was H. Shanks jun. (340 Kingfisher-JAP), with A. J. Luce (740 BAT-JAP) fifth, and Frank McNab (492 Trump-JAP)—whose machine had one of the latest 90-bore JAP engines—sixth.

The Long Handicap provided G. E. Stanley with the first of what was to be a long succession of wins at Brooklands. Limit man R. J. Bell (257 Moto Rêve) got away well and still led at the end of the first lap, with P. Weatherilt second. The next time past the Fork, Weatherilt led with Stanley second and McNab third. The finish was a close one, with scratch man Godfrey just failing to catch Stanley, who by then led the field.

LONG MOTOR CYCLE HANDICAP (up to 1000 cc).
Over three laps. Fork start and Long finish.

		H'cap start	
1.	G. E. Stanley (499 Singer)	1 min 30 sec	Speed unknown
2.	O. C. Godfrey (994 Indian)	scratch	
3.	P. Weatherilt (297 Zenith-Gradua-JAP)	2 min 15 sec	

Preparing for the Island races

Two days later on Wednesday, June 7th, the Bemsee held its Fourth Monthly Members' Race Meeting of the year. This was eagerly awaited as it included Junior and Senior One-Hour Brooklands' TT Races which could prove a pointer to the results of the Isle of Man TT Races in a few weeks time. Both races complied with the Isle of Man race requirements for 1911, regarding machine specifications.

In the Junior Race, Oliver Godfrey rode a 299 cc Zenith-Gradua-JAP, for the first time. All got away well except G. E. Stanley (295 Singer), who withdrew as his engine refused to fire.

At the end of the first lap, P. Weatherilt (299 Zenith-Gradua-JAP) led, Harry Martin (292 Martin-JAP) lay second, and Bert Colver (334 Enfield twin) and Godfrey followed in close order, while Sam Wright brought up the rear. Weatherilt stayed ahead until lap three, when Harry Martin grabbed the lead and in the fourth lap he rapidly increased it. Colver and Wright dropped further and further behind.

Godfrey was moving up rapidly and on lap five snatched the lead from Martin, never again losing it. His o.h.v. JAP engine ran reliably throughout, and he won easily, setting up a new one-hour record for Class B (350 cc) in the process. All the other riders had retired except for Weatherilt.

JUNIOR ONE-HOUR BROOKLANDS' TT RACE
(up to 300 cc singles and up to 340 cc twins). Fork start.

		Distance covered
1.	O. C. Godfrey (299 Zenith-Gradua-JAP)	54 miles 726 yd
2.	P. Weatherilt (299 Zenith-Gradua-JAP)	52 miles 774 yd

The Senior One-Hour Brooklands' TT Race followed.

All got away smartly, though Victor Surridge (499 Rudge) was the last, First time round G. E. Stanley (499 Singer) led easily, with Victor second and Frank McNab on the 90-bore (492 cc) Trump-JAP third.

Surridge was clearly out to beat his own record and actually led from laps four to nine. Then a broken valve put him out of the running. A. J. Sproston (499 Rudge) retired on the fourth, when the split pin came out of his exhaust camshaft.

By lap ten, Stanley had a firm lead, which he steadily improved upon until the end of the race. But for the fact that his engine occasionally misfired, due to an oily plug, he might well have beaten Surridge's record. As it was, Stanley was only 528 yd short of the record distance.

SENIOR ONE-HOUR BROOKLANDS' TT RACE
(up to 500 cc singles and up to 585 cc twins). Fork start.

		Distance covered
1.	G. E. Stanley (499 Singer)*	60 miles 255 yd
2.	J. R. Haswell (499 Triumph)	57 miles 1500 yd
3.	F. A. McNab (492 Trump-JAP)	57 miles 309 yd

(*Set up a new Class C 50-mile record at 61.70 mph).

Stanley's fastest lap was set up at 63.61 mph.

The last event of the day's programme was the Second Eliminating Handicap. This was a knockout competition on the lines of that held at the Third Members' Race Meeting. The result was a win for Sidney Tessier.

KNOCKOUT HANDICAP FINAL over a
standing-start one lap. Fork start and finish.

1.	S. T. Tessier (580 BAT-JAP)	Speed unknown
2.	A. J. Luce (738 BAT-JAP)	
3.	A. B. White (488 Trump-JAP)	

1911—AN INDIAN SUMMER

In the evening of the following day, Thursday, the Rudge-Whitworth Company gave a dinner party at the Savoy Hotel, London, in honour of Victor Surridge's achievement of being the first man to accomplish sixty miles in the hour on a "500".

The next day at Brooklands Charlie Franklin, riding a 254 cc single-cylinder Moto Rêve, broke the Class A (275 cc) six-hour record, averaging 26.60 mph for the distance covered. His mount was of standard pattern, except that he used racing handlebars and a larger-than-usual petrol tank.

The Annual ACU Race Meeting

Fine weather but a brisk breeze greeted competitors and spectators arriving at Brooklands, for the Second Annual ACU Race Meeting on Saturday, June 10th.

The first event, as with the 1910 meeting, was the one-lap scratch race for the *Automotor Journal* Challenge Cup, for machines with engines not exceeding 345 cc. P. Weatherilt (297 Zenith-Gradua-JAP) made a good start, but was passed by the trophy holder, Harry Martin, about a quarter-of-a-mile from the finishing line.

OPEN SCRATCH RACE FOR THE "AUTOMOTOR JOURNAL" CHALLENGE CUP over one lap, with a Fork start and finish.

1. H. Martin (344 Martin-JAP)   57.21 mph
2. P. Weatherilt (297 Zenith-Gradua-JAP)
3. W. D. Chitty (344 Frays-JAP)

The second man, Weatherilt, averaged 57.03 mph, and finished only four-fifths of a second behind Harry.

In the open scratch race for the *Motor Car Journal* Challenge Cup, Matchless machines did well. The event was over four laps, for any type of machine up to 1000 cc. Charlie Collier was riding a 986 cc 90-bore twin-cylinder Matchless-JAP fitted with an oil pump controlled by Bowden cable from the handlebars. He led easily at the end of the first lap, keeping this position to the end of the race. In fact he led so easily, that he even had time to look behind him in the third lap to see if he was threatened. Charlie was followed in by Charlie Franklin (994 Indian)—the Irish Champion, A. J. Luce (733 BAT-JAP) and A. J. Sproston (499 Rudge); he won by about 500 yd.

OPEN SCRATCH RACE FOR THE "MOTOR CAR JOURNAL" CHALLENGE CUP over 4 laps. Fork start and finish.

		Speed (mph)
1.	C. R. Collier (986 Matchless-JAP)	68.22
2.	C. B. Franklin (994 Indian)	65.83
3.	A. J. Luce (733 BAT-JAP)	57.30

For the first time in 1911, a passenger vehicle race was run and a scratch event at that. This was for machines up to 1000 cc over two laps. Trailers were banned.

There were only three starters and all were sidecar outfits. The runners were: J. T. ("Bizzy") Bashall (964 BAT-JAP s/car), Billy Wells (994 Indian s/car) and E. Webster (976 Matchless-JAP s/car). Of these, the only single-geared outfit—Bizzy Bashall's—led at the end of the first lap, followed closely by that of Billy Wells, while Webster brought up the rear. The positions remained unchanged on lap two and Bizzy won by about a hundred yards.

SIDECAR SCRATCH RACE (up to 1000 cc s/car) over two laps. Fork start and finish.
1. J. T. Bashall (964 BAT-JAP s/car)   48.44 mph
2. W. H. Wells (994 Indian s/car)
3. E. Webster (976 Matchless-JAP s/car)

Only three out of eight entries turned out for the International Open Scratch Race over 50 kilometres, despite the excellent prize money of £10 for a first, £3 for a second and £1 for a third. An unfortunate incident prior to this event put Oliver Godfrey (994 Indian) out of the race. Apparently, some ill-disposed person had sabotaged his engine by inserting a broken-off piece of workshop file into one of the auxiliary exhaust ports of his engine. This led to a broken piston on starting up.

The three starters: Charlie Franklin (994 Indian), Harry Collier (976 Matchless-JAP) and A. J. Sproston (499 Rudge), pushed off in the Railway Straight and finished at the Fork. At the end of the first lap the riders were in the previously mentioned order. In the next, Harry Collier led and Sproston withdrew. All that happened for the remainder of the race was that Harry gradually increased his lead. When at the end of the eleventh lap, he was over two miles ahead of Franklin.

INTERNATIONAL SCRATCH RACE (up to 1000 cc) over 50 km. Railway Straight start and Fork finish.
1. H. A. Collier (976 Matchless-JAP) ENGLAND 67.92 mph
2. C. B. Franklin (994 Indian) IRELAND 63.54 mph

According to Oliver Godfrey, one of his team mates in the 1911 Isle of Man TT Race, it was Franklin who had inadvertently discovered the socalled "squish" effect, whereby combustion turbulence is promoted, resulting in an increase in power. Apparently, in an attempt to raise the compression ratio of his o.h.i.v. engine, he had welded a lump of metal on to the underside of his cylinder head above the piston, and produced a pre-Ricardo "Ricardo-type" combustion space. This antedated the pioneer work of Sir Harry Ricardo on the effects of combustion, by almost ten years.

A week prior to this race meeting Jake de Rosier had arrived from the United States with Oscar Hedström, the designer of Indian Motor Cycles for the Hendee Manufacturing Company. Hedström was over here to look after the Indian entries in the Isle of Man TT Races. Jake, who was due to ride in The Island, was a spectator at this meeting, and was down in the race programme to attempt the Class E (1000 cc) five-mile record. This announcement was apparently unauthorised as Jake had no machine of his own available. Instead, he gave a demonstration run on Franklin's Indian during the tea interval, covering a lap at 64 mph.

The last event was the One-Hour Scratch Race for *The Motor Cycle* Challenge Cup (held by W. D. Chitty) for single-cylinder machines up to 500 cc and multis up to 585 cc conforming to Isle of Man TT regulations. Some of the entrants had mudguards fitted and refrained from competing for fear of subsequent disqualification. There was some misunderstanding on this point.

The race was an interesting one. At the end of the first lap Charlie Collier (580 Matchless-JAP) led, with G. E. Stanley (499 Singer) and Harry Collier (580 Matchless-JAP) almost neck-and-neck close behind. In the next lap Charlie Collier increased his lead, while his brother lapped Sidney Tessier (580 BAT-JAP) after pushing Stanley into third spot. Charlie increased his lead still further on lap three. On the fourth, Billy Elce (499 Rudge) retired through engine overheating. In the next round Percy Butler (582 DOT-JAP), whose engine had been misfiring, withdrew.

Harry Collier withdrew in the seventh lap with driving belt trouble, leaving Stanley in second place and Frank McNab (492 Trump-JAP) third. Meanwhile Jack Haswell (499 Triumph) and A. Baker White (492 Trump-JAP) fought for fourth place.

By the fifteenth lap Charlie Collier was three-quarters of a lap ahead and had lapped the third man, McNab, who was also running well, and who for some time afterwards followed in Charlie's slipstream.

The next lap saw the disappearance of Baker White (492 Trump-JAP) with valve trouble and the only runners left were: Charlie Collier who was about to lap Stanley, and McNab and W. O. Oldman (492 Zenith-Gradua-JAP), who were both nearly two laps behind. Stanley, who had been running well inside the hour record all the time, now began to lose ground, and left the honours of the day to Charlie Collier and Frank McNab.

ONE-HOUR FOR "THE MOTOR CYCLE" CHALLENGE CUP (up to 500 cc singles and up to 585 cc multis). Fork start.

		Distance covered
1.	C. R. Collier (580 Matchless-JAP)	64 miles 430 yd*
2.	F. A. McNab (492 Trump-JAP)	60 miles 640 yd
3.	G. E. Stanley (499 Singer)	59 miles 1386 yd

(*New Class D record).

Charlie Collier's winning machine was a TT model fitted with an expanding-pulley variable gear.

A colourful car meeting

One of the most colourful race meetings ever staged at Brooklands was that organised by the BARC on Saturday, June 17th, 1911. Shortly after 2.00 pm, several hundred richly-attired notables from the Far East, in England for George V's coronation, arrived at the track.

There was only one motor cycle race in this otherwise all-car meeting: the two-lap Third Short Motor Cycle Race—a handicap. At the end of the first lap, the order of the first three was: H. Shanks jun. (340 Kingfisher-JAP), A. Baker White (488 Trump-JAP) and then Capt. P. Y. Harkness (499 Triumph). Frank McNab (492 Trump-JAP), who lay fourth, gobbled up the places ahead of him to finish first, while Baker White and Victor Surridge (499 Rudge) gained second and third places respectively. The order of the remaining finishers was: Oliver Godfrey (994 Indian), P. Schmidt (796 NSU), J. Harrison Watson (499 Rudge), Jack Haswell (499 Triumph), J. Forgan-Potts (639 Indian), W. Johnson (331 Buchet), Capt. P. Y. Harkness, M. L. Ainslie (488 Zenith-Gradua-JAP) and A. J. Luce (740 BAT-JAP). Shanks retired. Result:

SHORT MOTOR CYCLE HANDICAP (up to 1000 cc) over two laps. Fork start and Long finish.

		H'cap start	
1.	F. A. McNab (492 Trump-JAP)	1 min 12 sec	58¾ mph
2.	A. B. White (492 Trump-JAP)	1 min 26 sec	
3.	V. J. Surridge (499 Rudge)	50 sec	

There was a strong wind blowing, which made the bulky McNab's task more difficult, but he won by three machine lengths from his team mate. Scratch man Godfrey was travelling at well over 80 mph down the Finishing Straight, but could only manage fourth place.

It had been noticed that some riders at previous meetings, had been travelling well-inside the 10-ft line and thereby completing a shorter lap distance. Officials observed the various riders at this meeting, and their particular course, to establish whether or not this was a widespread practice, and whether or not the lap distance for official race speed calculations should be taken in closer to the inside perimeter of the track.

It was found that the contrary was the case and the 10-ft line was retained. In fact, as some of the faster men remarked, around the Members' Banking it was physically impossible to ride anywhere near the 10-ft line at speed—the 20- or 30-ft lines up the banking being more appropriate.

Triumph and tragedy

Jake de Rosier had not just come over to England for the Isle of Man TT Races, but also for a series of match races at Brooklands against Charlie Collier. Matters had been agreed upon and the two riders were to compete for £130 in prize money. The races were scheduled for the next BMCRC race meeting at Brooklands, shortly after their return from the Isle of Man.

The last weeks of June saw most of the Brooklands' "regulars" practising over in the Island. There were exceptions, however, and on Wednesday June 21st following the June BARC meeting, Stanley (499 Singer) was out on the track attempting the Class C (500 cc) 50-mile record held by Surridge. This he successfully demolished with a time of 48 min 37 sec (an average speed of 61.7 mph).

The evening did not exactly favour record breaking, as a strong wind was blowing down the Railway Straight, and it was not until the eighth lap that Stanley got inside the average needed for the record. Sparking-plug trouble, however, took him outside it on the next. Gradually improving he was inside record again at the thirteenth lap and continued, to beat the 50-mile time.

June ended on rather a sad note for Brooklands' habitués, with the news of the death in practice in the Isle of Man, of the 500-cc hour record holder—Victor Surridge.

Jake shows his hand

Beautiful weather, at times unbearably hot, especially at the main spectator vantage point of the shadeless Fork enclosure, favoured the MCC's Third Annual Race Meeting at Brooklands on Saturday, July 8th. A large crowd of spectators had turned up, the principal attraction being Jake de Rosier's world record attempts later in the day.

The first two events on the race card were for touring machines. Both were over three laps and were handicaps. The first of these was for up to 560 cc machines and was won by E. A. Colliver (3½ hp Zenith-Gradua-JAP) at 50.69 mph. A. W. Brittain (499 Rudge) who ran into second place, was disqualified for not using mudguards. The second touring event was for machines of from 400 to 1000 cc. There was only two starters, C. Percival (6 hp Zenith-Gradua-JAP) winning by three-hundred yards after a good race. He averaged 45.92 mph.

The next race, for single-cylinder machines not exceeding 560 cc, was over three laps and was open to any member of the Motor Cycling Club (MCC). Frank McNab (492 Trump-JAP) looked like an easy winner in the early stages, but towards the end of the last lap his belt rim picked up a stone and his driving belt jumped off, putting paid to his chances. This gave the race to A. Baker White on a similar machine of 488 cc. Like all other events at this meeting, this race had a start and finish at the Fork.

The fifth race on the programme was intended to be an Oxford versus Cambridge match race, but unfortunately no Oxonians were present. A two-lap scrap was therefore staged between a dozen Cambridge men. This scratch race was won by A. E. Sheppard at 52.60 mph.

Sidney Tessier (580 BAT-JAP) was scratch man in the solo handicap over four laps, for MCC members riding machines in the 400-1000 cc category. He easily beat J. P. Le Grand (580 Rex) and V. Olsson (986 Oxted-JAP), the only other starters, to win at the very fine average of 74 mph.

The ten-lap MCC Championship for the "Harry Smith" Gold Challenge Cup, open to ordinary touring machines, attracted twenty-two starters.

B. M. Marians ($2\frac{1}{4}$ hp P & M), Oliver De Lissa and Jack Holroyd (both on $2\frac{1}{2}$ hp Motosacoches) were given a generous start, and went a considerable distance before the bulk of the field had even started. At the end of lap one, De Lissa was just leading Marians, but a lap later both Motosacoches had dropped out of the race.

N. D. Slatter (2 hp Alcyon) went very well, but the lap-and-a-half that he conceded to Marians was more than he could pick up. Fifteen minutes after the limit men had departed, a large bunch of single-cylinder machines were sent off. Of these A. W. Brittain (499 Rudge) was easily the fastest. The scratch man, Arthur Moorhouse (994 Indian), who was giving some minutes' start to Sidney Tessier (580 BAT-JAP), got into his stride immediately and was soon overhauling places galore. He finished an easy winner and was able to ease off considerably towards the end. Result:

MCC CLUB CHAMPIONSHIP FOR "HARRY SMITH" CUP. A handicap over 10 laps. Fork start and finish.

1. A. Moorhouse (994 Indian)   scratch   59.3 mph
2. B. M. Marians ($2\frac{1}{4}$ hp P & M)   19 min 30 sec
3. L. A. Baddeley ($3\frac{1}{4}$ hp Brown)   5 min 40 sec

Brittain ran into third place, but was again disqualified, this time on a technical point. Breakdowns were extremely common and barely half the competitors who had started completed the distance.

After the racing, some gymkhana events were staged. Then as a finale shortly after 6.00 pm, Jake de Rosier came out on his 994 cc chain-driven track-racing Indian, which he had brought over specially from the USA for his match races with Charlie Collier. He was to make an attempt at short-distance records in Class E (1000 cc). In this he was successful with the following speeds:

        fs 1 km   85.32 mph
        fs 1 mile   87.38 mph
        fs 5 miles   80.72 mph

All three performances counted as world records and the one-mile speed beat Henri Cissac's long-standing record.

Only the bare functional necessities found a place on Jake's machine. It had a 994 cc (82.5 × 92 mm) o.h.i.v. engine with non-adjustable tappets and auxiliary exhaust ports drilled in the cylinder walls. All touring accessories had been removed and the carburetter was completly devoid of throttle control. The only concession to comfort was the use of the latest pattern leaf-sprung Indian front fork. The exhaust pipes were only three-inches long and unsilenced. Final drive, as with all Indians at that time, was by chain, and a mechanically-driven oil pump was fitted, with an oil-tank-mounted hand pump for emergencies.

Battle of the champions

At the BMCRC's Fifth Monthly Race Meeting of 1911 on Saturday, July 15th, the much-heralded Collier-de Rosier match races were held. Three races were scheduled over two, five and ten laps, the overall winner to receive the purse of £130 put up for the competition.

Large crowds had gathered to witness what promised to be a historic Brooklands meeting. The weather was ideal for racing—fine but cool with little wind. As the sun was hidden by cloud there would be little glare from the track concrete: a blessing for riders and spectators alike.

Excitement became intense at 3.00 pm approached and the two great rivals appeared for the first of their match races.

Jake had fitted a 2.64-to-1 gear on his Indian and a new six-ply treaded American "Blue Streak" back tyre. He had a four-ply one of the same make on the front. Both tyres were of 28 × 2 in. Apart from these points, and the addition of wider handlebars and a pair of knee grips, to help handling, his machine remained unchanged since its previous outing.

Charlie Collier's red Matchless was fitted with a 998 cc (90 × 78.4 mm) o.h.v. JAP engine. It had no auxiliary exhaust ports and its two-foot long exhaust pipes had empty silencer shells at their ends. Its two cylinders were fed from an Amac carburetter via a T-junction manifold. In contrast to the Indian, final drive was by belt. Hutchinson 26 × 2¼ in tyres were used, front and rear, and a standard Matchless sprung fork was fitted.

Both machines used magneto ignition and ran on petrol for these races.

The riders' dress differed as much as their machines. De Rosier wore tight-fitting brown leathers and a helmet of a type similar to that used in modern cycle track-racing. Collier on the other hand wore riding breeches, a white pullover and a leather flying-helmet.

At the start, Harry Collier wheeled his brother's machine down past the Fork, to where the bridge crossed the River Wey. Sydney Garrett, a well-known Brooklands' rider of the time who was acting as host to Jake while he was in this country, did likewise with the Indian. Jake and Charlie walked down chatting from the paddock.

The procedure with all three match races, was to have a rolling start across the line at the Fork, abreast of the official track car. Standing in the back of this, Ebbie Ebblewhite, armed with a red flag, acted as the starter.

In this first two-lap race both machines were over the starting line together, with Charlie just a shade ahead. He appeared to be pulling a lower gear than Jake, for, climbing the Members' Banking, he had started to establish a few lengths lead. By the middle of the Railway Straight they were almost level again. Charlie, however, had a one-and-a-half lengths lead on passing the Fork.

It was clear that the Indian had speed in hand, for whereas Charlie was lying flat along his tank, Jake only needed to adopt a semi-crouch to keep up with him.

Again, coming under the Members' Bridge, Charlie was several lengths in front, but the American again drew level after half the length of the Railway Straight had been covered. He was introducing a new art to Brooklands' habitués—that of slipstreaming. After passing the Byfleet aeroplane sheds, the two machines seemed to spectators at the Fork to merge into one. But hopes for an English win were dashed when people saw that Charlie's white jersey was acting as a background to the crouching leather-clad Jake. They flashed over the line, with de Rosier winning by about a length, after one of the most exciting races ever witnessed at Brooklands. Result:

FIRST COLLIER-DE ROSIER MATCH RACE (5.43 miles). Rolling start at the Fork and a Fork finish.

		Speed (mph)
1.	J. de Rosier (994 Indian)	80.59
2.	C. R. Collier (998 Matchless-JAP)	80.53

A fifth-of-a-second separated the two men at the finish. Jake's laps were covered at 78.80 mph and 82.49 mph respectively.

The second race on the programme was a ten-lap open scratch event for up to 500 cc machines. This brought out six starters.

W. O. Oldman (493 Zenith-Gradua-JAP) was quickest away and, thanks to his variable gear, led the field easily until the Railway Straight, when G. E. Stanley (499 Singer), who was travelling well, got in front. He was followed by Frank McNab and A. Baker White (493 Trump-JAPs). At the end of the first lap Stanley led McNab by fifty yards, with Baker White third by a similar distance.

The positions were the same at the end of lap three, except for the third place which had been re-taken by Oldman, Baker White having lengthened an exhaust valve. This was the order at the end of the race, by which time the lead held by Stanley had increased to some one-hundred and twenty yards.

TEN-LAP SCRATCH RACE (up to 500 cc) over 27 miles. Fork start and finish.

		Speed (mph)
1.	G. E. Stanley (499 Singer)	60.31
2.	F. A. McNab (493 Trump-JAP)	60.05
3.	W. O. Oldman (493 Zenith-Gradua-JAP)	56.38

Now followed the second race in the Collier-de Rosier match series, this time over five laps or 13.6 miles. Once again Charlie lost his initial lead and the end of lap one found Jake hanging on to his rear wheel. The same story was repeated on lap two. In the middle of lap three a tremendous cry went up from the spectators, when they saw that Jake had slowed. Charlie had flashed out of sight behind the Byfleet aeroplane sheds, before his rival had completed the length of the Railway Straight! Continuing, Charlie completed the remaining two laps and crossed the line the winner. But what had happened to Jake?

Shortly after Charlie had finished, Jake motored in on a tyre-less front rim, the remains of his front cover dangling from the wheel hub. When the crowd realised what had happened, they gave Jake a great ovation. Apparently, when flat out on the Railway Straight, a small stone had pierced his front tyre and rapidly deflated it. With great skill he managed to keep his machine on an even keel, and motor in, to the pits minus front tyre on a badly bent rim. Result:

SECOND COLLIER-DE ROSIER MATCH RACE (13.59 miles). Rolling start at the Fork and Fork finish.

		Speed (mph)
1.	C. R. Collier (998 Matchless-JAP)	79.92
2.	J. de Rosier (994 Indian)	—

The All-Comers' Open Handicap which followed attracted nineteen starters and was over five laps. Oliver Godfrey (994 Indian) scratch man in this race, was clearly in winning form and was soon overhauling all-and-sundry. He took a different line to most riders when coming down past the Fork, as he cut across very close, literally under the noses of the lap scorers. Roaring home an easy winner, Godfrey finished seventeen seconds ahead of the second man, Harry Martin (345 Martin-JAP), whom he had passed on the Byfleet Banking on the final lap. Frank McNab (493 Trump-JAP) was a close third three seconds later. Result:

ALL-COMERS' HANDICAP (13.59 miles) with a Fork start and finish.

		H'cap start	Speed (mph)
1.	O. C. Godfrey (994 Indian)	scratch	74.46
2.	H. Martin (345 Martin-JAP)	2 min 55 sec	57.62
3.	F. A. McNab (493 Trump-JAP)	2 min 30 sec	59.15

Now came the great deciding third round of the Collier-de Rosier match series, this time over ten laps (or 27.18 miles). Excitement ran high as it was thought that, although Jake obviously had the faster machine, Charlie possibly had better staying powers, which might wear him down. Odds of 5-to-4 on Collier to win were freely offered by the bookmakers and equally freely taken. Soon Godfrey's two-inch Continental-tyred front wheel had been substituted for Jake's battered front rim and all was ready—or so it seemed. But after a false start, it was found that Jake's original front wheel cover, on bursting, had broken one of the carbon brushes of his Indian's forward-mounting magneto. A spare one was taken from Godfrey's machine, which was rapidly becoming depleted of its fittings. Then, off at last!

This time Jake pulled out of Charlie's slipstream to finish a wheel ahead at the end of lap one. Charlie just led again on lap two, with Jake in close company. A lap later Jake was ahead by two lengths on crossing the line at the Fork, but on the Railway Straight Charlie picked up this distance and as much again, to cover the flying-start half-mile in $21\frac{2}{5}$ sec (or at a speed of 84.1 mph). He was still leading at the end of lap four, and was going so well that hopes of an English victory ran high.

Then it happened! Shortly after the half-distance Charlie's handle-bar-mounted ignition switch jumped into the "off" position due to track vibration. By the time he had located and remedied this fault, Jake had gained a half-mile lead. To pick this up in the remaining four laps was a hopeless task. Nevertheless, Charlie went like a demon, to finish only twenty seconds behind Jake, who, leaving nothing to chance, went all out until the finish. So Jake de Rosier won on aggregate by two races to one. Result:

THIRD (AND DECIDING) COLLIER-DE ROSIER MATCH RACE (27.18 miles). Rolling start at Fork. Fork finish.

	Speed (mph)
1. J. de Rosier (994 Indian)	78.64
2. C. R. Collier (998 Matchless-JAP)	77.40

Jake's hand was bleeding at the finish, the skin having been chafed right through. His back and leggings were covered with engine oil, which had been thrown from his back tyre after being spewed from his auxiliary exhaust ports.

This meeting was certainly a traumatic one for the Brooklands' motor-cycle-racing fraternity: their champion had been beaten fair and square. Yet even then many refused to admit what the facts

1911—AN INDIAN SUMMER

had proved—namely, that a good chain-driven machine will always beat a good belt-driven one of equivalent horse-power development.

Midweek racing and records

Brilliant weather occurred for the BARC July Meeting on the following Wednesday, July 19th, and included the customary two motor cycle handicap events in an otherwise all-car programme. Nineteen riders turned out for the first of these, the Third Short Handicap over 5¾ miles. They included Jake de Rosier (994 Indian) at scratch, Charlie Collier (998 Matchless-JAP) with a 2-sec start, Harry Collier (580 Matchless-JAP), Gordon Bell the aviator, riding A. J. Luce's 580 cc BAT-JAP, and Sidney Tessier on a machine of the same capacity and make. Others included: G. E. Stanley (499 Singer), Jack Haswell (499 Triumph), Harry Martin (345 Martin-JAP), and the Trump-JAP team consisting of Frank McNab, R. N. Stewart and A. Baker White.

De Rosier had picked up forty yards on Charlie Collier by the time these two had reached the Railway Straight, and from there on a fine struggle developed. Charlie managed to take a leaf out of Jake's book and did a little slipstreaming on his own account. The TT BATs went very well, especially Gordon Bell's, for, despite his driving belt breaking when he was halfway down the Finishing Straight, he managed to win by a good forty yards, helped by a strong following wind.

SHORT MOTOR CYCLE HANDICAP (up to 1000 cc) over 5¾ miles. Fork start and finish.

		H'cap start	
1.	G. Bell (580 BAT-JAP)	1 min 6 sec	64½ mph
2.	S. T. Tessier (580 BAT-JAP)	1 min 6 sec	
3.	C. R. Collier (998 Matchless-JAP)	2 sec	

Jack Haswell finished fourth and Jake de Rosier fifth.

All but two of those who rode in the Short Race rode in the Long Handicap, over 8½ miles. Gordon Bell (580 BAT-JAP) was penalised 36 sec on handicap for winning the first motor cycle race of the day, and had to give away 3 sec to Harry Collier. The result was an easy win for Sidney Tessier, the others finishing in much the same order as before, except that Harry Collier was better placed, in fourth position.

LONG MOTOR CYCLE HANDICAP (up to 1000 cc) over 8½ miles. Fork start and Long finish.

		H'cap start	
1.	S. T. Tessier (580 BAT-JAP)	1 min 39 sec	63¼ mph
2.	J. R. Haswell (499 Triumph)	2 min 18 sec	
3.	G. Bell (580 BAT-JAP)	1 min 3 sec	

The Collier-de Rosier scrap in this event was a reversal of what had happened in the Short Handicap. Hanging behind Charlie, Jake slipstreamed the Matchless and, after a couple of laps, swung out at the Fork and got home twenty yards ahead of him.

During the late afternoon of July 25th, the Tuesday of the following week, Lieut. R. N. Stewart and Frank McNab set out on their 492 cc Trump-JAPs to try to break long-distance Class C records. Stewart was forced to retire by an oil tank leakage, but McNab went on successfully to set up a new two-hour record, with a distance of 110 miles 297 yd, and a record average of 54.9 mph for the hundred miles.

Clubmen go racing at "Royal" meet

Two motor cycle races were featured at the RAC and Associated Clubs' Brooklands' meeting on Saturday, July 29th. Just as the first of these, the ACU Short-Distance Handicap over 5½ miles, was about to start at the Fork, Prince Henry of Prussia arrived at the track. There was a brief pause while he was introduced to competitors, then the "off" was given.

All got away well except Geoffrey Smith (499 Triumph), who broke a driving belt fastener as soon as his engine fired. Malcolm Campbell (499 Triumph), the second man away, led at the end of the first lap. Charlie Collier (998 Matchless-JAP), the scratch man, was rapidly catching up the field until put out with a driving-belt fastener pulling through. The result was a win for H. Hunter, whose machine had been timed at 68 mph in practice.

ACU SHORT-DISTANCE HANDICAP (up to 1000 cc) over 5½ miles. Fork start and finish.

		H'cap start	
1.	H. Hunter (666 BAT-JAP)	1 min 10 sec	54.56 mph
2.	H. Martin (345 Martin-JAP)	1 min 25 sec	
3.	M. Campbell (499 Triumph)	1 min 45 sec	

1911—AN INDIAN SUMMER

The other two-wheeler event was the ACU Inter-Team Race, for teams of three motor cycles entered by clubs affiliated to the ACU. Each team comprised a 500 cc single, a 670 cc multi, and a 1000 cc passenger machine. All had to be standard touring machines fully equipped for the road. The result was a win for the Streatham & District MCC team consisting of Sidney Tessier (580 BAT-JAP twin), W. O. Oldman (498 Zenith-Gradua-JAP single) and A. R. Hunter (988 Zenith-Gradua-JAP s/car).

Jake's final fling

Starting in the early hours of Friday, August 4th, Jake de Rosier had a last fling at Brooklands before sailing for America the following day. He successfully set new Class E (1000 cc solo) records for the flying-start kilometre and mile with speeds of 88.77 mph and 88.23 mph.

During the evening of the same day Jake was the guest of honour at a farewell dinner held at Frascati's Restaurant in London by H. H. Collier senior, founder of the Matchless concern. There Jake tried to persuade Charlie Collier to undertake racing in the States, but to no avail.

The Saturday saw Jake's departure and, at Brooklands, a further unsuccessful attempt on the Class C hour record, this time by Lieut. R. N. Stewart (493 Trump-JAP).

August Bank Holiday Monday, August 7th set the scene for the customary monthly BARC meeting at the track. Unfortunately only one motor cycle event was included: a Short Handicap over 5¾ miles. In this Stanhope Spencer (499 Rudge) led the field home, pursued by A. J. Sproston on a similar machine. Jack Haswell (499 Triumph) finished a close third. The two Collier brothers were heavily handicapped and unable to get into the placings. Contemporary race reports, unfortunately, give no race speeds.

Charlie Collier breaks Jake's records

Everyone was taken aback on Friday, August 11th, when Charlie Collier went out on his 998 cc Matchless-JAP and blasted wide open Jake de Rosier's "impregnable" records of a week before.

The Friday evening, fine with little wind, was ideal for record breaking. After riding a lap to get up speed, Charlie was all set for an attempt on the flying-start 5 miles. He broke the British record, held by Jake, with an average speed of 83.72 mph.

The next attempt on the agenda was that of the flying-start kilometre. Starting from the Fork, Charlie was soon going well, but after coming off the Members' Banking and entering the Railway Straight, his engine seemed to lose some of its hum.

Afterwards, it was learnt that the throttle lever had shifted after the machine had struck a bad bump on the track. But Charlie's time for the kilometre gave an average of 89.48 mph—a world record.

After returning to the Fork to shorten his driving belt, he made an attempt on the world's mile record, which was duly taken with a speed of 91.31 mph. This was the first time that any British machine had officially exceeded 90 mph, and with belt drive at that. He claimed that the machine had not been fully "run-in" for the earlier match races against de Rosier, it having had only about a week on the road beforehand. This fact saddened the two Collier brothers, who felt that their machine could, but for this, have beaten de Rosier. Whatever the cause, it had certainly now acquired some extra power.

W. ("Bill") Ellis, an indentured apprentice to the Collier concern at this time, used to take Charlie Collier's machines down to Brooklands for track testing, with another apprentice. Bill did the timing from the Members' Bridge, whilst his companion carried out the riding and running-in of the engines. When interviewed in later years, Bill recalled some interesting details of these racers. Thus twin carburetters were tried out at one stage, but proved unsatisfactory and were never used in an actual race. Also, graphite was used in the oil and, to assist engine starting, ether in the petrol.

Harry Martin breaks the "500" record

The Sixth Monthly Members' Race Meeting of the BMCRC saw two events on the programme: the Second 1911 Record Time Trials and an Hour Race. Both events covered all the recognised solo classes of 1911.

This meeting was held on Saturday, August 26th, in fine but rather cloudy weather. A stiff breeze along the Railway Straight hindered competitors in the Hour Race, especially those on lightweights. The one-mile, five-mile and one-kilometre attempts in the

Record Time Trials, however, were run together in the reverse direction to normal track running, to take advantage of this wind and five new records were set up:

RECORD TIME TRIALS

Class			Speed (mph) over:		
			fs km	fs ml	fs 5 ml
A	(up to 275 cc)	W. D. Chitty (272 Frays-JAP)	60.11	58.26	47.11
B	(275-350 cc)	H. Martin (343 Martin-JAP)	66.42	64.75	42.00*
C	(350-500 cc)	H. Martin (498 Martin-JAP)	73.95*	72.89*	—
D	(500-750 cc)	S. T. Tessier (735 BAT-JAP)	74.37	73.83	—
E	(750-1000 cc)	C. R. Collier (998 Matchless-JAP)	91.23*	89.01	82.48

(*New Class records).

Harry Martin had a field day, setting up the fastest times in Classes B and C. He established a new 350-cc five-mile record and his 500 cc flying-mile speed beat the 72.58 mph average set up by W. Stanhope Spencer (499 Rudge) at the Nottingham MCC's Clipstone Speed Trials on August 19th. It is interesting to note that it was only early in that year that a five-hundred had for the first time exceeded 70 mph: a 490 cc s.v. Norton ridden at the Sheffield and Hallamshire MCC Sprint Meeting by Dan Bradbury.

Harry Martin's record-breaking machine in the 500-cc Class, was powered by a 498 cc V-twin JAP engine of bore and stroke 76 × 56 mm.

In Class A (up to 275 cc), W. D. Chitty made the fastest time. Harry Martin lost his driving belt while running well, and in the five-mile attempt his cylinder head blew off.

In the Hour Race, during which competitors in all classes were on the track simultaneously, Harry Collier (666 Matchless-JAP) at once took the lead and kept it for 16 laps until forced to retire with a cylinder head blown off. By this time he had lapped most of the other competitors.

The most exciting part of the event was the keen tussle between Jack Haswell (499 Triumph) and Oliver Godfrey (497 Indian).

First one led, then the other, and twice they passed the Fork neck-and-neck, but towards the end of the race Godfrey's inlet rocker broke, his valve then working automatically like that in an a.i.v. engine. Naturally his pace dropped, and though he could no longer keep up with Haswell, he did manage to beat the previous Class C (350-500 cc) hour record by upwards of two miles. G. E. Stanley (499 Singer) stopped at the end of the 21 laps (over 57 miles) half-a-minute before time, for want of oil. Bert Colver (340 Enfield), whose chain-driven twin ran very steadily, was only 604 yd outside the Class B (275-350 cc) hour record.

Class A (up to 275 cc) also produced two good performances, W. D. Chitty (272 Frays-JAP) and R. O. Clark (249 FN) both beating the old class record.

Frank McNab (493 Trump-JAP), who started well, suffered a puncture and had to retire after only two laps.

HOUR RACES

Class			Distance covered	
			Miles	Yards
A	(up to 275 cc)	1. W. D. Chitty (272 Frays-JAP)	50	239*
		2. R. O. Clark (249 FN)	41	1454
B	(275-350 cc)	1. H. V. Colver (340 Enfield)	54	122
		2. J. Cocker (295 Singer)	42	410
C	(350-500 cc)	1. J. R. Haswell (499 Triumph)	63	194*
		2. O. C. Godfrey (497 Indian)	62	1147
D	(500-750 cc)	1. A. Moorhouse (584 Indian)	55	1020

(*New class records).

Most of the machines were belt driven, the exceptions being the Indians and the Enfield which used chains and the Belgian FN which was gear driven. Several had no silencer or practically none. Colver had two long exhaust pipes on his machine, which extended to the back wheel hub.

To complete a month of record breaking, on Wednesday, August 30th, Arthur Moorhouse (994 Indian) beat the Class E (750-1000 cc) hour record, riding 70 miles 1388 yd. He covered fifty miles at an average speed of 73.19 mph.

More long-distance records and racing

Oliver Godfrey made several abortive attempts at the Class C hour record during the first two weeks of September. In one of these Arthur Moorhouse was on the track on his 994 cc Indian and attempted to act as pacemaker with Godfrey in his slipstream. Ebbie Ebblewhite, who was acting as timekeeper, promptly stopped the attempt. He considered this practice unethical.

On Monday, September 11th, Harold Cox, riding a 350 cc Forward, a machine of his own design and manufacture, succeeded in lowering the Class B two-hour and hundred-mile records, with average speeds of 45.76 mph and 47.84 mph. The following Friday, Harry Martin was out on Brooklands' Track for an attempt on the Class C hour record on his 498 cc twin-cylinder Martin-JAP. The north-westerly wind, however, blew so strongly that he could not maintain the required average speed.

A Junior Hour Race incorporating Classes A and B, and a Hundred-Mile Record Race, were the only two events on the programme of the Seventh 1911 Monthly BMCRC Race Meeting. Saturday, September 23rd was a cool day, and early in the afternoon attendance was sparse, but it improved later on.

All got away well in the Junior Hour Race except for Alan Woodman (340 Humber), who had some trouble getting his little V-twin to fire. But eventually he got going. The order of the first three at the end of lap one was, Bert Colver (338 Enfield), Harry Martin (272 Martin-JAP), then Sam Wright (340 Humber). This was Freddie Barnes' first and last circuit of the race on his 299 cc Zenith-Gradua-JAP: a seized tappet rocker caused his retirement. Peter Weatherilt (299 Zenith-Gradua-JAP) now took the lead and kept it for eight laps until a sooted sparking plug put him back a lap.

At half time Harry Martin led with Weatherilt second and Wright third. In the twelfth lap Sam Wright took second place and Weatherilt fell back to third. This order did not change till the last lap but two, when Weatherilt began to force the pace and got into second position again. Results:

JUNIOR ONE-HOUR RACE (Classes A and B). Fork start
                                                                Distance covered
1. H. Martin (272 Martin-JAP)   54 miles 310 yd*
2. P. Weatherilt (299 Zenith-Gradua-JAP) 51 miles 796 yd
(* New Class A record).

The next and last event of this final Bemsee meeting of the year was the Hundred-Mile Record Race for Classes C, D and E (not exceeding 500, 750 and 1000 cc respectively). Charlie Collier was mounted on his 998 cc Matchless-JAP record breaker, which had now been converted to chain drive via a countershaft clutch. His gear ratio was 2.6-to-1. Harry Collier rode a similar—but belt-driven machine.

Frank McNab had a new 493 cc Trump-JAP fitted with Hellesen and Hunt battery-and-coil ignition, and one of the recently-introduced CAP carburetters.

After an impressive start at the Fork, Charlie Collier had gained a considerable lead by the end of the first lap, which he turned in 2 min $22\tfrac{4}{5}$ sec (68.51 mph). His brother, Harry, came next and then Gordon Bell (riding A. J. Luce's 580 cc BAT-JAP), followed by the rest of the field.

Harry Collier took the lead in the fourth lap, but lost it again to his brother. Then Harry stopped. After twelve laps Charlie Collier was visibly slowing and eventually had to retire through a seized front piston. Then Harry, who had got going again, also retired through engine trouble. Just after the start of the race he attempted, whilst at speed, to tighten a nut on his carburetter. His spanner somehow fell from his hand into the spokes of his front wheel and he was brought off. Fortunately he was thrown on to the grass verge on the inside of the track.

With the Collier brothers' retirement, Billy Elce (499 Rudge) led with Jack Haswell (499 Triumph) second; the race developed into a Rudge-Triumph duel, Haswell winning on a flat tyre. Elce stopped to change his driving belt, which was getting oily, and thereby lost the race.

HUNDRED-MILE RECORD RACE (Classes C, D and E) over 37 laps or 100.56 miles. Fork start and finish.

		Speed (mph)
1.	J. R. Haswell (499 Triumph)	61.65
2.	W. H. Elce (499 Rudge)	61.40
3.	O. C. Godfrey (497 Indian)	58.76

Haswell completed the hour at an average speed of 62.66 mph, failing to beat his own record. Sidney Tessier (738 BAT-JAP) was fourth, W. Stanhope Spencer (499 Rudge) fifth, and E. B. Ware, on another 499 cc Rudge, sixth.

A Rudge record spree

On Tuesday, October 3rd, twenty-one year-old W. Stanhope Spencer (499 Rudge) captured several records at Brooklands. He started at 11.39 am, followed at minute intervals by Billy Elce and by W. L. T. Rhys, on similar machines. Billy soon retired through magneto trouble, while Rhys continued to lap at 62 mph or so, which was too low for record breaking.

But Spencer was going well, covering his second lap at 66.29 mph and settling down to a steady 66 mph average. Although it was a fine and rather cold day, windless at first, towards the end of the hour a gust sprang up to reduce Spencer's average to below 66 mph. During the second hour it dropped further, to about 64 mph, and at the forty-third lap, with only eight minutes to go before he was due to stop, an inlet cotter broke. Fortunately this jammed so that the valve spring did not come adrift and he was able to finish.

The records obtained were as follows: 50 miles at 65.83 mph (Classes C and D); 100 miles at 63.74 mph (Classes C, D and E); the hour at 65.45 mph (Classes C and D); and two hours at 61.60 mph (Classes C, D and E). Stanhope Spencer's fastest lap was his sixth, at 66.65 mph.

After lunch, Frank E. Pither set out to establish the first-ever 500 cc sidecar record for the hour. His machine was a standard single-geared belt-driven 499 cc Rudge, with mudguards removed, attached to a Portland sidecar fitted with a canoe-shaped wickerwork body. The combined weight of outfit, driver and passenger came out at 548 lb.

Pither kept up a steady average of 42 mph until a sparking plug blew out of his cylinder head, reducing the average for that particular lap to 25 mph. Despite this, he managed to cover 40 miles 1660 yd in the time.

The final record of that day was taken by Spencer, who, again riding his 499 cc Rudge, beat Victor Surridge's flying-start five-mile record time by $2\frac{2}{5}$ sec, averaging 65.79 mph (a new Class C record).

Last race meeting of the year

The next day, Wednesday, October 4th, the last Brooklands' race meeting of the year was held in cool, damp, dull weather. A BARC meeting, it included but one motor cycle race; the Fourth Long Handicap of the year, over $8\frac{1}{2}$ miles.

Frank Pither (this time mounted on a solo Rudge) shed his driving belt at the start and P. Schmidt (NSU) could not get his engine to fire. But the rest of the field got away well and by the end of the first lap Norman Slatter (247 Alcyon) led by almost a mile. Charlie Collier (998 Matchless-JAP) was the scratch man, while Oliver Godfrey (994 Indian) and Harry Collier had gone off together from the 6-sec mark.

In the second lap the order changed continuously: Peter Weatherilt (299 Zenith-Gradua-JAP) took the lead, followed by H. W. Hands on a similar machine. Charlie Collier now lay eighth. Meanwhile Slatter was put out by a broken driving belt.

Charlie Collier on the chain-driven Matchless was travelling well, but had a stiff job on to catch the leaders. He succeeded in gaining second position; another lap and he would have undoubtedly won easily, but Hands proved the eventual winner by virtue of his favourable start.

LONG MOTOR CYCLE HANDICAP (up to 1000 cc) over 8½ miles. Fork start and Long finish.

		H'cap start	
1.	H. W. Hands (299 Zenith-Gradua-JAP)	2 min 45 sec	55.5 mph
2.	C. R. Collier (998 Matchless-JAP)	scratch	
3.	P. Weatherilt (299 Zenith-Gradua-JAP)		

Fourth was Oliver Godfrey (994 Indian), fifth Harry Collier and sixth Harry Martin (498 Martin-JAP) twin.

End of the season record breaking

The period around that of the holding of the Olympia Motor Cycle Show was perennially one of record attempts and record breaking, and that of 1911 was no exception.

Oliver Godfrey, who was due to attempt the Class E (1000 cc) hour record, had to forget the idea, for he was involved in a road accident and landed in hospital with a broken arm and other injuries. On the other hand, Tuesday, October 24th, saw Norman Slatter (247 Alcyon) breaking Class A (up to 275 cc) records from two to six hours at speeds ranging from 42.44 mph down to 37.31 mph.

1911—AN INDIAN SUMMER

Ever since the Brooklands' Track had opened, there had been local residents who had complained of noise. Towards the end of October matters came to a head, with these people threatening to apply for an injunction against Mr Locke-King and the BARC, unless steps were taken to reduce the noise of motor cycles, which were considered by them to be the chief culprits. Accordingly the BARC issued a circular to all motor cycle manufacturers and track habitués, stating that no motor cycle would henceforth be allowed at Brooklands without an efficient silencer fitted. Cut outs were to be banned.

On the Wednesday, the first records to be attempted under the new silencing regulations were set up by Sam Wright riding a 340 cc (60 × 60 mm) twin-cylinder Humber. He and P. J. Evans, the 1911 Isle of Man Junior TT Race winner (on a similar machine), under the management of Bert Yates, set out to lower all Class B (up to 350 cc) record times in the space of two hours that they could. Evans retired at the twenty-fourth lap, but Wright steadily improved his speed and reeled off his fourteenth lap at 61.61 mph. With the fifty-mile record in his pocket at an average speed of 58.65 mph, Sam Wright then annexed the hour record at 58.80 mph. He stopped on lap 31 for petrol, and although he was doing well, a misfire slowed him down to a lap time of about 3 min 54 sec (45.72 mph) after his 36th circuit. At the fortieth lap he had to stop and replace a sparking plug; this done, he found time to complete another lap before the two hours were up. He thus gained the record for that period at an average speed of 54.77 mph.

Wright's machine had a standard TT-type exhaust pipe extending to the rear wheel, with its end flattened and holes drilled in it four inches from its outlet.

Not satisfied with his previous record performances, W. Stanhope Spencer (499 Rudge) was again out on the track, on Monday, November 6th. He took the 150-mile record in Class C at 57.00 mph, and in Classes C, D and E, the three-hour record at 57.03 mph and two-hundred miles at 57.47 mph. The weather was bitterly cold for Spencer's attempts, and the wind blew at 40 to 50 mph the whole time. When riding against it his speed dropped to some 25 mph and although he wore two waistcoats, two sweaters and a leather suit, he was unable to keep sufficiently warm and decided to call it a day.

H. T. Lloyd, who was preparing a 499 cc Triumph for record attempts, whilst practising on the track collided with a notice warning of repairs being carried out to its surface. He was taken to the Weybridge Cottage Hospital with a suspected broken jaw. Jack Haswell on his Triumph was more fortunate.

On Tuesday, November 14th, Haswell set out in poor weather, to create new Class C, D and E records up to six hours. His machine (his usual 499 cc s.v. Triumph) ran very consistently, and there was little difference on time between his fastest and slowest laps, which gave speeds of 63.53 mph and 60.77 mph respectively. Valve trouble and a loose exhaust silencer forced several stops *en route*, which kept his average speed down to well below 60 mph. Despite this he managed to secure the four-, five- and six-hour records and those for 250 and 300 miles as well, but decided to have a further attempt and try to improve on them before the year was out.

Thus it was that the following Tuesday saw Jack Haswell out on the track again after records, with W. L. T. Rhys (499 Rudge) and Bizzy Bashall (976 BAT-JAP s/car) to keep him company.

Rhys was first away, followed an hour later by Jack. At the end of three hours Haswell stopped for replenishments. Rhys, who had just beaten Jack's previous Class C four-hour record, pulled in at the same time and mentioned the fact to him. This stirred Jack into action, who remounted his machine and soon completed four hours with a new record distance of 239 miles 947 yd to his credit; equivalent to an average of 59.88 mph.

Haswell was inside the existing record at two hours, having averaged 62.07 mph. His records applied to Classes C, D, and E. The problem of accommodating a single bulky exhaust silencer on his Triumph, with its inherent tendency to vibrate and come loose had been obviated by using a branching exhaust pipe. Each branch led to a smaller separate silencer on either side of the machine alongside the rear wheel . This provided the required degree of silencing without any apparent diminution in performance. In fact the enforced use of long exhaust pipes with such a silencing system, as opposed to the short pipe to a "pepper pot" type of silencer, probably boosted his engine power unwittingly.

Despite his chagrin over losing his four-hour record so recently established, Rhys restarted and went on to beat Jack Haswell's five- and six-hour distances at new record averages of 53.61 mph and 53.73 mph. He also took Jack's 250- and 300-mile records, at 53.79 mph and 53.70 mph, in the process.

On the same day Bizzy Bashall, with his young brother Aubrey as passenger, established a one-hour record for 1000 cc sidecar outfits on his 976 cc BAT-JAP combination by covering 45 miles 639 yd in the time.

So ended one of the most eventful and significant years in the history of Brooklands' Track.

6

1912—TWO, THREE OR FOUR WHEELS?

SIDECAR Racing, which had started in 1911, was to have a real boom year in 1912. The then newly-introduced concept of the "cyclecar" which could have either three or four wheels, was rejected by the motor-car racing fraternity and fell under the organising envelope of the BMCRC and the ACU. It gradually gave rise to the three-wheeler category, for which the BMCRC accepted responsibility and the light four-wheeled motor car which was more properly the province of the BARC. That was not until after the 1914-18 War, however.

The increasingly aggressive expansion of German interests on the political scene abroad, culminating in the Agadir incident of August, 1911, had awakened the British Government to the possibility of a European conflict within the foreseeable future, and the need for mechanised transport in that eventuality. The War Office decided to investigate all the possibilities in that direction, including the use of motor cycles for the carrying of military despatches. So it was that the War Department held a special speed test for production machines at Brooklands, on Monday, January 29th, 1912, shortly after the Winter track repairs had been completed. All manufacturers were invited to send along examples of their current models, with riders, the carrot being the possibility of a government contract.

None of the competing machines was able to achieve the War Office's ideal of a 45 mph flying-start lap for a 500 cc machine. Freddie Barnes (493 Zenith-Gradua-JAP) did the best with a 43.2 mph standing-start lap and a 44.2 mph flying lap. But the 350 cc target of 40 mph for a flying lap was easily beaten by Gordon Fletcher (350 Douglas), whose two-speed machine achieved standing and flying laps of 42.8 mph and 42.0 mph. His flying lap actually being the slower. Barnes and Fletcher also shone in the timed runs up the

Brooklands' Test Hill, intended to assess hill-climbing capabilities. Overall, the War Office officials were reasonably pleased with the day's work.

Long-distance solo and sidecar records

Rain and generally foul weather conditions caused the First BMCRC Members' Race Meeting of 1912 to be postponed until Wednesday, March 27th. Three events were down for decision on that bright, sunny, yet windy day. The first, a Sidecar Scratch Race for machines up to 1000 cc fitted with touring sidecars and carrying passengers of over 8 stones in weight, provided an easy win for Freddie Barnes' big Zenith outfit:

SIDECAR SCRATCH RACE (up to 1000 cc s/car)
over 8½ miles. Fork start and finish.

		Speed (mph)
1.	F. W. Barnes (988 Zenith-Gradua-JAP s/car)	56.00
2.	C. R. Collier (964 Matchless-JAP s/car)	54.08
3.	S. T. Tessier (734 BAT-JAP s/car)	49.68

The Hundred-Mile Race which followed attracted some fifty-five entries. Its start was made at the Fork and its finish 975 yd short of the Fork, which with thirty-seven laps to cover gave a race distance of exactly a hundred miles. The race was for all classes, both solo and sidecar, competitors' times being taken over fifty miles, one hour and a hundred miles, for record purposes. Solo Classes A and B, and the sidecars, started first as a bunch, the rest of the solos an hour later. The winners were as follows:

HUNDRED-MILE ALL-COMERS' SCRATCH RACE
Fork start. Finish 975 yd short of Fork.

Solo classes			Speed (mph)
A	(up to 275 cc)	No finishers	—
B	(275-350 cc)	S. Wright (340 Humber)	48.83
C	(350-500 cc)	E. B. Ware (499 Rudge)	55.71
D	(500-750 cc)	No finishers	—
E	(750-1000 cc)	A. Moorhouse (994 Indian)	66.85

Sidecar classes
- C (350-500 cc)   G. Griffiths (499 Rudge s/car)   32.16
- D (500-750 cc)   No finishers   —
- E (750-1000 cc) F. W. Barnes (988 Zenith-Gradua-JAP s/car)*   48.50

(* Freddie Barnes, in addition to setting up this 100-mile record, also set new records for: 50 miles, at 49.74 mph; one hour, at 49.73 mph; and two hours, at 48.64 mph.)

Sidney Tessier (734 BAT-JAP s/car) was early in difficulties and valve trouble put him out of the running. Sidney Axford (988 Zenith-Gradua-JAP s/car) ran out of oil and petrol. Norman Slatter (247 Alcyon) ran well for 31 laps in Class A, and then, with a heart-rending screech, his overstressed engine blew up with a broken connecting rod.

Young P. J. Wallace (499 Rudge), a sixteen-year-old rider who was making his track debût in this race, had just completed his ninth lap and was approaching the end of the Railway Straight on his tenth, when his driving belt broke and became wedged between the belt rim and a rear frame member. The machine went into a violent skid and flung the rider off, fortunately on to the grass verge on the inside of the track. As one half of the belt-fastener had become stuck in the groove of the engine pulley, he was forced to walk his machine back to the paddock around the Byfleet Banking—a distance of almost 1½ miles. Wallace was to become well known after the 1914-18 War as a rider in sprint events and he eventually became Chief Test Plant Engineer with Napier Aero Engines, a post from which he retired in 1962.

Another rider to become well known at the track, A. G. Miller, rode a 988 cc Matchless-JAP in this race, but was forced to retire due to its somewhat poor handling. He accompanied Wallace back to the paddock.

The first cyclecar race

The last event of the day was the first-ever cyclecar race to be held at Brooklands. There was a capacity limit of 1100 cc and one of 600 lb on minimum unladen weight. The race provided a comparatively easy win for Harry Martin, driving an o.h.v. 90-bore JAP-

Founder of the Brough-Superior concern, George Brough, who on this 964 cc Brough of his father's manufacture won the 400-1000 cc Touring Handicap at the MCC race meeting on Saturday, July 6th, 1912.

The line-up at the Fork for the start of the Junior Brooklands' TT Race, on Saturday, September 14th, 1912. *Left to right:* No. 12 Sam Wright and No. 10 S. W. Phillpott (340 Humbers); and No.7, H. Greaves (350 Enfield). Standing behind Phillpott is a youthful Victor Horsman.

Jack Emerson (490 Norton) after winning the 150-mile Senior Brooklands' TT Race at 63.88 mph, on Saturday, September 14th, 1912.

Sydney Garrett (499 Regal-Green-Precision s/car). He finished third in the one-hour 1000 cc sidecar class at the BMCRC Open Championship Meeting, on Saturday, October 12th, 1912, thus establishing a new 500 cc sidecar hour record of 50 miles 1740 yd. Note the water-cooled engine.

engined Morgan three-wheeler. He covered his second lap at 59 mph. Result:

CYCLECAR SCRATCH RACE (up to 1100 cc c/car) over 8½ miles. Fork start and finish.

		Speed (mph)
1.	H. Martin (998 Morgan-Martin-JAP)	57.31
2.	E. D. Tate (1066 Sabella-JAP)	44.19
3.	J. Robinson (1066 Sabella-JAP)	

Most of the competing machines at this meeting were well silenced. Sam Wright's 340 cc Humber had a neat foot-operated oil pump, and a separate wedge-shaped oil tank below the rear of his fuel tank. This enabled him to travel the Hundred-Mile All-Comers' Race non-stop.

The first four-valve racer?

Ask even a knowledgeable motorcyclist: "What was the first four-valve racing motor cycle?" and the odds are that he will reply: "The Ricardo Triumph of the early 'twenties". This is not so, however, for as early as 1911, Louis Coatalen—the famous Sunbeam car designer—had been working on such a machine for the Singer Company. It made its first appearance at Brooklands early in 1912 in the hands of A. J. Dixon.

The machine had a 499 cc (85 × 88 mm) engine, with an air-cooled barrel and a water-cooled detachable cylinder head, both made of cast iron. The twin radiators were mounted one at each side of the single front down tube of the frame. Four vertical valves were used—two inlet, at the front of the cylinder head, and two exhaust at the rear—each pair having its own rocker, pushrod-operated from a common camshaft mounted in the front of the crankcase. The forward-facing inlet port diverged to the inlet valve seats inside the cylinder head casting and was fed by an updraught rearward-curving induction pipe from a single rear-facing carburetter. The exhaust ports merged within the head casting to feed a large diameter rear-facing and almost straight exhaust system mounted on the offside of the machine.

A. J. Dixon continued testing of this machine at Brooklands and the Singer Company hoped that an eventual 80-90 mph would be possible using it, but so far as is known it never appeared in a race.

One explanation for this may be that G. E. Stanley, the principal rider for Singer at that time, found that he could get all the speed he required in order to win races from his existing sidevalve engine. As a professional rider, dependent on race bonuses for his living, he could ill-afford the time necessary to sort out the bugs from such a new and complicated engine design.

Easter at Brooklands

The two motor cycle races included in the first BARC race meeting of the year on Easter Monday, April 8th, took place in boisterously windy conditions which made riding tricky.

Twenty started in the Short Handicap, which provided a surprise win for D. C. Bolton (499 Rudge). Result:

SHORT MOTOR CYCLE HANDICAP (up to 1000 cc) over $5\frac{3}{4}$ miles. Fork start and Long finish.

		H'cap start	
1.	D. C. Bolton (499 Rudge)	56 sec	$62\frac{1}{2}$ mph
2.	G. E. Stanley (299 Singer)	1 min 22 sec	
3.	M. Campbell (499 Triumph)	1 min 22 sec	

In the second race, the Long Handicap, Bolton's brilliant red Rudge was more heavily handicapped and could only finish third. The winner this time proved to be Stanley:

LONG MOTOR CYCLE HANDICAP (up to 1000 cc) over $8\frac{1}{2}$ miles. Fork start and Long finish.

		H'cap start	
1.	G. E. Stanley (499 Singer)	1 min 3 sec	$64\frac{1}{2}$ mph
2.	J. A. Manners-Smith (499 Triumph)	2 min 3 sec	
3.	D. C. Bolton (499 Rudge)	35 sec	

More records

Ten days later on Thursday, April 18th Arthur Moorhouse was out on the track attempting records on his 994 cc o.h.i.v. Indian. The weather was sunny and warm, and he reeled off consistent lap speeds of between 70 and 72 mph. Apart from tyre changes and tank re-fuelling, the only other stop was caused by an oil pipe breaking

1912—TWO, THREE OR FOUR WHEELS?

at the end of four hours. The new records obtained were: 150 miles at 66.03 mph; 200 miles at 66.01 mph; 250 miles at 63.69 mph; 2 hours at 65.29 mph; 3 hours at 65.90 mph; 4 hours at 62.24 mph; and 5 hours at the much lower average, because of oil-pipe breakage of 55.50 mph.

This was to be the last occasion on which Arthur was to attempt records at the track, for within forty-eight hours he was to die in the first motor cycling fatality at Brooklands since it opened five years before.

Meeting marred by a fatality

Four events were included in the programme of the BMCRC's Second Monthly Race Meeting of 1912 on Saturday, April 20th. The June-like and almost windless conditions proved ideal for the setting up of high speeds in the first event: the first in the 1912 series of Record Time Trials. These counted towards an aggregate award to be presented at the end of the racing season. The fastest speeds in each class were as follows:

RECORD TIME TRIALS

				Speeds (mph) over:	
				fs km	fs ml
Solo classes					
B	(350 cc)	1.	G. E. Stanley (299 Singer)	58.13	57.91
		2.	N. A. Ayres (299 Singer)	56.48	56.14
C	(500 cc)	1.	G. E. Stanley (499 Singer)	70.11	68.78
		2.	D. C. Bolton 499 Rudge)	68.74	68.30
D	(750 cc)	1.	S. T. Tessier (741 BAT-JAP)	70.84	69.72
		2.	H. Hunter (750 Corah-JAP)	67.77	66.00
E	(1000 cc)	1.	C. R. Collier (998 Matchless-JAP)	79.73	78.75
Sidecar classes					
E	(1000 cc)	1.	G. F. Hunter (988 Zenith-Gradua-JAP s/car)	64.85	59.02

G. F. Hunter's sidecar outfit was the only one entered in the Time Trials. Collier's machine was fitted with a special oil pipe to the front cylinder, which could be closed by means of a tap; Stanley's 499 cc Singer was provided with a foot-operated oil pump.

The three-lap 500 cc Scratch Race, the second event in the list, had a Fork start and finish. The first prize was a cup presented by the Singer Company. Pushers were barred except in the cases of Alan Woodman (340 Humber), the one-legged New Zealand rider, and that of Alan Hill (499 Rudge), who was lame.

Stanhope Spencer (499 Rudge) got away first, but by the end of the first lap G. E. Stanley (499 Singer) had established a good lead with D. C. Bolton (499 Rudge) coming up fast. By the start of the second lap they were battling for first place, with Spencer and W. O. Oldman (498 BAT-JAP), some way behind, struggling for third.

The finish provided a close exciting win for Bolton, who beat Stanley by barely a length:

500 CC SCRATCH RACE FOR SINGER CUP
over 8 miles 269 yd. Fork start and finish.

	Speed (mph)
1. D. C. Bolton (499 Rudge)	64.18
2. G. E. Stanley (499 Singer)	64.12
3. W. S. Spencer (499 Rudge)	61.18

The five-lap Cyclecar Handicap Race over 13 miles 1035 yd (Fork start and finish) resulted in a win for G. Wadden (964 Autotrix-JAP) at 45.92 mph. Harry Martin (984 Morgan-JAP) clearly had the fastest vehicle in the race, but he was handicapped out of the first three places by being sent off from scratch. He could finish no higher than fourth.

There then came the tragic hour race in which Arthur Moorhouse was killed. The event was for all classes, machines of various capacities running simultaneously on the track.

The engine of Moorhouse's 994 cc Indian was running badly before the start, and he was the last man to line up. Nevertheless he got away fairly well and was soon in the lead, reeling off laps at around the 70 mph mark. By the seventh lap the leading four were Moorhouse, G. E. Stanley (499 Singer), Harry Collier (741 Matchless-JAP) and Sidney Tessier (741 BAT-JAP). The next thing seen by spectators at the Fork was a big blaze at the start of the Railway Straight and a column of smoke. The first facts came from W. O. Oldman, who said Moorhouse was seriously injured in a crash and that the race had been stopped. Later it was learnt that he had been killed.

Years afterwards Harry Bashall, who rode a 340 cc Humber in

the race, recounted what had in fact happened: "In the course of the race Moorhouse's Indian had lapped my Humber several times. When it passed me on the seventh lap, I noticed that its back wheel was canted over in the frame fork ends, as if the spindle nuts had worked loose. It seemed as if the pull of the driving chain was the only thing keeping the wheel in position. Then, as Moorhouse went up the Members' Banking prior to sweeping down on to the Railway Straight, the wheel must have come loose, for he went at full speed into a telegraph pole on the inside of the track and was killed outright. His machine burst into flames."

It is part of the Brooklands' folklore that Moorhouse's machine was buried by his friends beneath the telegraph post that killed him, and which was said to bear the imprint of his goggles from the impact. If true, the machine may still be there to this day.

The event was a tragedy, in a lesser sense, for G. E. Stanley. His machine was performing so well that he might have set up a new 500 cc (Class C) hour record, if the race had not been cancelled. As it was he established new 500 cc standing- and flying-start Brooklands' lap records at 63.12 and 67.38 mph respectively. For the nine laps (24 miles 808 yd) he had completed, he averaged $65\frac{1}{2}$ mph.

The discoverer of valve overlap?

During his travels to various race meetings around the country, Stanley had befriended a keen young Singer rider named Victor Horsman*. Whilst tuning his own engine, Horsman decided that interchanging the inlet and exhaust camshafts would give the valve lift curves he was looking for in his search for increased performance. He confided his ideas to Stanley, who ingeniously modified his own engine to test the theory. The result was a considerable boost in power.

On examination, they found that the inlet and exhaust valve "open periods" overlapped—probably the first time that valve overlap had been utilised on a motor cycle engine. Anyway, Stanley was taking no chances on the secret being discovered, for on those

---

* Real name Vincent Edward Horsman: someone early on in his racing career had made a bad guess at the meaning of his first initial and the name "Victor" had stuck.

occasions when he had to leave his machine unattended, he took good care to alter the valve settings.

The merry month of May

Unfortunately, rain spoiled the Second BARC Race Meeting of the year on Wednesday, May 1st, and it was abandoned, but not before the running of the first of the two scheduled motor cycle races—the Seventh Short Handicap.

As usual with Short Handicaps, this race was over two laps, with a Fork start and a Long finish on the straight by the paddock. It provided a win for Sidney Axford (498 Martin-JAP twin) from the 54-sec mark, at 58½ mph. Second was G. E. Stanley (299 Singer) and Malcolm Campbell (499 Triumph) was third. Amongst the finishers was a Japanese rider—K. Yano—on a 998 cc BAT-JAP.

On the Friday, L. N. Palmer was out on the track in a Bedelia cyclecar fitted with a 8 hp V-twin Bourbeau-Devaux engine. He set up a new class record of 43 miles 1034 yd in the hour.

The BMCRC's May meeting on Saturday, May 11th gave a clear indication of G. E. Stanley's new-found speed, when he set up new flying-start mile and kilometre records for Class C in the Record Time Trials.

RECORD TIME TRIALS

			Speed (mph) over:	
Solo classes			fs km	fs ml
A	(up to 275 cc)	H. Martin (272 Martin-JAP)	59.18	60.20
B	(275-350 cc)	G. E. Stanley (299 Singer)	63.91	63.16
C	(350-500 cc)	G. E. Stanley (499 Singer)	75.45*	73.02*
D	(500-750 cc)	H. Hunter (746 Corah-JAP)	77.80*	76.04*
E	(750-1000 cc)	C. R. Collier (998 Matchless-JAP)	85.38	82.19
Sidecar classes				
E	(750-1000 cc)	G. F. Hunter (988 Zenith-Gradua-JAP)	72.15*	64.75

(*New class records).

H. Hunter's fine performance in Class D, was achieved with an engine specially built for him by the JAP engine concern.

The second event was the 500 cc "Car Challenge" Race over three laps, the first and second placemen qualifying for an invitation race with a selected car at the next month's Brooklands' meeting.

G. E. Stanley (499 Singer) took the lead from the start and was never seriously challenged, although W. Stanhope Spencer (499 Rudge) was hard on his heels at the end of the first lap. But the gap between them steadily increased until Stanley won by some two hundred yards.

500 CC "CAR CHALLENGE" SCRATCH RACE
over 8 miles 269 yd. Fork start and finish.
1. G. E. Stanley (499 Singer)   65.93 mph
2. W. S. Spencer (499 Rudge)
3. N. A. Ayres (499 Singer)

Billy Elce (499 Rudge) was fourth. Stanley covered his first lap at 62.71 mph.

The Cyclecar Handicap (over five laps or 13 miles 1035 yd) provided a win for J. T. Wood (1070 GWK), by twenty yards over F. Hill (723 AC), at an average speed of 47.3 mph. Scratch man Harry Martin (990 Morgan-JAP) could do no better than finish third. The winning GWK employed a form of "infinitely-variable gear". The drive from the engine to the rear wheels, was via two large friction discs whose axes were set mutually at right angles. The gear ratio was altered by moving one disc across the face of the other, whilst the two were rotating.

Run on similar lines to the 500 cc race, the 750 cc "Car Challenge" event resolved into a procession with Harry Collier (741 Matchless-JAP) at its head. The order of the first three remained the same throughout.

750 CC "CAR CHALLENGE" SCRATCH RACE
over 8 miles 269 yd. Fork start and finish.
1. H. A. Collier (741 Matchless-JAP)   64.2 mph
2. R. L. Printz (746 BAT-JAP)
3. H. Hunter (746 Corah-JAP)

The Matchless clearly had speed in hand for, on the third lap when challenged by Printz, Harry Collier had no difficulty in increasing his lead to something like three hundred yards by the finish.

Charlie Collier (998 Matchless-JAP) had an easy win in the 1000 cc "Car Challenge" Scratch Race. At the start W. L. T. Rhys (499 Triumph) gained an initial lead with a smart piece of acceleration from the Fork. But by the end of the Railway Straight, Charlie had overtaken him and he romped home an easy winner by two minutes, with plenty of power in hand.

1000 CC "CAR CHALLENGE" SCRATCH RACE
over 8 miles 269 yd. Fork start and finish.
1. C. R. Collier (998 Matchless-JAP) 68.42 mph
2. H. Hunter (998 Corah-JAP)
3. W. L. T. Rhys (499 Triumph)

Rhys finished with his engine misfiring badly.

The final event of the day was the Fifty-Mile Senior Brooklands' TT Race (up to 500 cc), for the "Alec Ross" Cup. There were only six starters.

S. C. W. Smith, who had entered a Singer, instead elected to ride a 216 cc SIAMT, the smallest machine in the race. G. E. Stanley (499 Singer) took the lead from the start, which was at the beginning of the timed half-mile stretch on the Railway Straight. This gave an exact fifty-miles' race distance.

At the end of lap one Stanley was leading and drawing away from Billy Elce (499 Rudge), N. A. Ayres (499 Singer) and Jack Haswell (499 Triumph) who were closely bunched, with Smith on the little SIAMT (an Italian machine) bringing up the rear. Another lap saw Haswell in second place. The gap between first and second steadily increased, and at the end of his tenth circuit Stanley lapped Elce the third man, Ayres having retired. Haswell gave up after twelve laps with a leaking oil tank.

On his sixteenth lap, an already-punctured back tyre eventually stopped Stanley. Elce also stopped, but got going again a lap-and-a-half behind the leader. Meanwhile, Smith on the SIAMT had stopped and come to Stanley's aid with a cycle pump. But the puncture was too serious and "G. E." had to retire. Stanley's average speed for the thirteen laps he had completed, prior to the onset of his puncture, was 66.6 mph. His fastest lap was set up at 67.47 mph.

Smith restarted his small mount and continued, to finish second to the only other survivor in the race: Billy Elce.

FIFTY-MILE SENIOR BROOKLANDS' TT RACE
(up to 500 cc). Start at the ½-mile post. Fork finish.
1. W. H. Elce (499 Rudge) (No speed reported)
2. S. C. W. Smith (216 SIAMT)

1912—TWO, THREE OR FOUR WHEELS?

Altogether this was one of the most contrary long-distance races ever witnessed at Brooklands.

To add to his execrable luck, on the following Friday, May 17th, when he attempted the 500 cc (Class C) hour record—Stanley's machine was stopped with a broken valve spring. He did succeed, however, in setting up a new class flying-start five-mile record with a speed of 67.51 mph.

The final meeting of the month to incorporate motor cycle events, was the BARC one on Whit Monday, May 27th.

In the Short Handicap, all got away well from the Fork start, except for E. F. Remington (998 Matchless-JAP), whose machine was slow starting. When he did eventually get going, he lost his driving belt and had to retire.

SHORT MOTOR CYCLE HANDICAP (up to 1000 cc)
over 5¾ miles. Fork start and Long finish.

		H'cap start	
1.	W. Dewar (499 Triumph)	1 min 42 sec	Speed unknown
2.	M. Campbell (499 Triumph)	1 min 26 sec	
3.	G. E. Stanley (499 Singer)	1 min 30 sec	

A newcomer to the track in this event was S. M. Friedlander's 499 cc Calthorpe, fitted with a side-valve engine.

The other motor cycle race of the day—the Seventh Long Handicap of 1912—provided another second place for young Malcolm Campbell, who was to do so well in later years in cars at Brooklands and in world record attempts on four wheels.

The winner proved to be Peter Weatherilt riding a 494 cc 90-bore Zenith-Gradua-JAP.

LONG MOTOR CYCLE HANDICAP (up to 1000 cc)
over 8½ miles. Fork start and Long finish.

		H'cap start	
1.	P. Weatherilt (494 Zenith-Gradua-JAP)	1 min 24 sec	65¼ mph
2.	M. Campbell (499 Triumph)		
3.	E. Kickham (350 Douglas)		

Fourth Bemsee race meeting of the year

At the Fourth Monthly Race Meeting of the BMCRC, held on Saturday, June 1st, were staged the series of "Car Challenge" races for which the eliminating trials had been run off on Saturday, May 11th. The first of these was for 500 cc machines.

Run over a distance of three laps, there were two competitors: G. E. Stanley (499 Singer) and G. C. Pullen (24 hp four-cylinder Cameron car). At the start, Stanley got well ahead, but by the end of the second lap Pullen was leading and eventually finished five seconds ahead. Result:

500 CC "CAR INVITATION" CHALLENGE SCRATCH RACE over 8 miles 269 yd. Fork rolling start. Fork finish.

1. G. C. Pullen (24 hp 3047 cc Cameron)   66.38 mph
2. G. E. Stanley (499 Singer)   65.64 mph

All the other "Car Invitation" events used the same rolling-start technique, in which competitors dressed-in-line abreast of the timekeeper's moving car and thus had a low-speed flying-start at the Fork.

The five-lap Cyclecar Handicap over 13 miles 1035 yd, which provided yet another win for J. T. Wood and his 1070 cc GWK (at 64.9 mph), was followed by the other two "Car Invitation" events. First of these was for 750 cc motor cycles and brought to the line: R. L. Printz (746 BAT-JAP), Harry Collier (741 Matchless-JAP) and H. Petit (driving A. Lambie's 22.4 hp four-cylinder 2694 cc Bedford car). Both motor cycles left the car at the start. By the end of lap one Collier held a useful lead, with the car second. Printz had stopped with sparking-plug trouble. In the last lap the Bedford forged ahead on the Byfleet Banking near the aeroplane sheds and won by two-hundred and fifty yards.

750 CC "CAR INVITATION" CHALLENGE SCRATCH RACE over 8 miles 269 yd. Fork rolling start. Fork finish.

1. H. Petit (22.4 hp 2694 cc Bedford)   64.90 mph
2. H. A. Collier (741 Matchless-JAP)

In the 1000 cc three-lap "Car Invitation" event, Charlie Collier (998 Matchless-JAP) had a stiff challenge in the form of F. R.

Samson (driving Gordon Watney's 48.6 hp four-cylinder 9237 cc Mercédès). Charlie's chances were not improved by the fact that he was still suffering the after-effects of a recent accident. Spectators were, therefore, not altogether surprised with the result—a win for Samson by three-quarters of a mile.

1000 CC "CAR INVITATION" CHALLENGE SCRATCH RACE over 8 miles 269 yd. Fork rolling start. Fork finish.
1. F. R. Samson (48.6 hp 9237 cc Mercédès)   74.70 mph
2. C. R. Collier (998 Matchless-JAP)

Stanley had much better luck in the final event of the day, the All-Comers' Hour Race, compared with previous such events. Both his machine and that of the Australian Les Bailey (350 Douglas) were on top form, finishing first and second respectively.

ALL-COMERS' HOUR RACE

	Distance covered
1. G. E. Stanley (499 Singer)	60 miles 1552 yd
2. S. L. Bailey (350 Douglas)	56 miles 755 yd
3. A. E. Woodman (340 Humber)	53 miles 1250 yd

G. F. Hunter (988 Zenith-Gradua-JAP s/car) finished fourth with his brother as passenger.

One-design races

The June Meeting of the BARC on Saturday the 15th, was a pleasant surprise for racing motorcyclists: in addition to the usual Short and Long Handicaps, there had been organised a series of three "one-design" handicap races for particular makes of motor cycle.

In the first motor cycle event, the Ninth Short Handicap over two laps, a strong wind blew, reducing speeds. Freddie Edmond (198 Humber), the limit man, made a good start and was never caught. Eddie Kickham (350 Douglas), who also made a good getaway, came in second.

Harry Martin (268 Martin-JAP) had a small-bore pipe leading from his exhaust, coiling around his intake, and entering the carburetter on the engine side of the main jet. The intention was to increase petrol vaporisation and augment air speed into the engine.

Any advantage, however, probably arose from the now well-established "anti-knock" properties of re-inspired exhaust gas.
Result:

SHORT MOTOR CYCLE HANDICAP (up to 1000 cc) over 5¾ miles. Fork start and Long finish.

		H'cap start	
1.	F. G. Edmond (198 Humber)	2 min 32 sec	46 mph
2.	E. Kickham (350 Douglas)	1 min 6 sec	
3.	W. H. Elce (499 Rudge)	20 sec	

Harry Martin finished fourth.

In the Long Handicap over three laps, J. H. Whitlark's driving belt came off his 610 cc V-twin Rex, just after pushing off from the starting line. Rex Mundy (294 Singer) failed to start owing to sparking-plug trouble.

The race provided a second win for Freddie Edmond (198 Humber) with G. E. Stanley (499 Singer) second about a kilometre behind. Result:

LONG MOTOR CYCLE HANDICAP (up to 1000 cc) over 8½ miles. Fork start and Long finish.

		H'cap start	
1.	F. G. Edmond (198 Humber)	4 min	48 mph
2.	G. E. Stanley (499 Singer)	39 sec	
3.	E. Kickham (350 Douglas)	2 min 15 sec	

The "one-design" races had been suggested by F. P. Armstrong, a member of the BARC Committee and a prominent member of the Royal Motor Yacht Club. They were based on the same principles which he had suggested and which the last named organisation had so successfully used, for yacht racing. There were such races: A, for 2½ hp (69 × 80 mm) solo Singer machines; B, for 3½ hp (85 × 88 mm) solo Rudges; and C, for up to 8 hp (1000 cc) twin-cylinder Zenith-sidecar outfits. They were sprint handicaps of about two miles in length, with starts on the Railway Straight and finishes at the Long Finishing Line by the Clubhouse. The winners were: Race A, W. A. Jacobs at 48 mph; Race B, A. G. Walker at 55 mph; and Race C, R. Charlesworth (771 Zenith-Gradua-JAP s/car) at 47¼ mph.

The Thursday of the following week, June 20th, saw Charlie

Franklin (998 Indian) out on Brooklands' Track after records. He started at 11.00 am in windy conditions, and by 5.00 pm he had set up new Class E (1000 cc solo) records from two to six hours and from 250 to 350 miles inclusive, at speeds ranging from 66 mph down to 62 mph. No mechanical troubles were experienced with his o.h.i.v.-engined machine, the only stop being one for refreshment and two for precautionary tyre changes.

MCC race day at Brooklands

Fine weather greeted the Motor Cycling Club's Fourth Annual Race Meeting, held on Saturday, July 6th. Ten races were run off, all of which started and finished at the Fork.

The first two events were three-lap handicaps for touring machines. N. O. Soresby (499 Rudge) won the first, which was for singles up to 560 cc, at a speed of 60.54 mph. Second home was Dudley Noble (499 Rover) and third, H. C. Mills the scratch man, riding one of the new Regal-Greens fitted with a 499 cc water-cooled Precision engine manufactured by F. E. Baker. In this the thermosiphon principle was used, the radiators being fitted pannier-fashion each side of the cylinder.

Making his track debût in this race was the youthful Herbert ("Bert") Le Vack, riding a Motosacoche of unspecified capacity. Le Vack was to prove one of the greatest—if not the greatest—rider-tuner of them all during the Brooklands' golden era, the twenties.

Another young rider, later to achieve fame as a designer and manufacturer of motor cycles, won from scratch the other touring event, for twins of 400-1000 cc, at 66.1 mph. He was George Brough, the man who was to build the Brough-Superior, and who had gained renown in motorcycling circles by winning the London-to-Edinburgh Reliability Trial the previous two years in succession. He was mounted in this race on a 964 cc s.v. twin Brough of his father's manufacture. It proved to be the fastest machine at the meeting. Second man was R. E. Guest, riding a "semi-works' supported" 974 cc Matchless-JAP.

The two three-lap Open Handicaps that followed, for 560 cc and for 350 cc machines, provided wins respectively for Tom Peachy (499 Premier) and for Freddie Barnes (299 Zenith-Gradua-JAP).

In the 400-1000 cc Open Handicap, George Brough was again at scratch on his 964 cc Brough. The 499 cc Rovers ridden by Dudley Noble and Chris Newsome were fast, but too heavily handicapped to get placed in only four laps, and the result was a win for Croucher. Sydney Garrett came in second on the water-cooled Regal-Green.

400-1000 CC OPEN HANDICAP over four laps. Fork start and finish.

		H'cap start	
1.	R. Croucher (499 Kerry-Abingdon)	4 min 4 sec	
2.	S. F. Garrett (499 Regal-Green-Precision)	1 min 36 sec	
3.	E. B. Ware (494 Zenith-Gradua-JAP)	1 min 36 sec	

Winning speed = 53.64 mph.

Ware's machine was powered by a V-twin JAP engine.

Two two-lap Sidecar Handicaps followed, the first for single-cylinder machines up to 560 cc and the second for twins from 400 to 1000 cc. In the first (up to 560 cc) sidecar race, Croucher again came in first, having attached a sidecar to his machine, at 42.30 mph. F. C. North (499 Ariel s/car), who was troubled with disengaging gears, had a very close finish with F. J. Watson (499 Swift s/car). Freddie Barnes travelled at a great pace from scratch in the larger capacity sidecar race, and nearly caught E. B. Ware (494 Zenith-Gradua-JAP s/car) who had 2-min start over him. Ware came in first, however, at an average of 44.39 mph.

The final motor cycle race of the day was the MCC Championship for the "Harry Smith" Gold Challenge Cup. This was a closed-to-club ten-lap handicap for solo touring machines up to 1000 cc. The event drew thirty entries, which made life difficult for the lap scorers. R. E. Guest proved the eventual winner. Result:

MCC CLUB CHAMPIONSHIP FOR "HARRY SMITH" GOLD CHALLENGE CUP. Handicap over ten laps. Fork start and finish.

		H'cap start	
1.	R. E. Guest (974 Matchless-JAP)	2 min 40 sec	63.95 mph
2.	H. C. Mills (499 Regal-Green-Precision)	2 min 40 sec	
3.	E. B. Ware (494 Zenith-Gradua-JAP)	4 min	

Thus ended a most successful and well-organised race meeting.

The following Wednesday, July 10th, H. Ward, driving a 90 × 100 mm V-twin-engined Bedelia cyclecar, successfully broke the hour record, held by Wood's GWK, for his class of vehicle. He covered 45 miles 278 yd in the time.

There was only one motor cycle race at the BARC Brooklands' race meeting held three days later on Saturday, July 13th. This, the Tenth Short Handicap of 1912, resulted in a win for E. B. Ware (494 twin-cylinder Zenith-Gradua-JAP). He, and A. G. Walker and S. Day Timson (both on 499 Rudges), set off from the 36-sec mark. G. E. Stanley, Jimmy Cocker and D. R. O'Donovan all rode 294 cc Singers in this event, but could not get placed. Contemporary accounts of the race unfortunately do not give Ware's speed.

A fast Norton

Brooklands habitués were really staggered, when at the BMCRC's Fifth Members' Meeting of the year on Saturday, July 20th, track newcomer Percy Brewster cracked Stanley's 500-cc flying-start mile record during the Record Time Trials. Well known in the Midlands as a hill-climb and sprint expert riding James ("Pa") Norton's long-stroke motors, he had made his Brooklands' debut with a vengeance. His kilometre speed was the fastest time of the day in these sprints, including the 1000 cc class.

The fastest speeds set up in each class were as follows:

RECORD TIME TRIALS

Solo classes		Speed (mph) over:	
		fs km	fs ml
A (up to 275 cc)	H. Martin (270 Martin-JAP)	63.50	62.72
B (275-350 cc)	H. Martin (345 Martin-JAP)	67.90	67.85*
C (350-500 cc)	P. Brewster (490 Norton)	73.95	73.57*
D (500-750 cc)	H. Printz (746 BAT-JAP)	62.48	64.00
E (750-1000 cc)	E. C. E. Baragwanath (998 Winit-JAP)	73.58	73.47
Sidecar class			
E (750-1000 cc)	G. F. Hunter (998 Zenith-Gradua-JAP s/car)	62.84	63.60

(*New class records).

Interviewed in later years, Percy Brewster recalled some interesting details of his machine. It was basically a standard 79 × 100 mm bore and stroke fixed-head 490 cc s.v. Norton, single-geared with belt-drive at 4-to-1, and with its frame lengthened to render it more controllable around Brooklands. Harold Cox, maker of the CAP carburetter and a personal friend of Brewster, had supplied him with a special 1¼-in. bore component (the standard bore was 1⅞in). It made possible the use of high-volatility petrol of 0.680 specific gravity in the record-breaking run.

There were many advanced features associated with the engine, including: a roller bearing big-end (the standard 1912 Norton used a plain big-end) and a connecting rod of Duralumin machined from the solid. This aluminium alloy had only been brought on to the market 18 months before, by Vickers Ltd. These points and the use of a light steel piston, permitted in excess of 4000 rpm to be maintained during the mile record: a very high engine speed for a 1912 500 cc single.

Another interesting feature of these Record Time Trials, was that the other record breaker—Harry Martin—was using a much longer exhaust pipe than anyone else; but it proved his undoing in the next event: the Junior Five-lap Scratch Race for machines up to 350 cc.

Les Bailey (350 Douglas) got away well at the Fork start, and by the Railway Straight had a lead of twenty to thirty yards. Harry Martin steadily closed up, passing Bailey on the Byfleet Banking. By the end of the lap he had a lead of three yards over Bailey. Third was G. E. Stanley (299 Singer). In the second lap, the same order was maintained, but on passing the Fork again at the start of the third circuit—it happened! Harry Martin's exhaust pipe came adrift and that finished him for the race.

Stanley steadily caught up the Douglas in the remaining two laps, eventually coming level on the Byfleet Banking and winning by a mere two-fifths of a second. Result:

JUNIOR SCRATCH RACE (up to 350 cc)
over 13 miles 1035 yd. Fork start and finish.

1. G. E. Stanley (299 Singer)   59.4 mph
2. S. L. Bailey (350 Douglas)
3. A. E. Woodman (340 Humber)

Australian Les Bailey. With this special 349 cc o.h.v. Douglas, he became on Tuesday, December 17th, 1912, the first rider of an under-350 cc machine to exceed 70 mph. His engine was built by Granville Bradshaw.

Freddie Barnes (986 Zenith-Gradua-JAP s/car) after winning the Sidecar Handicap at the BMCRC meeting on Wednesday, April 2nd, 1913. He won from scratch at 60.92 mph, with Sam Wright the Humber rider as his passenger. The engine he used had twin carburetters.

A. J. McDonagh (499 Rudge) winner of the Short Motor Cycle Handicap at the BARC race meeting on Whit-Monday, May 12th, 1913.

G. E. Stanley (499 Singer) after gaining first place in the *Daily Express* sponsored Benzole Handicap, on June 21st, at $69\frac{1}{2}$ mph over three laps.

1912—TWO, THREE OR FOUR WHEELS? 145

After his fine performance in the Record Time Trials, Percy Brewster (490 Norton), naturally started firm favourite in the Senior Five-lap Scratch Race (up to 500 cc). As in the Junior Race, there were only six starters.

G. E. Stanley (499 Singer) moved into an early lead. Brewster was in second place for the first three laps, but increasing magneto trouble then slowed him so much that he was overtaken by Sydney Garrett (499 Regal-Green-Precision) and he eventually finished last. On the fourth lap, Sidney Axford (498 Martin-JAP) dropped out with sooted sparking plugs. The final result was:

SENIOR SCRATCH RACE (up to 500 cc)
over 13 miles 1035 yd. Fork start and finish.
1. G. E. Stanley (499 Singer)   Speed unknown
2. S. F. Garrett (499 Regal-Green-Precision)
3. S. D. Timson (499 Rudge)

Eleven starters came to the line for the All-Comers' Handicap, a five-lap race for solos and combinations up to 1000 cc, and for cyclecars up to 1100 cc. Interest centred on the Carter three-wheeler, which was appearing for the first time in this event. It had two wheels at the front and a single belt-driven back wheel. Its engine constituted one half of an enormous 2102 cc 90° V-twin—one of the cylinders having been removed! This vehicle retired on its second lap.

Percy Brewster, riding his Norton, again retired with magneto trouble, this time on his first lap. The scratch man, E. C. E. Baragwanath ("Barry") rode a 998 cc Winit-JAP and retired on his third lap. The result was a relative walkover for the Australian rider Les Bailey:

ALL-COMERS' HANDICAP (up to 1000 cc)
over 13 miles 1035 yd. Fork start and finish.
                                                H'cap start
1. S. L. Bailey (350 Douglas)   2 min 5 sec
2. S. F. Garrett (499 Regal-Green-Precision)   1 min 20 sec
3. H. C. Mills (499 Regal-Green-Precision)   1 min 20 sec
Winner's speed unknown

The day's sport concluded with the Brooklands' Test Hill event, competitors starting on the level some fifty yards from the hill's foot. Les Bailey's 350 cc Douglas made the fastest climb, averaging 33.36 mph.

New 500 cc sidecar record

During the afternoon of Thursday, July 25th, while the ACU was conducting its Special Silencer Trials, W. Stanhope Spencer (499 cc single-geared Rudge s/car) was busy attempting Class C (500 cc) sidecar records. His first attempt was abortive due to carburation trouble. A second attempt proved more successful, and despite a 7½-minute delay to replace a broken valve, he managed to complete 43 miles 356 yd in the hour to beat Frank Pither's old record. He continued to circulate the track. Despite the disintegration his sparking plug insulation and the lodging of a piece of it under his exhaust valve causing it to stay open, he went on at reduced speed to set new fifty-mile and two-hour records as well, at around the 40 mph mark. His fastest lap, his fourteenth, was at 52.50 mph.

The second clubmen's meeting

On Saturday, July 27th, 1912, the Second Annual Gala Day of those clubs associated with the RAC was held. The first motor cycle event was so over-subscribed that it had to be run in two heats and a final, each of two laps duration. It was the Short-Distance Handicap for *The Motor Cycle* Cup, covering any class of machine (up to 1000 cc), owned by a member of the ACU or any of its affiliated clubs. Pushers were allowed and machines could be stripped for racing. In each race the start was at the Fork, and the finish was at the Long Finishing Line.

Charlie Collier broke his driving belt on the way to the Fork from the Paddock for the First Heat, and so could not compete.

Limit man H. P. Beasley (299 Singer) maintained his lead past the Fork at the end of lap one. The winner, however, proved to be Sydney Garrett (499 Regal-Green-Precision), who gobbled-up five places in the last lap to finish comfortably ahead on his water-cooled engined machine. The first eight to finish were eligible for the Final.

FIRST HEAT: SHORT-DISTANCE HANDICAP
(up to 1000 cc) over 5¾ miles. Fork start and Long finish.

H'cap start

1. S. F. Garrett (499 Regal-Green-Precision)   56 sec   64¼ mph
2. H. P. Beasley (299 Singer)   2 min 22 sec
3. R. E. Guest (726 Matchless-JAP)   34 sec

At the start of the Second Heat, there were six limit men away from the 1-min 16-sec mark. Harry Reed (998 DOT-JAP), riding a machine of his own manufacture, romped through the field from the 12-sec mark and was in the lead by the end of the first lap, with Les Bailey (345 Douglas) second. Harry remained unchallenged, and kept his lead until the end. But H. C. Mills (499 Regal-Green-Precision) passed Bailey on the finishing line to gain second spot. Again, the first eight moved on to the Final, which was held over until the end of the meeting.

SECOND-HEAT: SHORT-DISTANCE HANDICAP (up to 1000 cc) over 5¾ miles. Fork start and Long finish.

		H'cap start	
1.	H. Reed (998 DOT-JAP)	12 sec	73 mph
2.	H. C. Mills (499 Regal-Green-Precision)	56 sec	
3.	S. L. Bailey (345 Douglas)	56 sec	

There now followed the Inter-club Team Race, for club teams each comprising: a single-cylinder machine up to 500 cc, a multi up to 750 cc, and a passenger machine up to 1000 cc. All had to be touring models fully-equipped, and pushers were allowed.

The race was a two-lap scratch event and points were awarded in accordance with the order of finishing, the club team with the least number of points being adjudged the winner. This turned out to be the Streatham & District MCC team.

First past the post was Sidney Tessier (580 BAT-JAP) at an average speed of 67 mph. Second, was Harry Reed (998 DOT-JAP) and third F. C. Jones (998 Zenith-Gradua-JAP s/car).

The Final of the Short-Distance Handicap rounded off the meeting with a well-deserved win for Harry Reed (998 DOT-JAP), who passed H. P. Beasley (299 Singer) almost on the finishing line: a tribute to good handicapping.

FINAL: SHORT-DISTANCE HANDICAP (up to 1000 cc) over 5¾ miles. Fork start and Long finish.

		H'cap start
1.	H. Reed (998 DOT-JAP)	unknown
2.	H. P. Beasley (299 Singer)	
3.	S. F. Garrett (499 Regal-Green-Precision)	

Bank holiday racing

Billy Elce and F. H. Arnott (both on single-geared Rudges) were the Short and the Long Handicap winners, averaging 62¼ mph and 60½ mph respectively, at the BARC Bank Holiday Monday, August 3rd, race meeting at Brooklands. A Zenith rider at this meeting, C. Townsend, running on a badly worn tyre front which burst, was thrown from his machine. Fortunately he was only concussed.

Arnott's win qualified him to run in the so-called Winners' Handicap, with 53 sec start (over one lap) with the following car competitors: K. Yano (25.8 hp Bedford), 49 sec start; C. H. Bird (15.9 hp Sunbeam), 10 sec start; L. N. Straight (15.9 hp SCAR), 36 sec start; Louis Coatalen (30.1 hp Sunbeam), scratch; Turner-Smith (13.9 hp Stoewer) and G. W. Hands. Arnott led easily and would have won but, instead of turning off down the straight to the finish, he unaccountably continued to the Members' Banking on the Outer Circuit. He thereby lost a cup to the value of £12 10s—a small fortune in 1912.

The 500 cc sidecar hour record again broken

Routine testing of machines continued at Brooklands, but no further race meetings took place during August. Of particular regret was the postponement due to rain of the BMCRC meeting originally scheduled for August 24th, until Saturday, September 14th. People were all the more disappointed because they had been looking forward to the two 150-mile Brooklands' TT Races on the 24th.

As if to make up for this dearth of activity, W. Stanhope Spencer decided to have another crack at the 500 cc sidecar hour record riding his 499 cc single-geared Rudge outfit. He succeeded not only in breaking his old hour distance, but also in setting up two other long-distance records as well, covering: in one hour, 46 miles 587 yd; in two hours, 87 miles 115 yd; and in three hours, 112 miles 900 yd. The hundred-mile record also succumbed with an average of about 42 mph.

Junior and Senior Brooklands' TT Races

The weather was fine and cool with little wind for the two postponed 150-mile Races on the 14th.

1912—TWO, THREE OR FOUR WHEELS?

Fifteen runners came to the line for the first of these, the Junior Race (up to 350 cc), which started at 11.00 am from the Fork.

A keen struggle had been forecast between the Douglas team of Bizzy and Aubrey Bashall, Frank McNab, Les Bailey and Victor Wilberforce; and the Humber team comprising Alan Woodman (the one-legged rider), S. W. Phillpott, Freddie Edmond and Sam Wright. And a keen struggle it proved to be.

At the start Bizzy Bashall and Les Bailey shot ahead on their two-speeders, and after passing under the Members' Bridge the field behind them had sorted itself out into a sizeable procession. The order at the end of lap one was Bailey, Edmond, Woodman, with Howard Newman (346 Ivy-Precision) fourth. Then Edmond's engine began to misfire and on the next circuit Sam Wright gained second place, followed by Woodman, with Edmond fourth, Bizzy Bashall fifth and Newman sixth. The two leaders Bailey and Wright were constantly swapping positions and slip-streaming each other. Both riders were lapping at around the 55 mph, but since 60 mph was well within their capabilities, they were obviously keeping their engines well-in-hand in view of the race distance.

Now the troubles started. Bert Colver (348 Enfield) stopped in the pits at the Fork to clean a sparking plug, while Frank McNab rode in on a flat back tyre.

The twelfth lap saw Bailey with a substantial lead over Wright. Colver had to call it a day because of a broken exhaust valve, and Howard Newman dropped out with a broken valve rocker.

At the end of the first hour Les Bailey still led, with a distance of 52 miles 3 yd to his credit. He at once came in to his pit to refuel and change his driving belt. Frank McNab came in with yet another burst tyre, this time fitting a new wheel from Bizzy Bashall's machine, which had dropped out earlier with engine trouble.

Hugh Mason (350 NUT-JAP), his o.h.v. V-twin going extremely well after an indifferent start, had now crept up the field to third place.

Aubrey Bashall (350 Douglas) came in with a flat back tyre which had blown off the rim and almost thrown him from his machine. W. A. Jacobs (299 Singer) also came in, with a stretched valve. Then, Sam Wright blew up the rear cylinder on his Humber, leaving Bailey with the race in his pocket failing any mischance—Mason being most three laps behind due to time lost at the start.

The numbers were now further reduced; Aubrey Bashall, who had restarted with a fresh tyre, retired with a leaking fuel tank. Freddie Edmond got a stone in his belt rim, which threw the driving belt off, jamming the back wheel of his machine and causing him to crash into the inside banking of the track, fortunately without injury.

Bailey's Douglas continued to circulate consistently and he finished the winner in record time by two complete laps or exactly eleven minutes. Being informed that the three-hour Class B (350 cc) record lay within his grasp, he hastily refuelled, shot off again and succeeded in gaining that as well, at an average speed of 53.18 mph.
Result:

JUNIOR BROOKLANDS' TT RACE (up to 350 cc) over 150 miles. Fork start. Finish short of the Fork.

		Av. speed (mph)
1.	S. L. Bailey (350 Douglas)	53.02*
2.	H. Mason (350 NUT-JAP)	49.83
3.	A. Woodman (340 Humber)	39.03

(*New Class B Record).

Phillpott was fourth, Frank McNab fifth and A. J. Jenkins sixth on a Douglas which was in full touring trim, and which he had ridden down from Liverpool the day before.

The stragglers in the Junior Race were so long in finishing, that a start had to be made with the Senior (500 cc) event.

At the drop of the flag all twenty-six starters got away smartly, but Sidney Axford (494 Martin-JAP) collided with another rider and had to retire with a damaged machine. L. Hill (499 Rudge) led first time round, with Jack Emerson (490 Norton)—a newcomer to Brooklands—close behind. Great things were expected of Emerson, who had ridden his Norton down from Hull earlier in the week and had been lapping consistently at 68 mph in practice. Sydney Garrett (499 Regal-Green-Precision) was next, Percy Brewster (490 Norton) fourth and Harold Petty (499 Singer) fifth.

On lap two Garrett lost his oil filler cap and dropped back; Oliver Godfrey (498 Indian) and Charlie Collier (498 Matchless-JAP) crept up several places, then came Jack Woodhouse (499 Regal-Green-Precision), Petty, Jack Haswell (on a new experimental o.h.i.v. 499 cc Triumph), C. R. Martin (on Haswell's old 1911 record-breaking s.v. 499 cc Triumph) and Victor Horsman (499

Singer). Hill and Emerson had set up a cracking pace, completing lap after lap in 2 min 28 sec (66.11 mph). The question was: would this pace last without someone's engine blowing up?

Emerson, if anything, speeded up and gradually drew ahead, until by the fourteenth lap he was a full half minute in front.

In the fifteenth lap Hill dropped out, leaving an even bigger gap between Emerson and the field. Charlie Collier was now second on the Matchless. In this round, there was a general shuffling of positions. Several now stopped to replenish their oil and fuel tanks. They included Emerson, a fact which caused his supporters some disappointment, as he had stood a chance of taking the 500 cc hour record if he had kept going. He appeared to be playing safe, however, so far as the race was concerned. H. C. Mills (499 Regal-Green-Precision) retired with a seized engine due to a leaky radiator causing overheating and Sydney Garrett, on a similar machine, with a loose driving belt pulley.

At the twentieth lap the order was Emerson, Collier, T. A. Carter (498 Martin-JAP), Haswell, Godfrey and the rest. Peter Weatherilt (498 Zenith-Gradua-JAP) had fallen back due to a stop for petrol. Jack Haswell, who was going well, rode his experimental machine because his original side-valve entry had been damaged in practice.

H. Huckle (498 Zenith-Gradua-JAP) dropped out with a broken cam lever. Percy Brewster also had engine trouble. At the end of the first hour, Emerson led with 63 miles to his credit, while Charlie Collier and E. B. Ware (498 Zenith-Gradua-JAP), who had picked up a lot of ground, fought for second place. C. R. Martin stopped to change a valve on his Triumph and Jack Woodhouse retired with a seized engine.

After one-and-a-half hours of riding Jack Emerson had completed 35½ laps, and was 2½ laps ahead of the rest of the field! Of course everyone was asking who this new rider was, who was showing the older Brooklands' hands the way round. One thing was certain, he knew a thing or two about making a Norton go fast and last in a long-distance race.

As the fifty-sixth lap drew nearer, the result was regarded as a foregone conclusion for Emerson, whose Norton had run regularly throughout. With his exhaust note as crisp as at the start, he finished an easy winner and continued for the three-hour record, but had to give up due to tyre trouble.

Unfortunately for Weatherilt, who had picked up to second place, his oil tank split towards the end of the race, pouring oil over the engine and over his driving belt causing it to slip. He was much slowed by this and was soon passed by Haswell and Godfrey. Result:

SENIOR BROOKLANDS' TT RACE (up to 500 cc) over 150 miles. Fork start. Finish short of Fork.

		Av. speed (mph)
1.	J. L. Emerson (490 Norton)	63.88*
2.	J. T. Haswell (499 Triumph)	58.39
3.	O. C. Godfrey (498 Indian)	57.96

(* New Class C record).

Emerson also took the hundred-mile and two-hundred-mile records at average speeds of 64.22 mph and 63.68 mph respectively. He finished 13 min $16\frac{3}{5}$ sec ahead of the second man Haswell. Peter Weatherilt finished fourth, Ware fifth, Carter sixth and Billy Elce (499 Rudge) seventh.

Throughout the day Jack Emerson's lap speeds steadily improved and his fastest, achieved before the onset of tyre trouble, was completed at 67.94 mph.

Dangers of the Long Finish

The last BARC meeting of the year, held at Brooklands on Saturday, September 28th, demonstrated yet again the potential dangers associated with the use of the Long Finishing Line by the paddock. It was in the one-and-only motor cycle event on the race card, the Short-Distance Handicap over $5\frac{3}{4}$ miles, that the first man across the finishing line E. F. Remington (986 Matchless-JAP) went straight up the Members' Banking and over the top because of the failure of his front brake. Fortunately he was unhurt, but both wheels of his machine were buckled. His average speed for the race was $73\frac{3}{4}$ mph despite his mishap.

Major Lloyd reported the incident to the race stewards, who took the view that Remington should have ensured that his brakes were in good order. They disqualified him for not stopping within the prescribed distance.

Thus the declared result was as follows, with the second finisher being declared the winner:

SHORT-DISTANCE HANDICAP (up to 1000 cc)
over 5¾ miles. Fork start and Long Finish.

		H'cap start	
1.	L. Hill (499 Rudge)	42 sec	65¼ mph
2.	W. H. Elce (499 Rudge)	42 sec	
3.	S. L. Bailey (350 Douglas)	1 min 4 sec	

More record breaking

During the next week a minor but mostly successful bout of record attempts took place.

On the Wednesday, October 2nd, J. T. Wood, driving his 1068 cc GWK cyclecar set new records for the hour (at 47.79 mph) and for the 50 miles (at 47.97 mph) during the afternoon. He was prevented from going for longer distance records because of a cracked water jacket on his engine.

G. E. Stanley decided to attempt the Class C (500 cc solo) hour record on his 499 cc Singer later in the afternoon, but this had to be postponed until 5.30 pm due to the wind. He covered his first twelve laps at an average of 69.75 mph, but oiling difficulties were slowing him. He carried on, however, beating the fifty-mile record with an average speed of 68.70 mph, but it became too dark to see and he could not complete the hour. Stanley's fastest lap was his third at 69.98 mph.

While Stanley was waiting for the wind to abate, Les Bailey (350 Douglas) went out and set up a new flying-start five-miles' average of 61.81 mph for Class B (350 cc solo).

Forty-eight hours later, on the Saturday, Stanley went for the flying-start five-mile records in Classes C and D, and got them at 70.75 mph.

Bemsee Championship meeting

Thick fog in the morning nearly forced a cancellation of the BMCRC Open Championship Meeting, held on Saturday, October 12th. Fortunately at 11.00 am, an hour after the scheduled starting time, the fog started to lift and by midday all was blue skies and sunshine.

The first race on the agenda was an hour race for cycle cars (up to 1100 cc). It provided an easy win for J. T. Wood (1068 GWK), who covered 47 miles 30 yd, with R. Bourbeau (1008 Bedelia) second and Cyril Pullin (1080 Sabella) third.

The next event was an hour race for sidecar machines (up to 1000 cc). For this passengers had to weigh over 10 stones.

Freddie Barnes (988 Zenith-Gradua-JAP s/car) held the lead during the first lap, with G. F. Hunter on a similar outfit following and Sidney Tessier (736 BAT-JAP s/car) third. Running well in fourth place was Sydney Garrett (499 Regal-Green-Precision s/car). Barnes shed his driving belt at the Fork opposite the timekeepers' box, at the end of lap one. Tessier and Garrett then ran neck-and-neck for first place in the second lap, while Billy Wells (994 Indian s/car) lay third and Freddie Barnes, who had restarted, fourth.

Garrett maintained a lead for the first eight laps, and then Barnes on his bigger motor regained the premier position, which he never afterwards relinquished. Garrett held second spot until lap 15, when Billy Wells took it over on the big Indian outfit, which was fitted with a two-speed gear and clutch.

Both Freddie Barnes and Sydney Garrett set up new class records.
Result:

SIDECAR HOUR RACE (up to 1000 cc). Fork start.

		Distance covered
1.	F. W. Barnes (988 Zenith-Gradua-JAP s/car)	52 ml 300 yd*
2.	W. H. Wells (994 Indian s/car)	51 ml 840 yd
3.	S. F. Garrett (499 Regal-Green-Precision s/car)	50 ml 1740 yd*

(* New class records).

In the Junior Hour Race, Les Bailey (350 Douglas) led at the end of lap one, followed in second place by Billy Newsome who was making his debut on a Douglas. Next came Peter Weatherilt (299 Zenith-Gradua-JAP), with G. E. Stanley (299 Singer) in the unusual position, for him, of fourth.

Stanley took first place in the next lap and right up until the fourteenth circuit it was a ding-dong affair for the lead between him and Bailey, when the latter retired with a broken valve. There were many mechanical breakdowns, which thinned out the field considerably. The final order was as follows:

1912—TWO, THREE OR FOUR WHEELS?

JUNIOR HOUR RACE (up to 350 cc). Fork start.

	Distance covered
1. G. E. Stanley (299 Singer)	55 miles 1260 yd
2. H. V. Colver (348 Enfield)	53 miles 10 yd
3. E. Kickham (350 Douglas)	52 miles 1390 yd

Billy Newsome finished fourth with 50 miles 36 yd, and Harry Bashall (350 Douglas), the winner of the 1912 Junior TT Race in the Isle of Man, fifth with 48 miles 85 yd covered.

The *Motor Car Journal* had put up its Challenge Cup as first prize in the next event; the Five-Lap ACU Championship Race for machines up to 1000 cc. The 1911 winner was Charlie Collier, and he again came in first for this 1912 event. The race distance had been increased by one lap over the previous year.

ACU CHAMPIONSHIP FOR THE "MOTOR CAR JOURNAL" CUP (up to 1000 cc) over 5 laps. Fork start and finish.

1. C. R. Collier (998 Matchless-JAP)   74.65 mph
2. O. C. Godfrey (994 Indian)
3. H. Hunter (738 Zenith Gradua-JAP)

The last event of the day, was the Senior Hour ACU Championship Race (up to 500 cc) for *The Motor Cycle* Challenge Cup.

G. E. Stanley (499 Singer) established an early lead, but was put out in the third lap with lubrication trouble and a puncture. After Stanley's retirement Jack Emerson (490 Norton) struggled with L. Hill (499 Rudge) for the lead, until the latter retired also. Thereafter, with no other challenger in sight and his motor running perfectly, Jack went on to finish the hour three miles ahead of his nearest rival: Charlie Collier (497 twin-cylinder Matchless-JAP). Result:

SENIOR HOUR RACE FOR "THE MOTOR CYCLE" CHALLENGE CUP (up to 500 cc). Fork start.

	Distance covered
1. J. L. Emerson (490 Norton)	63 miles 1289 yd
2. C. R. Collier (497 Matchless-JAP)	60 miles 1660 yd
3. C. R. Martin (499 Triumph)	60 miles 1650 yd

Fourth was Oliver Godfrey (497 Indian).

Stanley breaks the hour record

Immediately after the Championship Meeting, G. E. Stanley returned to the Singer Works at Coventry and spent Monday working on his 499 cc machine. The intention was to return to Brooklands early on Tuesday, October 15th, for an attack on the Class C (500 cc solo) hour record held by Stanhope Spencer's 499 cc Rudge.

On arrival at the track, he did a lap to see that his machine was in good fettle and then put it away until late in the afternoon, when the weather conditions would be more to his liking.

Starting his record attempt, he averaged 64 mph for his first lap and 70.48 mph for his second, which was to prove his fastest. His first five laps were completed at an average of over 70 mph, and at fifty miles he had achieved a record average of 69.44 mph. He had started to slow on his seventeenth lap to avoid a cyclecar practising on the track, and for that circuit he averaged only 68.70 mph, his slowest flying lap.

It was nearly dusk when Stanley finished. At the start of his last lap, it looked as though he would average over 69 mph for the hour, but just as he got to the end of the Railway Straight the inlet valve, which was not new, broke at the cotter hole. The engine continued to fire intermittently, the valve working automatically, but Stanley had to paddle the machine along with his feet over the final distance. This one-and-only contretemps, apart from the cyclecar incident, reduced his hour distance to 67 miles 782 yd—which nevertheless handsomely beat Spencer's record.

Pulling a $3\frac{3}{4}$-to-1 single gear by belt drive, the 85×88 mm (499 cc) s.v.-engined Singer maintained an estimated steady 3400 rpm for most of the distance. The machine, which was fitted with a Brown & Barlow carburetter, gave a total petrol consumption of 60 mpg, which meant that the $1\frac{3}{4}$-gallon fuel tanks was more than adequate.

The following day, Stanley went for the flying-start mile and kilometre records in Class C, but was thwarted by severe crosswinds on the Railway Straight. The attempts therefore were abandoned.

To celebrate his success, on Friday, October 25th, Stanley was entertained by Singer and Company Ltd to a dinner in his honour at the Queen's Hotel, Coventry.

More cyclecar records

With the Motor Cycle Show in the offing, a number of other firms had their sights on records at Brooklands. Several Rudge exponents were preparing their machines at the track. On Wednesday, October 30th, L. de Peyrecave and J. McArthur succeeded in setting up new long-distance records in their 976 cc Duocar. These were over periods of from three to nine hours and distances of from 150 to 300 miles, at average speeds ranging from 39 mph down to 35 mph.

Final race meeting of the year

Making their first public appearance at Brooklands at the last BMCRC Race Meeting of the year, on Saturday, November 9th, were the new four-valve single-cylinder and eight-valve twin-cylinder racing Indians. These had two inlet and two exhaust valves per cylinder, operated by forked rockers. Each cylinder had its own individual exhaust pipe and auxiliary exhaust ports drilled in its base. Mechanical oil pumps were used, as on the 1911 o.h.i.v. Indian machines.

The first event was the fourth of the 1912 series of Record Time Trials. The fastest speeds in each class were as follows:

RECORD TIME TRIALS

			Speed (mph) over:	
			fs km	fs ml
Solo classes				
A	(275 cc)	H. Martin (270 Martin-JAP)	50.97	50.57
B	(350 cc)	P. Weatherilt (298 Zenith-Gradua-JAP)	65.16	64.89
C	(500 cc)	C. R. Collier (498 Matchless-JAP)	69.04	62.23
D	(750 cc)	C. R. Collier (738 Matchless-JAP)	75.29	74.05
E	(1000 cc)	C. R. Collier (999 Matchless-JAP)	80.47	79.87
Sidecar classes				
C	(500 cc)	S. F. Garrett (499 Regal-Green-Precision)	46.93	48.03
D	(750 cc)	A. Mago (554 Bradbury)	43.45	48.42
E	(1000 cc)	F. W. Barnes (988 Zenith-Gradua-JAP)	59.02	59.02

| Cyclecars | A. W. Lambert (1082 Morgan-JAP) | 58.94 | 58.86 |

Although the weather conditions were extremely mild for the time of the year, a strong south-westerly wind prevented any records being set up.

Racing began in earnest at 11.45 am with the Olympic Cyclecar and Olympic Sidecar Races, which were run concurrently over one hour.

In the cyclecar race H. F. S. Morgan, on a three-wheeler of his own manufacture, soon established a lead which he never relinquished. He finished a winner by over eight miles.

Freddie Barnes (998 Zenith-Gradua-JAP s/car) won the sidecar race by over two miles. Charlie Franklin, with one of the new eight-valve Indians, finished third.

Various troubles wrought havoc in both races. Sidney Tessier's flywheels came adrift in the engine of his 736 cc BAT-JAP s/car, Oliver Godfrey's o.h.i.v. 994 cc Indian s/car broke a piston and one of the cylinder heads of E. B. Ware's Zenith blew off. Harry Martin sheared a transmission key on his Morgan-JAP three-wheeler and had to retire.

The final results were as follows:

OLYMPIC PASSENGER MACHINE HOUR RACES
(Fork start).
Sidecars (up to 1000 cc)

1. F. W. Barnes (988 Zenith-Gradua-JAP s/car)	51 miles 897 yd
2. S. F. Garrett (499 Regal-Green-Precision s/car)	49 miles 420 yd
3. C. B. Franklin (994 Indian s/car)	47 miles 210 yd

Cyclecars (up to 1100 cc)

1. H. F. S. Morgan (966 Morgan-JAP)	55 miles 329 yd*
2. F. E. Readwin (1096 Sabella)	47 miles 1540 yd
3. J. T. Wood (1068 GWK)	46 miles 1202 yd

(*New class record).

The next event, a 500 cc three-lap scratch race, provided the first win for a four-valve 497 cc Indian, in the hands of Oliver Godfrey. He led right from the start, followed by Percy Brewster (490 Norton), L. Hill and Frank Bateman (499 Rudges), Peter

Weatherilt (494 Zenith-Gradua-JAP), Stanhope Spencer and Billy Elce (499 Rudges), H. Greaves (425 Royal Enfield) and Jack Woodhouse (499 Regal-Green-Precision). In the second lap Godfrey led by about three-hundred yards from Brewster; Weatherilt had picked up to third place, then came four Rudges, Woodhouse and lastly Greaves on the Enfield twin. The final result was:

500 CC SCRATCH RACE (over 8½ miles.)
Fork start and finish.

	Av. speed (mph)
1. O. C. Godfrey (497 four-valve Indian)	65.60
2. P. Brewster (490 Norton)	64.27
3. P. Weatherilt (494 Zenith-Gradua-JAP)	63.90

For the first three laps of the Junior Hour Race (up to 350 cc) Harry Martin (340 Martin-JAP) led, then his petrol pipe broke, putting him out. Next, Les Bailey went to the front on his 350 cc Douglas, but a broken tappet delayed him for a while in the pits, the lead being taken over by Hugh Mason on the little V-twin 350 cc o.h.v. NUT-JAP. Mason held it for the rest of the race. All the Douglases, except for Newsome's, were plagued by small, delaying troubles of various kinds. Results:

JUNIOR HOUR RACE (up to 350 cc). Fork start.

	Distance covered
1. H. Mason (350 NUT-JAP)	52 miles 625 yd
2. W. F. Newsome (350 Douglas)	51 miles 688 yd
3. L. Temple (340 Moto Rêve)	41 miles 688 yd

The up to 1000 cc three-lap scratch race provided plenty of excitement. Charlie Collier (999 Matchless-JAP) slipped and fell just as his big twin began to fire, and he was dragged along for a yard or two. He managed to recover himself and by a supreme effort reached the saddle. But despite help from a pusher-off he had to retire, as the driving belt broke when the engine fired again.

Harry Bashall (988 Zenith-Gradua-JAP) led at the end of lap one, followed by Charlie Franklin on the eight-valve 994 cc Indian, E. F. Remington (988 Matchless-JAP), Harry Reed (988 DOT-JAP), H. Hunter (988 Zenith-Gradua-JAP) and T. Rogers (988 Matchless-JAP), who brought up the rear.

On the second lap, Franklin assumed the lead, with Reed second and Bashall third. Reed's DOT-JAP was running really well, and he soon displaced Franklin, coming home an easy winner. Meanwhile Remington had gained third position and Harry Bashall finished fourth.

1000 CC SCRATCH RACE (over $8\frac{1}{2}$ miles). Fork start and finish.

		Av. speed (mph)
1.	H. Reed (988 DOT-JAP)	74.97
2.	C. B. Franklin (994 Indian)	74.60
3.	E. F. Remington (988 Matchless-JAP)	70.56

Harry Bashall made an outstanding first lap in this race, averaging 74.12 mph; a standing-start lap record for the track.

The last race of the day was one of the most exciting. It was the Senior One-Hour event for machines up to 500 cc. Jack Emerson (490 Norton) led for many laps until he had to stop, because the top of his float chamber came unscrewed. The race then became a duel between Oliver Godfrey (497 four-valve Indian) and Sydney Garrett (499 water-cooled Regal-Green-Precision).

Anticipating difficulty in determining who would be the race leader at the completion of the hour, Ebbie Ebblewhite, the senior time-keeper, sent his assistant George Reynolds with a synchronised stop watch and a pair of strong field glasses to the top of the tower over the club buildings in the paddock. He was to observe the relative positions of the race leaders at the termination of the hour.

Godfrey and Garrett crossed the line together at the Fork on the last lap, after which Garrett shot ahead. Sydney Garrett was thought by the crowd to be a certain winner and all were delighted. A dozen or so joined hands and danced around Frank Baker, the maker of the water-cooled Precision engine which had powered Garrett's machine. When Garrett arrived he was carried shoulder high. But the news came that, as the hour had expired Godfrey was judged to be leading by eight yards, so friends persuaded Garrett to lodge a formal protest—which he did.

The protest was heard by the BMCRC Committee but was disallowed, and the method of hour race determination by direct observation was upheld. So the race result stood as follows:

SENIOR HOUR RACE (up to 500 cc). Fork start.

		Distance covered
1.	O. C. Godfrey (497 Indian)	60 miles 1370 yd
2.	S. F. Garrett (499 Regal-Green-Precision)	60 miles 1362 yd
3.	J. L. Emerson (490 Norton)	58 miles 1047 yd

End of season record-breaking

Tuesday, November 19th, saw J. T. Wood on the track with his 1070 cc GWK cyclecar regaining the hour record in his class, with a distance of 56 miles 76 yd. He completed the fifty miles at an average speed of 56.45 mph. Later the same day, Les Bailey secured records up to six-hours' duration in Class B (350 cc) on his s.v. Douglas, averaging between 44 and 45 mph.

The following Friday, November 22nd, Hugh Gibson (554 Bradbury s/car) set up new two-hour and 100-mile Class D (750 cc) sidecar records at 45.99 mph and 46.04 mph respectively. On the same day H. F. S. Morgan (988 Morgan-JAP) blasted J. T. Wood's Tuesday's cyclecar records wide open, with a distance of 59 miles 1123 yd in the hour and an average speed of 59.43 mph for the fifty miles.

The final bout of record-breaking was the most sensational of all. Les Bailey had persuaded Granville Bradshaw, designer to the All British Engine Company (ABC), which made the ABC aero-engine and whose works were near the Flying Ground, to make up some special parts for his 350 cc Douglas. These included steel cylinders, overhead valves and valve gear with cylinder head to suit, cast-iron pistons and steel connecting rods. One piston used two connecting rods, the other a single connecting rod equal to their combined weights. The horizontally-opposed engine, which in all other respects used Douglas parts, did away with any twisting couple on the crankshaft, which had no overhang. On Tuesday, December 17th, all was completed and the machine was taken on to the track with a view to attacking Class B (up to 350 cc solo) flying-start kilometre and flying-start mile records.

The first attempt was frustrated by misfiring due to too high a compression ratio (7.5-to-1), so compression plates were fitted and the ratio on each cylinder brought down to 6-to-1. Bailey then went for the flying-start kilometre and accomplished it in 30.8 sec (72.63 mph) beating Harry Martin's old record by over 4 mph.

On attempting the mile Bailey averaged 70.04 mph; but was still accelerating at the end of the distance because too short a run-in had been used. On his second attempt, the screws holding his carburetter worked loose and his average fell to 67.67 mph. A third attempt resulted in the disintegration of a sparking plug, so he decided to call it a day. This was to be his last ride in England for a while as he was due to sail for Australia on the Thursday, to establish agencies there for the Douglas concern.

The new engine had a bore and stroke of 60.9 × 60 mm, and later on-test at the ABC works showed a horsepower development of 13 bhp at its peak engine speed of 5000 rpm.

So ended the 1912 racing season on a most auspicious note and the Brooklands Track closed down for its period of Winter repairs.

7

1913—SPEEDS MOUNT

THE first event of the year at Brooklands Track was the ACU Silencer Trials, in which various makes of silencer were tested for their efficacy. Out of these, that of Chris Newsome's $3\frac{1}{2}$ hp Rover emerged with flying colours.

The first motor cycle races were held on Bank Holiday Monday, March 24th, during the Easter BARC Race Meeting. Kenneth Holden (499 BSA) made his début on the track with a surprise win from the 1-min 14-sec mark, in the Short Motor Cycle Handicap. This was run over the usual two laps ($5\frac{3}{4}$ miles) with a Fork start and Long finish, and he averaged $60\frac{3}{4}$ mph. Second was Frank Bateman (499 Rudge) with 46 sec start and third, Harry Collier (666 Matchless-JAP) who had a 20-sec start.

The Long Handicap over three laps or $8\frac{1}{2}$ miles was the second motor cycle race and both scratch man Charlie Franklin (994 Indian), and Harry Collier (666 Matchless) again on the 20-sec mark, had difficulty starting their machines. As it turned out neither was placed. Cyril Pullin (499 Rudge), going off from the 1-min 50-sec mark, led from the end of the first lap to the finish. He won at an average speed of $60\frac{1}{4}$ mph, with Frank Bateman and L. Hill (499 Rudges), both from the 1-min 9-sec mark, filling second and third places. The fastest lap was made by Franklin at 76.79 mph.

This fine one-two-three finish by the Rudge riders was witnessed by that marque's managing director, John Vernon Pugh, who was watching the meeting.

Twin carburetters

The last motor cycle race of the day was a handicap for sidecar combinations up to 1000 cc, with passengers weighing not less than

9½ stones, and cyclecars as defined by the RAC, with passengers optional. Run over two laps (5¾ miles), it had a Fork start and Long finish as with the previous two events.

The finish was most exciting, as J. T. Wood (1068 GWK) only beat Freddie Barnes (986 Zenith-Gradua-JAP s/car) by a yard. Barnes probably would have won, despite his conceding 34 sec to Wood, if one of his two carburetters had not come loose and induced a misfire. A. W. Lambert (1082 Morgan-JAP), who finished third, ended the race with one cylinder out of action due to an HT lead coming adrift. Wood averaged 54 mph for the two laps.

Rain spoils first Bemsee meet of the year

Saturday, March 29th saw the start of the First BMCRC Race Meeting of the 1913 season. Shortly after the start of the first scheduled event, a Hundred-Mile High-Speed Reliability Trial, it began to rain. At the finish of this race, which was restricted to cyclecars and which provided a win for G. W. Hands (1095 Calthorpe), the weather became so bad that the remaining races had to be postponed until the following Wednesday.

The postponed Bemsee meet

A full programme of eight three-lap races—four scratch and four handicaps—enlivened the postponed remainder of the BMCRC First Monthly Race Meeting, held on Wednesday, April 2nd. All races were held over 8 miles 269 yd, with a Fork start and finish in each case.

The first lap of the 350 cc Scratch Race concluded with a fierce struggle for the lead between G. E. Stanley (349 Singer) and Hugh Mason (347 NUT-JAP). On the second lap Mason broke a valve cotter on his o.h.v. twin, leaving Stanley with an easy victory at an average speed of 58.66 mph. Harry Martin (345 Martin-JAP) finished second and Max Heinzel (324 NSU twin) third.

Only nine out of eighteen entries came to the starting line for the 500 cc Scratch Race, which provided another victory for Stanley (499 Singer) at an average of 67.94 mph. He also made fastest lap at 70.18 mph. Rudges were second and third, in the hands of Frank Bateman and S. Heales.

In the Sidecar Race, open to outfits up to 1000 cc engine capacity, H. C. Mills (499 Regal-Green-Precision s/car) was using a G. H. countershaft gear and chain drive. Freddie Barnes's 986 cc Zenith-Gradua-JAP sidecar outfit again had a carburetter to each cylinder, and two drip oil feeds. Barnes had it all his own way from the start and was never really pushed, winning at an average of 54.84 mph and making fastest lap at 56.35 mph. Second was Jack Woodhouse (965 Regal-Green-Precision s/car) and third L. Hill (499 Rudge s/car).

There were only three competitors in the next event, the 1000 cc Scratch Race, all using o.h.v. twin JAP engines. Charlie Collier proved unhappy riding his new six-speed 986 cc Matchless and could only finish second. Harry Reed (986 DOT-JAP) won at an average speed of 72.68 mph by almost 35 sec. Third was T. V. West (986 BAT-JAP).

As with the scratch event, scratch man Stanley (349 Singer) won easily the 350 cc Handicap—averaging 56.49 mph. The 24-sec start men, Harry Martin (345 Martin-JAP) and Max Heinzel (324 NSU), came in second and third. Fourth was Tudor Thompson (350 Douglas).

Stanley was not so lucky in the 500 cc Handicap, Vernon March (499 single-geared Rudge) coming in first from a 54-sec start at an average speed of 64.46 mph. S. Heales, with a 30-sec start, was second on a similar machine and Stanley who was again the scratch man was relegated to third position.

The Sidecar Handicap was a very fine race, Freddie Barnes as scratch man having all his work cut out for him to gain first place. This he did, giving his big Zenith outfit its first-ever win at over 60 mph (60.92 mph to be exact). He overhauled the limit man L. Hill (499 Rudge s/car) within sight of the finishing line after a close fight for the lead. Hill's outfit proved faster even than A. J. McDonagh's big 750 cc (85 × 132 mm) Rudge combination in this event. The third finisher proved to be Jack Woodhouse (965 Regal-Green-Precision s/car).

Freddie also set up a new fastest lap for sidecars, with a speed of 62.32 mph.

A Rudge "Multi" in the hands of P. F. Glover won the 1000 cc Solo Handicap—the first *recorded* victory for a multi-geared Rudge at Brooklands. Although introduced in 1911, two years earlier, just before the Isle of Man TT Races, the Rudge "Multi" gear had not been much used at the track. Regular Rudge-riding habitués seemed to prefer single-geared machines for track work. Glover averaged 56.29 mph for the three laps of the race. Second was T. V. West (986 BAT-JAP) and Harry Martin (345 Martin-JAP) was third. The winner's fastest lap was set at 58.94 mph.

The principle of operation of the Multi gear was quite ingenious and a definite improvement on the Gradua gear fitted to Zenith machines. A long tank-side-mounted lever opened the inner flange of the engine shaft pulley by means of a face cam, and at the same time contracted the outer flange of the rear wheel belt rim. The device gave a gear-ratio variation of from 7-to-1 up to 4-to-1, the lever being moved by hand through a series of usually about twenty notches on a tank-mounted ratchet.

New 500 cc solo and sidecar records

Instead of returning to the Singer works at Coventry, as was his usual practice after a BMCRC race meeting, G. E. Stanley decided to stay on at Brooklands and the following day, Thursday, he occupied himself in setting up new solo records in Classes C (500 cc) and D (750 cc). Riding his 499 cc Singer, he covered the flying-start kilometre and flying-start mile at new record averages of 78.22 mph and 76.27 mph. These speeds were achieved using a $3\frac{3}{4}$-to-1 fixed gear which, ignoring belt and tyre slip, gave an engine speed of 3780 rpm. He also used a Senspray carburetter.

On the same day, L. Hill (499 Rudge s/car), with Frank Bateman as his passenger, set up new 500 cc sidecar records with speeds of 53.77 mph and 54.22 mph for the flying-start kilometre and flying-start mile.

Granville Bradshaw, inspired by the success of Les Bailey's 350 cc record-breaking Douglas, using parts he had supplied, had set to and designed a 500 cc fore-and-aft horizontally-opposed twin engine. During April, 1913, Freddie Barnes appeared on the track testing one of these units in a Zenith frame. The engine had a bore and stroke of 68 × 68 mm and used the one-large and two-small connecting-rod three-throw crankshaft arrangement employed on Bailey's motor.

Brooklands' TT Races

Two major long-distance races plus an innovation, Old Public School Boys' Races, were down in the programme for the Second BMCRC Members' Meeting of the year at Brooklands on Saturday, April 26th.

The two long-distance Brooklands' TT races created much interest and gave competitors some idea of how their machines might fare in The Island. Many of those ridden in the Junior (350 cc) event, the first race, were very noisy and the ACU officials indicated that this would not be tolerated in the Isle of Man.

A silver cup was the first prize for the twenty-two-lap Junior Brooklands TT Race, which had a total distance of 59 miles 1388 yd. At the end of the first lap, after the Fork start, G E. Stanley (349 Singer) led, with Billy Newsome (350 Douglas) second and Hugh Mason (350 NUT-JAP) third.

Freddie Edmond (340 Humber) was early in trouble, as his machine caught fire near the Members' Bridge, while E. Elwell (350 Douglas) broke an exhaust valve shortly after completing his first lap. Stanley rapidly increased his lead over Newsome, Mason still retaining third position. Freddie Barnes stopped on his little 240 cc Zenith-Gradua-JAP at the end of his second lap, with a blocked main jet and silencer trouble. Mason then crept up to second place displacing Newsome to third.

Later Elwell restarted and ran consistently thereafter. Stanley kept far ahead until he started to slow, and was overtaken by Mason on his twenty-first lap. Bert Colver (350 Enfield), had a machine with mechanical lubrication which ran very consistently and finished second, while Freddie Barnes, who had restarted with a leaky oil tank, stopped yet again in his seventeenth lap to clear his main jet and finished third. Eddie Kickham (350 Douglas) and D. R. O'Donovan (349 NSU) both retired on their sixteenth laps with broken valves and a broken petrol pipe respectively. Result:

JUNIOR BROOKLANDS' TT RACE (up to 350 cc) over 59 miles 1388 yd. Fork start and finish.

		Av. speed (mph)
1.	H. Mason (350 NUT-JAP)	54.29
2.	H. V. Colver (350 Enfield)	48.92
3.	F. W. Barnes (240 Zenith-Gradua-JAP)	48.09

Stanley finished fourth with a sick engine.

The Junior TT was followed by the twenty-six-lap Senior event (up to 500 cc). For this a silver cup had been put up as first prize by the Singer Company.

Sidney Axford started on a new 499 cc o.h.v. (85 × 88 mm) single-cylinder Precision-engined Martin, having a cylinder with pear shaped finning. A blockage in his oil feed forced a retirement at the end of the first lap.

The sixteen starters got away well despite much jostling for position. L. Hill (499 Rudge) led at the outset, followed by S. Heales (499 Rudge), G. E. Stanley (499 Singer), Frank Bateman (499 Rudge), Victor Horsman (499 Singer) and the rest of the field. In the second lap Stanley took the lead, which he held till lap five when Hill took over again. Stanley dropped back to fifth place with temporary engine trouble. Frank Bateman was now second and Horsman third. In lap 14 Hill dropped out and Stanley, who in the meantime had picked up to second place, was once again first man.

The finish was exciting, as in the twenty-third lap Stanley had dropped back to third place owing to a stop for petrol. Horsman was first and Heales second at this stage. Stanley was not beaten, however, and on his twenty-fifth lap, after restarting, he was soon running second. On the last lap he passed Horsman to romp home the winner. Results:

SENIOR BROOKLANDS' TT RACE (up to 500 cc) over 70 miles 1161 yd. Fork start and finish.

		Av. speed (mph)
1.	G. E. Stanley (499 Singer)	57.82
2.	V. E. Horsman (499 Singer)	57.72
3.	S. Heales (499 Rudge)	55.55

Several runners had mechanical troubles.

The two-lap 1000 cc Old Public School Boys' Race over 5 miles 766 yd was very much over-subscribed, attracting no fewer than sixty entries. It was therefore decided to run this handicap event in two two-lap heats, the first fifteen finishers in each qualifying for a two-lap final.

The first of these heats was won easily at 71.45 mph by E. L. Moxey (986 Zenith-Gradua-JAP), whose machine boasted one of the latest Binks racing carburetters. Victor Wilberforce (350 Douglas) was second and A. G. Miller (986 Martin-JAP) third.

The next heat provided plenty of excitement. All the Douglas machines started together, and their riders all appeared to change into top gear simultaneously. C. O. Hayward (350 Douglas) led at the outset, but Sir Robert Arbuthnot on another Douglas, who was racing at Brooklands for the first time after a lapse of two years, took the pole position. He kept it until the finish. Archie Fenn (499 Triumph) was second and Hayward third. Arbuthnot's speed was 51.28 mph.

In the Final, Miller who was recovering from a recent hospital operation was allowed a pusher. Moxey, who had done so well in the first heat, could not run due to a broken valve.

Sir Robert led from the outset, hard pressed by Wilberforce, while Hayward followed close behind. Result:

OLD PUBLIC SCHOOL BOYS' RACE (up to 1000 cc).
A handicap final over 2 laps. Fork start and finish.

		H'cap start	
1.	Sir R. K. Arbuthnot RN (350 Douglas)	1 min 36 sec	51.34 mph
2.	V. Wilberforce (350 Douglas)	1 min 20 sec	
3.	C. O. Hayward (350 Douglas)	1 min 36 sec	

The race meeting ended with the Inter-Public-School Team Race over four laps. The result was a win for the Eton team, which comprised: Victor Wilberforce (350 Douglas), Gordon McMinnies (499 Triumph) and A. J. Luce (350 Douglas). The Bradfield and Rugby teams dead-heated for second place.

Track testing for The Island

The TT Rudges were undergoing strenuous testing at Brooklands prior to the Isle of Man Races. This testing was apparently carried out more with a view to discovering whether any parts were likely to shake loose, than for assessing speed. Each of the TT engines had to develop, it was reported, at least 10 bhp on the bench before being passed for use. The Multi gear had been somewhat modified, a $17\frac{1}{2}$-in belt rim being substituted for the standard 20-in one, so as to give a range of higher ratios. These were from $6\frac{1}{4}$-to-1 up to $3\frac{1}{2}$-to-1. No clutches were fitted and handlebar magneto controls were used.

Whitsun racing

The BARC race meeting on Whit-Monday, May 12th 1913, was held in very dull weather, and the final car events had to be postponed due to heavy rain. There were two motor cycle races: a Short and a Long Handicap, then an event for cyclecars. All three races had Fork starts and Long finishes.

The Short Handicap over two laps or $5\frac{3}{4}$ miles, was won easily by A. J. McDonagh (499 single-geared Rudge) from the 34-sec mark, at $65\frac{3}{4}$ mph. Freddie Edmond (340 Humber) was second with 1 min 14 sec start and Kenneth Holden (499 BSA) third off the 46-sec mark.

Using the Multi gear of his 499 cc Rudge to advantage, Frank Bateman, who had 45 sec start, passed Billy Newsome (350 Douglas) on the last lap of the three-lap $8\frac{1}{2}$-mile Long Handicap to win at $67\frac{1}{4}$ mph. Freddie Edmond (340 Humber) was again second, this time after having been put back to the 1-min 51-sec mark. Third was G. E. Stanley (499 Singer) who had a 36-sec start over the scratch man.

The Cyclecar Handicap was a walkover for the two GNs at scratch, with Archie Frazer-Nash winning at $53\frac{1}{2}$ mph from his team mate C. M. Whitehead. J. F. Buckingham (Chota) came in third from the 28-sec mark.

Cyclecar activity at Brooklands was becoming quite feverish and only the previous Saturday, B. H. Haywood and G. Baker, whilst taking turns driving a 1096 cc four-cylinder Singer light car, had set up new cyclecar records from 50 to 150 miles and from one to three hours, at speeds around the 60 mph mark. The hour-record average was set at 62.64 mph.

During the week following Whit-Monday, quite a fleet of TT machines was on the track, carrying out final preparations before going over to the Isle of Man. Douglas riders, who were experiencing valve troubles, were particularly in evidence.

A newcomer on a new Triumph, the South African Percy Flook, made an appearance at the track. He was also bound for the Isle of Man shortly.

The Enfield team packed up and left for The Island on the Thursday afternoon, evidently satisfied with their track testing. But Freddie Edmond (340 Humber) continued, averaging around 62 mph for lap after lap.

1913—SPEEDS MOUNT

The 340 cc TT Humbers being track-tested had each a primary chain drive to a countershaft, and a final belt drive over large diameter pulleys to an Armstrong three-speed gear enclosed in the hub of the rear wheel. The Humber concern was determined to overcome the problem of driving-belt slip which had afflicted them in the wet conditions of the 1912 Isle of Man TT Races.

First Record Time Trials of the year

Several records were set up during the Record Time Trials, the first event of the day on Saturday, May 17th, at the BMCRC's Third Members' Brooklands' Race Meeting of the year. The class winners were as follows:

RECORD TIME TRIALS

	Speed (mph) over:	
Solo classes	fs km	fs ml
A (275 cc) S. R. Axford (247 Martin-JAP)	48.21	48.65
B (350 cc) G. E. Stanley (349 Singer)	67.79	66.91
C (500 cc) G. E. Stanley (499 Singer)	77.19	76.69*
E (1000 cc) E. C. E. Baragwanath (986 Matchless-JAP)	81.05	80.72
Sidecar classes		
C (500 cc) H. C. Mills (499 Regal-Green-Precision)	51.78	52.17
D (750 cc) H. Hunter (738 Zenith-Gradua-JAP)	53.85	53.17*
E (1000 cc) F. W. Barnes (986 Zenith-Gradua-JAP)	71.35	70.11*
Cyclecar class		
(1100 cc) B. Haywood (1096 Singer)	66.50*	65.85*

(*New class records)

Other noteworthy performances included those of Frank Bateman (499 Rudge-Multi) who covered the flying-start kilometre at 74.57 mph and the flying-start mile at 73.47 mph.

The rest of the meeting was devoted to three separate long-distance races, of which the twenty-two-lap Second Junior Brooklands' TT Race (up to 350 cc). There were only five starters and they finished the first lap in the following order: G. E. Stanley (349 Singer), then Howard Newman (347 Ivy-Green-Precision), Max

Heinzel and D. R. O'Donovan (324 NSUs), and last but not least, A. M. N. Holzapfel (347 Regal-Green-Precision). Stanley stayed in front throughout, but in the third and fourth laps Newman pressed him very hard. After that Stanley steadily increased his lead, and romped home an easy winner by over half-a-minute. In lap three, Heinzel nearly fell whilst dismounting to investigate some trouble with his machine, but he got going again almost immediately.

This was to no avail, however, as he had to retire with tyre trouble on his sixteenth lap. Result:

JUNIOR BROOKLANDS' TT RACE (up to 350 cc) over 59 miles 1388 yd. Fork start and finish.

		Av. speed (mph)
1.	G. E. Stanley (349 Singer)	58.10
2.	H. Newman (347 Ivy-Green-Precision)	57.56
3.	D. R. O'Donovan (324 NSU)	55.60

(*Flagged off after 17 laps, as race had finished)

Stanley covered the flying-start fifty miles at an average speed of 58.41 mph in this race.

The next race was the Second Senior Brooklands' TT Race over twenty-six laps (up to 500 cc). Again the Singer Company was awarding a silver cup to the winner.

Stanley again led throughout, this time on his larger 499 cc machine. Frank Bateman (499 Rudge-Multi) lay second and S. Heales (499 single-geared Rudge) third until lap five, when Heales assumed second place and Bateman dropped back, eventually retiring through tyre trouble. Lap seven saw Vernon March (499 single-geared Rudge) third, whilst A. J. McDonagh on a similar model shed his driving belt and stopped. In the eighth lap L. Hill (499 single-geared Rudge) took second place and Heales dropped back to third. Then these two had a ding-dong struggle for second place up until lap 16, when Hill dropped out of the running. In the eleventh lap Sidney Axford (493 Martin-Precision) stopped with oil on his driving belt and on the next McDonagh, who had restarted, came in to his pit to refuel and change a belt.

By the seventeenth circuit, Harry Reed (490 DOT-JAP twin) had crept up to second place. Lap 19 saw Heales stop for petrol and Stanley did likewise three laps later. From this point onwards the race order remained unchanged, Stanley finishing the winner, over three minutes ahead of second man Heales. Result:

SENIOR BROOKLANDS' TT RACE (up to 500 cc) over 70 miles 1161 yd. Fork start and finish.

		Av. speed (mph)
1.	G. E. Stanley (499 Singer)	63.44
2.	S. Heales (499 Rudge)	60.77
3.	H. Reed (490 DOT-JAP)	56.17

Victor Horsman (499 Singer), who stopped after twenty-one laps, finished fourth at 45.06 mph and Sam Witham (499 Singer) fifth.

The long-distance Sidecar and Cyclecar race was also run over twenty-six laps and provided a comparatively easy win for B. Haywood (1096 Singer cyclecar). Two GNs were entered, driven by Archie Frazer-Nash and Ron Godfrey (cousin of Oliver Godfrey), but both retired with tyre troubles. Result:

SIDECAR AND CYCLECAR LONG-DISTANCE RACE over 70 miles 1161 yd. Fork start and finish.

		Av. speed (mph)
1.	B. Haywood (1096 Singer cyclecar)	59.09
2.	G. Hands (1096 Calthorpe cyclecar)	57.55
3.	F. W. Barnes (986 Zenith-Gradua-JAP s/car)	56.39

The Essex Club go racing

With eleven events on the race card, including two for sidecar outfits, four for solos and one for cyclecars, the motorcyclists at the Essex MC Race Meeting at Brooklands—held in fine weather on Saturday May 24th—found much to interest them.

Amongst the competing solos, the most successful of the day was L. G. Brown's 493 cc (90 × 77½ mm) Corah-JAP, which carried off four prizes. All the races involved a Fork start and finish, like BMCRC events.

The first race of the day was the Two-Lap Sidecar Open Handicap over 5¾ miles. G. T. Gray (750 Rudge s/car), whose big 85 × 132 mm single-cylinder outfit went off from the 1-min 44-sec mark, won at 47½ mph by over one hundred yards from Freddie Barnes (986 Zenith-Gradua-JAP s/car). The scratch man Albert A. Knight, on another Zenith outfit, was third.

A similar race for Essex MC members only, this time over three laps or 8½ miles, attracted six competitors and was won easily by Gray's combination with four hundred yards in hand over Freddie Barnes. Third, nearly half-a-mile behind Freddie, was Frank Applebee (499 BSA s/car). Gray's winning speed was 47¾ mph.

Eighteen starters took the field for the three lap, 8½-mile, All-Comers' Open Handicap (up to 1000 cc); A. J. Dixon (499 Singer) and L. G. Brown (493 Corah-JAP), both from the 2-min 33-sec mark, finished first and second, with S. Crawley (499 Triumph) third. Dixon averaged 57¾ mph. The bookmakers' favourites: F. Roberts (499 Singer), J. Chapman (499 Triumph) and B. Alan Hill (496 Motosacoche) could get nowhere.

Brown confirmed his form by winning the "Restricted to Essex MC Members' Only Handicap" at 38½ mph over three laps and he came third in the two-lap All-Comers' Open Handicap which followed. In this J. P. Le Grand and W. A. Jacobs finished first and second on their 348 cc Singers, both from the 2 min-mark. Le Grand's average speed was a creditable 55¼ mph. There was a large field of twenty runners in this race and the result was almost a dead-heat.

Of the six entries for the two-lap Cyclecar Handicap, only three came to the line. Alan Hill's Humberette retired early on and trouble with A. W. Lambert's usually-fast 964 cc Morgan-JAP three-wheeler presented Henry Jones' 964 cc Super with a comparatively easy win by over fifty yards, at 37½ mph.

It was quite evident that L. G. Brown (493 Corah-JAP) had been disguising his machine's true capabilities throughout the meeting, for he won the final race—a two-lap "Essex MC Members' Only Handicap"—by a good hundred yards at an average speed of 57½ mph, some 19 mph faster than his previous winning performance. The handicappers were not at all pleased with him over this! Second, also from the 1-min 34-sec mark, was A. J. Dixon (499 Singer). Third from the 1-min 52-sec mark was E. H. Lees (350 Douglas).

RAC Brooklands' Gala Day

Poor organisation and poor crowd control did nothing to improve the quality of the RAC Gala Race Meeting, held on Saturday, May 31st. Only two motor cycle events figured in the programme: the All-Comers' Cyclecar Handicap and a Motor Cycle Inter-Club

Team Race between RAC/ACU affiliated club teams. Crowds coming on to the track before the end of the meeting, plus mechanical troubles with the competing machines, rendered these team races something of a fiasco.

The Cyclecar Handicap which had a Fork start and Long finish was over three laps or $8\frac{1}{2}$ miles, and provided a win for B. Haywood (1096 Singer cyclecar) the scratch man at 60 mph. Second was Archie Frazer-Nash driving an 8 hp GN and third J. T. Wood (1068 GWK).

Possibly the most interesting machine at Brooklands that day, was G. F. Hunter's 986 cc water-cooled V-twin BAT-JAP sidecar outfit, which had one of the latest 90×77.5 mm engines. The honeycomb radiator for the engine was placed behind the rear cylinder alongside the rear down tube of the frame, and a Senspray carburetter was fitted. It was withdrawn from the team race owing to a blown out sparking plug.

Most of the well-known Brooklands' habitués were over in the Isle of Man for the TT Races at this time, which accounted for the paucity of entries for this meeting.

Stanley on a winning streak

In line with their policy of holding a series of short-distance races at their ordinary monthly meetings, the BMCRC at their Fourth Members' Meeting of 1913 on Saturday, June 14th, had no fewer than ten three-lap (8-mile 269-yd) races down on the race card. Each had a Fork start and finish. During the afternoon G. E. Stanley, the Singer exponent, proved to be on a winning streak, for he carried off four first prizes.

The first event, the 350 cc Scratch Race, attracted seven starters. D. R. O'Donovan (349 NSU twin) made a poor start. He had trouble owing to a choked main jet and the jamming of his throttle slides. On the first lap G. E. Stanley (349 Singer) led, with Billy Newsome (350 Douglas) second and Rear Admiral Sir Robert Arbuthnot (350 Douglas) third. Lap two saw the first and second runners the same, but Arbuthnot displaced by O'Donovan. But the latter dropped back, due to his carburation troubles and the final order of the first three was Stanley, Newsome, Arbuthnot. Stanley won easily at an average of 54.90 mph.

In the next race, the 500 cc Scratch Race, Stanley (499 Singer) established an early lead in the first lap, followed by Charlie Collier (496 Matchless-MAG) and Sidney George (497 Indian). On lap two Collier took the lead, but Stanley passed him on the Members' Banking. A little further on Charlie Collier's front tyre burst and he was lucky to stop without serious injury. This handed the race to Stanley, who came home an easy winner at an average speed of 67.56 mph, with George second.

The third event was a 1000 cc Scratch Race, a relative rarity at Brooklands, where most 1000 cc events were run as handicaps. E. F. Remington (986 Matchless-JAP) was an easy first-lap leader, with A. G. Miller (986 Martin-JAP) in second berth and Oliver Baldwin (986 BAT-JAP) third. The fourth man L. McLeod (770 Matchless-JAP), was flooding his carburetter and wobbling badly in the process. In the second lap Remington was still ahead, but had slowed somewhat. He crossed the line to average 71.31 mph. Miller and Baldwin followed in that order. It is of interest to note that Remington was running on motor benzole, the commercial grade of benzene, whereas the others were on petrol.

At the end of the first lap in the 350 cc Handicap which followed, Max Heinzel (349 NSU) was in the lead with a 1-min start, having overtaken the limit man A. M. N. Holzapfel (347 Regal-Green-Precision)—now fifth in the running order. Percy Newbold (340 Zenith-Gradua-JAP) lay second and Billy Newsome (350 Douglas) third. During the second lap Newsome had acquired a useful lead, with Heinzel second and Arbuthnot (350 Douglas) third. G. E. Stanley (349 Singer), who was rapidly overhauling the field, had moved up to fifth place by the end of that lap.

Well in sight of the finishing line, Stanley the scratch man caught Newsome, who had been given a 54-sec start over him. Meanwhile for the second time that afternoon Rear Admiral Arbuthnot finished third. Stanley's speed worked out at 62.24 mph, with a fastest lap at 63.36 mph: a good speed for a "three-fifty" in those days.

Stanley's fourth win of the day came in the 500 cc Handicap, which he won at 67.84 mph by three-quarters-of-a-mile, easing his throttle shut as he did so. He again started at scratch, catching by the end of the next circuit the first lap leader A. G. Miller (493 Martin-JAP), to whom he had conceded 33 sec at the start. It was Miller who turned up without number plates and, much to the amusement

The Fork start of the great Six-Hour Race held at the BMCRC's Fifth 1913 Race Meeting, on Wednesday, July 16th. Fifty riders took part. The smoke is coming from the Scott two-strokes of Tim Wood and Frank Applebee, in the front rank.

E. F. Remington (986 Matchless-JAP) won the Five-Lap ACU Brooklands' Championship at 76.43 mph on Saturday, October 18th, 1913. He clocked 85.38 mph over the flying kilometre at the same race meeting.

Two 499 cc Rudge exponents: *left*, Tommy Greene and *right*, Cyril Pullin shaking hands with S. A. Rowlandson. They have just finished third and first in the One-Hour Race for *The Motor Cycle* Cup, held on Saturday, October 18th, 1913. Pullin covered just over 64 miles.

of fellow competitors, had to have his numbers whitewashed on to the back of his leather riding jacket.

The sixth event, the 1000 cc Handicap, provided the 9 sec mark man Sidney George (997 Indian) with his comparatively easy first Brooklands' win at 75.50 mph. The scratch man E. F. Remington (986 Matchless-JAP) came in second with J. Hellaby (997 Indian) third after a 42-sec start.

There were only three runners in the Cyclecar Scratch Race. J. T. Wood (1068 GWK) led easily at the end of the first lap, but dropped out with sparking plug trouble, leaving only B. Haywood (1096 Singer cyclecar) and A. W. Lambert (1082 Morgan-JAP). The former steadily increased his lead and won at 57.34 mph.

Sidecar scratch races

By the second lap of the 500 cc Sidecar Scratch Race, Sydney Garrett (499 Regal-Green-Precision s/car) had established a lead followed by E. Folwell (499 BSA s/car), Freddie Barnes (493 Zenith-Gradua-JAP s/car), H. C. Mills and Howard Riddell (both on 499 Zenith-Gradua outfits fitted with water-cooled Green-Precision engines). Garrett won at 48.39 mph. Barnes took second place with Folwell third.

Pushers were allowed in this race, and some entries had three; in one instance the passenger assisted, leaping into the sidecar as soon as the engine fired.

Only four starters turned out for the 1000 cc Sidecar Scratch Race and one of these, Riddell (499 Zenith-Gradua-Green-Precision s/car), was late as he had taken part in the previous event. It was Freddie Barnes's race from start to finish. On his 986 cc Zenith-Gradua-JAP sidecar outfit he won at 58.24 mph, with Sidney George (994 Indian s/car) second and Sydney Garrett (499 Regal-Green-Precision s/car) third.

During the tea interval between the racing G. E. Stanley (349 Singer) made a successful attempt on the Class B (350 cc solo) five-mile record. He averaged 64.93 mph for the distance.

Sidecar beats cyclecar

The last event of the day, the Sidecar and Cyclecar Handicap, was very keenly contested. The scratch man was B. Haywood (1096 Singer cyclecar), while Freddie Barnes (986 Zenith-Gradua-JAP s/car) had a start of 15 sec over him.

Both J. T. Wood (1068 GWK) and Archie Frazer-Nash (GN) retired with sparking-plug troubles in the first lap. Barnes had a terrific struggle with 27-sec-start-man A. W. Lambert (1082 Morgan-JAP), to win at the fine average speed of 62.32 mph. Third man was E. Folwell (499 BSA s/car). With his heavy handicap, the best Haywood could do was fourth.

Racing on benzole

The Midsummer race meeting of the BARC, held on Saturday, June 21st, 1913, featured two motor cycle events. There was the usual Short Handicap over two laps, and a special Long Handicap over three laps sponsored by the *Daily Express* newspaper. In this race the competitors had to run their engines on motor benzole, supplied free for the occasion. Each race had a Fork start and a Long finish. The weather was ideal for racing, it being fine and warm with a complete absence of wind.

The first race, the Fifteenth Short Motor Cycle Handicap to be held at Brooklands, was started at 2.25 pm. By the time that the machines had reached the Members' Bridge on the first lap, Rear Admiral Sir Robert Arbuthnot (350 Douglas) had established a lead, with R. G. Parker (340 Humber) running a good second, and D. R. O'Donovan (349 NSU) third. G. E. Stanley was doing well on his 349 cc Singer, as were Sidney George (497 Indian) and Vernon March (499 Rudge), both off the 24-sec mark. On lap two J. A. Manners-Smith (499 Triumph) took the lead followed by O'Donovan and by J. P. Le Grand (349 Singer).

Cyril Pullin (499 Rudge) was moving up fast and had taken the lead by the start of the Finishing Straight, to win at $66\frac{1}{2}$ mph, with Manners-Smith second and Stanley third.

March's engine suffered a bad blow-up and he came into the pits with his cylinder and parts of his crankcase missing.

For the eight-and-a-half-mile Benzole Handicap, the *Daily Express* had put up, as first prize, a cup to the value of £37 10s with prizes of £8 and £5 for second and third finishers. The race itself originated as a result of the great interest being shown at that time in promoting the sales of home-produced motor fuels. Benzole was such a fuel, being a by-product of the gas industry.

The limit man was R. J. Bell (349 NSU) and E. F. Remington (986 Matchless-JAP) was at scratch. G. E. Stanley (499 Singer), who had conceded 3 min 15 sec to Bell, was moving up through the field rapidly. Bell still held the lead at the end of lap one, with Arbuthnot (350 Douglas) second and O'Donovan (349 NSU) third. But he was pressed hard by W. A. Jacobs (349 Singer) at the end of lap two. Freddie Edmond (340 Humber) was now running third, his little twin showing a surprising turn of speed.

Stanley, whose machine was going particularly well, gradually took the lead and crossed the line first at an average speed of $69\frac{1}{2}$ mph. He was followed home by Cyril Pullin (499 Rudge) and Jacobs. S. Yano (499 Triumph), the Japanese rider, was fourth and scratch man Remington fifth.

Apart from pulling a slightly lower main jet than when running on petrol, as did all the competitors, Stanley's machine remained unaltered for this race. It pulled a gear ratio of $3\frac{3}{4}$-to-1.

More sidecar records

On the Monday, June 23rd, Howard Riddell driving a Zenith-Gradua sidecar outfit fitted with a water-cooled single-cylinder 499 cc Green-Precision engine, was out on the track after Class C and D (500 cc and 750 cc) sidecar records.

He first went for the short distances achieving 56.78 mph for the flying-start kilometre, 54.88 mph for the flying-start mile, and 49.05 mph for the flying-start five miles. New 100-mile, 150-mile, two-hour, three-hour and four-hour averages were set up at speeds ranging from 44.5 mph down to 40 mph. A valve breakage, however, put paid to any longer distance or duration attempts.

MCC's Fifth Annual Race Meeting

Always keenly contested, the Annual MCC Brooklands' Race Meeting had no fewer than eleven events down for decision, all starting and finishing at the Fork.

Of the fourteen riders in the two-lap 350 cc Handicap, all the Douglas machines got away well. In fact three of them held the lead positions at the end of the first lap, but soon the two inseparables W. A. Jacobs and J. P. Le Grand (348 Singers) were gobbling up places galore and moving towards the front. The result was a win for Jacobs (8-sec start) at 55.72 mph from Sir Robert Arbuthnot (350 Douglas) by twenty-five yards, with Le Grand third.

The second race, another two-lapper, was a 350-500 cc Handicap. In this C. W. Meredith (499 Bradbury), better known as a rider in reliability trials, got into a wobble at speed and fell from his machine. Fortunately he was not badly hurt. P. Shaw (499 P & M) got away well, as did Oliver Godfrey (497 Indian) whose machine still had road-race gearing and which was really too low for serious track work. Oliver De Lissa's 496 cc Motosacoche, which was fitted with his patented exhaust valve, also appeared too low-geared for serious track work.

At the end of the first lap Chris Newsome (499 Rover) had worked his way to the front, and was riding magnificently. But his lead did not last, for Harry Collier (496 Matchless-MAG twin) soon moved to the front to win, off the 8-sec mark, at a speed of 62.87 mph. Second was R. E. Guest (493 Matchless-JAP—a 90-bore single) and P. Shaw was third.

As usual, Douglas machines were away first in the three-lap 350 cc Scratch Race, but were soon overhauled by W. A. Jacobs and J. P. Le Grand on their 348 cc Singers, and by Sam Wright on his 340 cc Humber, who were bunched together throughout the first lap. Le Grand's driving belt came off in lap two enabling Sir Robert Arbuthnot (350 Douglas) to move into third place behind Wright. This order was maintained until the finish, Jacobs averaging 55.72 mph for the distance.

Le Grand managed to restart and finish fifth, thus qualifying for the "Harry Smith" Gold Challenge Cup Race for the MCC Club Championship later in the meeting. The first five finishers were eligible for this race. The fourth man was Victor Wilberforce (350 Douglas).

The three-lap scratch race for machines of 350-560 cc had a good entry, but unfortunately there were six non-starters. Everyone got away well except for N. O. Soresby (499 Rudge), who had quite a struggle getting his motor to fire. Harry Collier (496 Matchless-MAG) assumed the lead at once, followed by Chris Newsome (499 Rover), R. E. Guest (493 Matchless-JAP single), Cyril Pullin (499 Rudge) and Oliver Godfrey (497 Indian). This order was unchanged at the end of the first lap.

During the second lap Collier increased his lead, and Guest ran second followed by S. A. Rowlandson (499 Rudge), whose engine was misfiring slightly due to sparking-plug trouble. Then came Pullin.

Newsome's Rover was obviously slowing and Soresby suffered both driving-belt and sparking-plug troubles. But Collier romped home an easy winner at 61.30 mph, with Pullin second, Rowlandson third, Guest fourth and Dudley Noble—on the other Rover—fifth.

Harry Collier scored his third win of the day in the 750-1000 cc Scratch Race over three laps, in which he rode a 986 cc Matchless-JAP. Second was A. V. Sumner (986 Zenith-Gradua-JAP) and third A. Mariani (994 Indian). Harry's average speed was 67.38 mph. Sumner's machine was rather new and showed signs of incipient seizure and drying up of oil. Mariani's Indian was not on its best form and misfired due to over-lubrication.

Benzole-only was the order of the day for machines in the next event, a two-lap scratch race for machines up to 650 cc. This provided Harry Collier, this time on his 496 cc Matchless-MAG twin, with his fourth win. He averaged 60.46 mph. Chris Newsome (499 Rover) was second.

Event seven was a Cyclecar Handicap and was won by Chris Halsall (Wilton cyclecar) at 52.10 mph. This was followed by a two-lap Sidecar Race for outfits up to 500 cc. Harold Karslake (499 Rover s/car) was the limit man, with a minute start over Sydney Garrett (499 Regal-Green-Precision s/car) who was at scratch. He retained his lead until the end of the first lap. Chris Newsome on the other 499 cc Rover outfit then became front runner, while Garrett moved up rapidly in pursuit. Newsome appeared to be an easy winner at the start of the last lap, but then his engine slowed and just before the finish Garrett swept past to win by about forty yards, at 47.96 mph. Harold Karslake was third.

Only three runners appeared on the line for the two-lap 1000 cc Sidecar Handicap, Oliver De Lissa (496 Motosacoche s/car) and R. J. Bell (496 FN s/car) receiving 1 min 38 sec start from A. V. Sumner (986 Zenith-Gradua-JAP s/car). This handicap proved insufficient, for Sumner soon took the lead and won with great ease at 52.0 mph, with De Lissa second.

Chris Halsall scored another victory with his little Wilton cyclecar, in the ten-lap Car Handicap for the "Albert Brown" Challenge Trophy. His average speed was 54.31 mph. There then followed the pièce-de-résistance of the day—a handicap—the ten-lap Club Championship for the "Harry Smith" Gold Challenge Cup.

The starters were: at scratch—A. V. Sumner (986 Zenith-Gradua-JAP); with 1 min 10 sec start—Harry Collier (496 Matchless-MAG), Cyril Pullin and S. A. Rowlandson (499 Rudges), and Dudley Noble (499 Rover); and on the limit mark with 4 min 50 sec start—W. A. Jacobs and J. P. Le Grand (348 Singers), Sam Wright (340 Humber), and Victor Wilberforce (350 Douglas). Everyone got away well, particularly Sumner. The smaller machines completed well over a lap before the scratch man started, Jacobs, Le Grand and Wright being all together in a bunch. Pullin dropped out of the race in the fourth lap, and the order at the fifth was: Jacobs, Wright, Le Grand, Collier, Rowlandson and Sumner. Collier was picking up rapidly and looked like a potential winner.

In lap seven, Sam Wright dropped back due to driving-belt slip. In the next Harry Collier took the lead, and Sumner, who was making a game fight of it, picked up two more p'aces. Jacobs was now lying second and Le Grand third. This order was maintained until the last lap, but with Collier steadily increasing his lead. In the last lap Jacobs and Le Grand changed places, after riding consistently throughout. Result:

MCC CLUB CHAMPIONSHIP FOR "HARRY SMITH" GOLD CHALLENGE CUP. Handicap over ten laps. Fork start and finish.

		H'cap start	
1.	H. A. Collier (496 Matchless-MAG)	1 min 10 sec	65.22 mph
2.	J. P. Le Grand (348 Singer)	4 min 50 sec	
3.	W. A. Jacobs (348 Singer)	4 min 50 sec	

Sumner, the scratch man, came in fourth and Rowlandson fifth.

So ended a fine day's racing, particularly for Harry Collier who had won every race in which he had started. Five in all.

The great six-hour race

Excitement and anticipation had been building up for weeks

amongst Brooklands' riders, ever since the announcement that a marathon six-hour multi-class scratch race would be run at the BMCRC's Fifth 1913 Meeting, on Wednesday, July 16th.

On the day, hot sultry weather with scarcely a breeze greeted the fifty riders as they assembled for the start in two lines at the Fork. It promised to be the Brooklands' event of the year, with most of the leading riders of the day taking part. The exceptions were the Collier brothers and the unfortunate Frank Bateman—who had died as result of a crash on his Rudge during the Isle of Man TT Races.

The six-hour race had been organised to give everyone a chance of breaking class records. It was split into three categories: *Division 1*, for solo motor cycles, Classes A to E (275cc to 1000 cc); *Division 2*, for sidecar outfits and three-wheeled cyclecars in Classes F to I (350 cc to 1000 cc); and *Division 3*, for four-wheeled cyclecars in Classes J and K (750 cc and 1100 cc). In contrast to previous events, the sidecar outfits and cyclecars now had recognised categories designated by letters like solo machines. This system of classification for racing persisted until the First World War.

Replenishment pits were set up at the Fork, and during the race, riders were only allowed to stop for refuelling and repairs at their own particular pit or depôt. Stopping for machine repair or refuelling at any other point on the circuit was strictly forbidden. In fact the race regulations had been tightened up all round. Thus they called for firmly attached and clearly marked number plates, if disqualification was to be avoided. The white-washing of numbers on to the backs of riders' leather riding jackets would most definitely not be tolerated!

At 11.38 am Major Lloyd signalled the "off". With a mighty roar all but two of the engines on the starting grid sprang into life and the throng got under way, amidst dense clouds of smoke from the exhausts of the two-stroke Scotts of H. O. ("Tim") Wood (the 1913 TT Race winner) and Frank Applebee, both in the front rank. The two machines remaining were not long dormant and R. J. Bell (349 NSU) and Howard Riddell (499 Zenith-Gradua-Precision s/car), were soon in pursuit of the departing multitude.

At the end of the first lap J. J. Cookson (986 Matchless-JAP) led by several lengths from Jimmy Cocker (499 Singer). Third was Oliver Godfrey (497 Indian), fourth G. E. Stanley (349 Singer), fifth W. G. Howard (496 Matchless-MAG twin), and sixth Tim Wood

(486 Scott two-stroke twin). The rest followed in a long drawn-out procession.

The first to stop at the pits was E. E. Elwell (350 Douglas) on his fifth lap, where he was delayed with a stretched valve. On the next circuit Sidney Axford (738 Martin-JAP) came in to change his driving belt. Then Bell (349 NSU) stopped for oil and Howard Newman (347 Ivy-Green-Precision) did likewise to fix a silencer which had come loose, and to change his driving belt. S. Halsall (499 Veloce) was the first to retire, with the cylinder of his side-valve motor cracked. Percy Newbold (345 Zenith-Gradua-JAP) stopped with a flat front tyre, on his eighth lap and then Elwell came in again for a brief spell. Freddie Barnes (986 Zenith-Gradua-JAP s/car), who was using a new untried engine—he had seized his usual one in a recent French road race—had to drop out with a cracked cylinder. A. V. Sumner (499 Zenith-Gradua-Green-Precision) was forced to retire because his flywheels had come adrift due to a loose crankpin nut.

Pit organisation varied enormously, the most elaborate being that of the Singer Company, which had no less than four helpers operating stop watches, signalling and generally attending to its riders interests.

Albert Knight (986 Zenith-Gradua-JAP) came into his pit too fast, applied his brakes too violently, skidded and fell. In an instant his machine was ablaze. The flames were quickly extinguished, however, and in about ten minutes Knight was once again back in the running, none the worse for wear. Godfrey retired on his tenth lap with a broken piston, and then G. W. Hands (1088 Calthorpe cyclecar) came in, changed both rear wheels and was quickly away again. On his sixteenth lap, Harry Martin (268 Martin-JAP), the sole runner in Class A (up to 275 cc), retired with a split cylinder. His machine had also been on fire earlier.

By the end of the first hour the leaders were:

Class B: 1. G. E. Stanley (349 Singer), 26 laps.
2. H. Mason (350 NUT-JAP), 25 laps.
Class B: 1. J. R. Haswell (499 Triumph), 27 laps.
2. H. O. Wood (486 Scott), 26 laps.
Class D: 1. S. R. Axford (738 Martin-JAP), 24 laps.
2. F. A. McNab (745 Trump-JAP), 17 laps.
Class E: 1. J. J. Cookson (986 Matchless-JAP), 25 laps.
2. A. A. Knight (986 Zenith-Gradua-JAP), 23 laps.

Class G: 1. J. Holroyd (496 Motosacoche s/car), 17 laps.
2. H. Le Vack (496 Motosacoche s/car), 16 laps.
Class H: 1. E. B. Ware (750 Zenith-Gradua-JAP s/car), 20 laps.
2. H. Gibson (554 Bradbury s/car), 18 laps.
Class I: 1. N. F. Holder (986 Morgan-Blumfield), 21 laps.
Class K: 1. G. W. Hands (1088 Calthorpe cyclecar), 23 laps.
2. A. Francis (1075 Duo cyclecar), 21 laps.

Tim Wood (486 Scott) came in with a flat back tyre and, assisted by Alfred Scott, the designer of the marque, he was quickly away again. Knight, who had been going well, was now put out by a split cylinder. It was announced that G. E. Stanley—"Wizard Stanley" as he was now known on account of his prowess at engine tuning—had become the first rider of a "350" to achieve more than sixty miles in the hour. His actual distance was 62 miles 920 yd.

R. E. Guest (742 Matchless-JAP s/car) retired with a broken inlet valve rocker; A. Francis (1075 Duo cyclecar) stopped to have a valve spring replaced, while L. F. De Peyrecave (985 Duo cyclecar) broke a chain. Howard Newman (347 Ivy-Green-Precision) came in and screwed up a leaky water union on his water-cooled engine, and later Jack Haswell (499 o.h.i.v. Triumph), now leading on his forty-fifth lap, stopped to replace a flat back tyre. Percy Brewster (490 Norton) dropped out with a broken piston ring.

Stanley gave up after covering fifty-eight laps owing to his back tyre being worn down and to his having "had enough", as he put it. Next to retire was Frank Applebee (486 Scott) in his thirty-sixth lap, owing to the petrol pipe union coming out of the tank.

The mechanical toll was becoming heavy, the pits never being free from riders coming in for repair or to retire.

George Baker (499 Peerless) stopped and wound string round the projecting end of his engine shaft to prevent oil leaking out of the crankcase bearing on to his driving belt. W. G. Howard (496 Matchless-MAG twin) retired because an exhaust valve broke and its head fell into the cylinder.

After riders had completed fifty laps, pink scoring cards with their numbers were used to show their race positions on the indicator board set up for that purpose at the Fork.

N. F. Holder (986 Morgan-Blumfield) at full speed down the Railway Straight, dropped his low-speed driving chain, which whittled dangerously along the track; fortunately no one was hit by it. Jack Holroyd's Motosacoche sidecar outfit was going well, but he had continually to raise the valve lifter to get oil to the piston rings.

At one stage Hugh Mason, on the little 350 cc NUT-JAP twin, led the whole field.

The first to complete fifty laps was Cyril Pullin (499 Rudge-Multi), who now led Class C, Haswell having dropped back slightly. Mason followed and Haswell was next, but when Mason developed sparking plug trouble, he let Haswell up into second position. Freddie Edmond (340 Humber twin) was now forced to retire, a stone breaking the barrel of his lubricator. Tim Wood was not at all happy, and stopped several times. Haswell took the lead on his fifty-third lap, and thereafter led the field, though he had to stop to tie his carburetter in position. Tudor Thompson's 350 cc Douglas suffered from overheating, so it was withdrawn. Jimmy Cocker (499 Singer) had retired owing to a fire, but "E. H. Victor" on the remaining Singer was going well in third place in Class C. Nobody was fooled by this nom-de-plume—for the rider was the erstwhile Victor Horsman. Apparently he, a travelling maintenance engineer engaged in cinema electrics, should strictly speaking have been working elsewhere that day and he did not wish to advertise his presence at Brooklands to his employers. His official working schedule made it difficult for him to be in the Weybridge area on Saturday race days of the BMCRC. Thus he was to enter a number of races under the name of "E. H. Victor". Mason stopped in his seventieth laps to adjust his tappets and fill up, whilst E. Gwynne (998 Indian) came in to his pit and stripped down his carburetter.

Almost all the competitors were being sponsored, but Horsman, being a pure amateur, was a notable exception. When asked in recent years about this, Victor Horsman recalled how he had mentioned the fact shortly before the race to an amazed Sidney Axford, who could scarcely believe that anyone would go in for such a long-distance event without some form of remuneration.

At half time, after three hours, the leaders were:

Class B: 1. H. Mason (350 NUT-JAP), 64 laps.
          2. H. V. Colver (350 Enfield), 58 laps.
Class C: 1. J. R. Haswell (499 Triumph), 68 laps.
          2. C. G. Pullin (499 Rudge-Multi), 68 laps.

Class D: 1. S. R. Axford (738 Martin-JAP), 61 laps.
2. F. A. McNab (745 Trump-JAP), 54 laps.
Class E: 1. J. J. Cookson (986 Matchless-JAP), 56 laps.
2. E. Gwynne (998 Indian), 53 laps.
Class G: 1. H. Riddell (499 Zenith-Gradua-Green-Precision s/car), 45 laps.
Class H: 1. E. B. Ware (750 Zenith-Gradua-JAP s/car), 51 laps.
2. H. Gibson (554 Bradbury s/car), 48 laps.
Class I: 1. N. F. Holder (986 Morgan-Blumfield), 53 laps.
Class K: 1. G. W. Hands (1088 Calthorpe cyclecar), 60 laps.
2. L. F. De Peyrecave (985 Duo cyclecar), 47 laps.

Howard Riddell's front tyre blew right off the rim, yet he managed to continue to his pit at some 20 mph. He was soon away again with a new one.

Horsman got ahead of Mason in the seventy-fourth lap. Newman retired as he could not prevent oil getting on to his driving belt, which he had already changed several times.

Bert Le Vack (496 Motosacoche s/car), who lay third in his class, had two tyre bursts early on but now circulated reliably. The numbers of those riders who had completed a hundred laps were now posted in green by the lap scorers.

In his sixty-ninth lap Riddell stopped to fill up with petrol and oil, and it was noticed that the racing body of his sidecar was beginning to disintegrate. Mason at this stage had several stops owing to the central electrode of one of his machine's sparking plugs coming loose.

At the fifth hour both Mason and Haswell, who had accomplished record distances in their respective classes, stopped at their pits for replenishment. Mason was first away, as Haswell had to change a wheel again.

On the eighty-eighth lap, near the end, Tim Wood thought it advisable to ream out the main jet of his carburetter which was getting choked up, whilst Haswell pulled up in his 124th lap for a few seconds owing to his carburetter working loose again. Mason stopped to replace a missing valve cotter, in his 118th circuit. The final results were as follows:

SIX HOUR RACE (Fork Start)

Class		Position	Rider (Machine)	Speed (mph)
Solos				
B	(350 cc)	1.	H. Mason (350 NUT-JAP)	54.27
		2.	H. V. Colver (350 Enfield)	50.48
		3.	E. Keyte (350 Enfield)	47.55
C	(500 cc)	1.	J. R. Haswell (499 Triumph)	58.62
		2.	C. G. Pullin (499 Rudge-Multi)	55.82
		3.	"E. H. Victor" (499 Singer)	51.49
D	(750 cc)	1.	F. A. McNab (745 Trump-JAP)	47.07
E	(1000 cc)	1.	J. J. Cookson (986 Matchless-JAP)	49.78
Sidecars and three-wheelers				
G	(500 cc)	1.	H. Riddell (499 Zenith-Gradua-Green-Precision)	41.19
		2.	J. Holroyd (496 Motosacoche)	36.69
		3.	H. Le Vack (496 Motosacoche)	29.67
H	(750 cc)	1.	E. B. Ware (750 Zenith-Gradua-JAP)	44.19
		2.	H. Gibson (554 Bradbury)	37.80
I	(1000 cc)	1.	N. F. Holder (986 Morgan-Blumfield)	—
Four-wheeled cyclecars				
K	(1100 cc)	1.	G. W. Hands (1088 Calthorpe)	51.78
		2.	A. Francis (1075 Duo)	41.48
		3.	L. F. De Peyrecave (985 Duo)	36.57

The team prize was won by Enfield machines. H. Greaves (350 Enfield) finishing fourth in Class B. Despite his troubles Tim Wood (486 Scott) managed to finish fifth in Class C, at an average speed of 49.60 mph. In addition to his hour record, G. E. Stanley (349 Singer) also set up a new fifty-mile record for Class B at 63.88 mph. Hugh Mason set up new records in Class B from two to six hours and from 100 to 300 miles, at speeds ranging from 59 mph down to 56 mph. Jack Haswell set up new five- and six-hour records and 250- and 300-mile records in Class C at 58 to 59 mph.

Howard Riddell (Class G) set up new 500 cc sidecar records for 5 and 6 hours, 250 and 300 miles, all at around the 41-mph mark. E. B. Ware (Class H) did likewise for 750 cc sidecars for periods of from two to six hours, and distances of from 100 to 250 miles. Finally, G. W. Hands (Class K) set new records from four to six hours and 200 to 300 miles, in his 1088 cc Calthorpe cyclecar, at speeds ranging from 54 mph down to 51 mph.

1913—SPEEDS MOUNT

Bank Holiday racing

Two solo events, one sidecar and one cyclecar, were included in the BARC August Bank Holiday programme at the race meeting held on Monday, August 4th. All had a Fork start and a "Long Finishing Line" finish near the clubhouse.

The first event, The Thirteenth Long Motor Cycle Handicap of 1913 over three laps (8½ miles), had forty-one entries, of whom thirty-three faced the starter. The scratch man was Sidney George (994 eight-valve Indian), while at the other end of the scale the limit man, with 3 min 51 sec start, was R. J. Bell (190 NSU single). It resulted in an easy win by forty yards for E. E. Elwell (350 Douglas), with 3 min 31 sec start, who averaged 53½ mph. Second was Victor Horsman (499 Singer) and third, Percy Brewster (419 Zenith-Gradua-JAP twin), both from the 1-min 36-sec mark. Harry Collier (496 Matchless-JAP twin) retired with a broken valve.

Kenneth Holden (499 BSA) with 56 sec start from Sidney George, who was again scratch man on the big eight-valve Indian, had a runaway win by 150 yd in the Short Handicap over two laps (5¾ miles). He averaged 65½ mph. Two newcomers, A. J. Brewin (986 Zenith-Gradua-JAP) and J. W. Tollady (499 Singer), with starts of 26 sec and 1 min 4 sec, finished second and third.

Before many minutes' running the result of the August Sidecar Handicap, a two-lap affair, became a foregone conclusion barring accidents. A. V. Sumner (499 Zenith-Gradua-Green s/car) and H. Jepson (493 Zenith-Gradua-JAP s/car), both with a 40-sec start, had obviously fooled the handicappers. They finished first and second in that order, Sumner's speed being 51¼ mph. A hundred-and-fifty yards separated the two at the finish, while there was a gap of three hunded yards or so between Jepson and the third man Kenneth Holden (499 BSA s/car). A. J. Luce (986 Zenith-Gradua-JAP s/car), the joint scratch man with A. J. Brewin on an identical outfit, finished fourth and set up the fastest lap at 54.51 mph.

In the two-lap Cyclecar Handicap H. E. Dew, driving a 964 cc DEW cyclecar of his own manufacture, was the limit man and led from start to finish at an average speed of 53½ mph. His only threat came from the scratch man B. Haywood (1096 Singer cyclecar) who finished second.

The Bemsee August meeting

A relatively short programme was on the agenda for the BMCRC's Sixth 1913 Monthly Race Meeting at Brooklands. Held during the afternoon of Saturday August 9th, in dull, rather cool weather, it offered three ten-mile races, specifically intended to enable riders to attempt new class records for the distance, and a three-lap All-Comers' Handicap. The ten-mile races were all scratch events and started at the beginning of the Railway Straight. The finish was at the Fork. The All-Comers' Handicap had a Fork start and finish. Each of the scratch events also had a sealed handicap, for which prizes were awarded.

The first event was the 350 cc Ten-Mile Record Race. Hugh Mason (350 NUT-JAP) led, the first time past the Fork, with G. E. Stanley (349 Singer) second and Cyril Williams (348 AJS), third. Then after a gap came Howard Newman (346 Ivy-Green-Precision), Bert Colver and D. Iron on their 350 cc Enfields, and lastly Percy Newbold (345 Zenith-Gradua-JAP). Harry Martin (340 Martin-JAP) had to retire with a faulty magneto. In the next lap Stanley surged ahead and gained a commanding lead, with Mason second and Williams third. Newbold dropped out. In the third lap Stanley greatly increased his lead and on the next came in to finish with his engine shut off, before the others were even in sight. Result:

350 CC TEN-MILE RECORD RACE
Railway-Straight start and Fork finish.

		Av. speed (mph)
1.	G. E. Stanley (349 Singer)	60.56
2.	H. Mason (350 NUT-JAP)	56.91
3.	C. Williams (348 AJS)	55.03

Cyril Williams won the sealed handicap on his side-valve AJS, which was making its Brooklands racing debut.

In the 500 cc event, Stanley again had things all his own way, this time riding his larger (499 cc) model.

The first time past the Fork the order was: G. E. Stanley (499 Singer), Percy Brewster (498 Zenith-Gradua-JAP), "E. H. Victor" (our old friend Victor Horsman) riding his 499 cc Singer, L. Hill and A. J. McDonagh (499 Rudges), Leon Cushman (482 NLG-JAP), Bert Le Vack (496 Motosacoche), George Baker (499 Peerless) and J. P. Nicholson (493 Zenith-Gradua-JAP).

In the second lap Stanley was way ahead, with Horsman second and Hill third. In the next Stanley greatly increased his lead, and on the final lap again, as in the 350 cc race, he shut off and glided in well ahead of everyone else. Hill beat Horsman for second place by a mere three-and-a-fifth seconds. Result:

500 CC TEN-MILE RECORD RACE
Railway-Straight start and Fork finish.

		Av. speed (mph)
1.	G. E. Stanley (499 Singer)	66.27
2.	L. Hill (499 Rudge)	63.62
3.	"E. H. Victor" (499 Singer)	63.26

The third man, Horsman, won the sealed handicap. Third prize winner in the sealed handicap was Percy Brewster (498 Zenith-Gradua-JAP), who averaged 60.13 mph.

At the start of the 1000 cc Ten-Mile Record Race, Harry Martin (986 Martin-JAP) slipped and fell whilst mounting his machine, injuring his hip and having to retire. E. F. Remington (986 Matchless-JAP) led the first time past the Fork, followed by Sidney George (994 eight-valve Indian), W. G. Howard (738 Matchless-JAP), Oliver Baldwin (986 BAT-JAP) and E. C. E. Baragwanath (986 Matchless-JAP).

In the second lap Remington forged ahead, Howard ran second with George third.

In the third and final circuit Remington increased his lead still further, Howard lay second and Baragwanath third. George retired first and Baldwin later in this lap. The result was an easy win for Remington.

1000 CC TEN-MILE RECORD RACE
Railway-Straight start and Fork finish.

		Av. speed (mph)
1.	E. F. Remington (986 Matchless-JAP)	74.04
2.	W. G. Howard (738 Matchless-JAP)	67.74
3.	E. C. E. Baragwanath (986 Matchless-JAP)	66.27

Remington also made the fastest lap, at 80.45 mph. The sealed handicap was won by Howard.

The last motor cycle race of the day was the All-Comers' Handicap. As Remington, Horsman and Williams had excelled in previoul races, their handicaps were altered accordingly. All got off wels except for George Baker (499 Peerless) and Baragwanath. The result was a win for the limit man Percy Newbold (345 Zenith-Gradua-JAP), who averaged 52.60 mph. Remington, who also made the fastest at 76.31 mph, came in second and G E. Stanley (349 Singer) third. The tenth finisher was a newcomer, Jack Granville Grenfell (496 Norton), who was to become a well-known Brooklands habitué in later years and an expert on supercharging.

The scratch man Sidney George (994 eight-valve Indian), could do no better than sixth place.

Cyclecar exceeds seventy

The BMCRC were treated to fine sunny weather for their Seventh Monthly Meeting of the year held on Saturday, September 13th. A strong south-westerly wind blew down the Railway Straight, providing high speeds in the first event: the Record Time Trials. The event began at 11.30 am, competitors starting at the Fork and gathering speed along the Byfleet Banking prior to entering the timed kilometre and mile. The best performances were as follows:

RECORD TIME TRIALS

	Speed (mph) over:	
Solo classes	fs km	fs ml
B (350 cc) G. E. Stanley (349 Singer)	64.21	63.60
C (500 cc) G. E. Stanley (499 Singer)	71.65	69.77
D (750 cc) W. G. Howard (744 Matchless-JAP)	69.43	68.44
E (1000 cc) E. C. E. Baragwanath (986 Matchless-JAP)	77.08	76.92
Sidecar classes		
G (500 cc) K. Holden (499 BSA)	51.28	51.72
H (750 cc) F. W. Barnes (748 Zenith-Gradua-JAP)	60.42	50.99
E. B. Ware (748 Zenith-Gradua-JAP)	46.38	51.43
I (1000 cc) F. W. Barnes (986 Zenith-Gradua-JAP)	60.42	60.00
Cyclecar classes		
K (1100 cc) B. H. Haywood (1096 Singer)	71.70*	71.18*

(*New class records)

Jack Emerson (498 ABC) after covering the flying kilometre at 80.47 mph, on Tuesday, January 13th, 1914; the first rider officially to exceed 80 mph on a machine under 500 cc.

F. G. Ball on the new 349 cc o.h.v. Douglas after carrying out track tests at Brooklands during February 1914.

Charlie Franklin (994 eight-valve Indian) on Saturday, March 28th, 1914, at the first BMCRC race meeting of the year. He has just won the 1000 cc Three-Lap Scratch Race at 79.90 mph. Note the leaf-sprung front fork.

A. J. Luce (986 Zenith-Gradua-JAP s/car) on Saturday, April 18th, 1914, after winning the three-lap Sidecar Handicap at 52.84 mph.

1913—SPEEDS MOUNT

D. R. O'Donovan seemed to have found some extra speed from his 490 cc Norton, coming in third in Class C with average speeds of 67.34 mph and 66.91 mph over the flying-start kilometre and mile respectively.

In attempting records all competitors had to stay outside the fifty-foot line, as the timing tapes did not exceed this width. Some of the sidecar bodies used were, it seems, "weird-and-wonderful" contraptions. Ware's, which had been christened "The Earwig" by other competitors, was tailored to fit the passenger and so offer little head resistance. Jimmy Cocker (499 Singer s/car), who came in second in the 500 cc sidecar class, with 51.04 mph and 51.43 mph for the flying-start kilometre and mile, used a sidecar chassis that was sprung with four vertically enclosed springs.

Events two, three and four, were one-lap sprint races, run in the following manner: competitors started about a quarter-of-a-mile from the official starting line, accompanied by the BARC car driven by Major Lloyd and carrying Ebbie Ebblewhite as the starter. Near the timekeeper's box they formed a line, and at the drop of the flag got away from a rolling start.

Event two, for Classes A and B, provided an easy win for G. E. Stanley (349 Singer) at 60.77 mph, with V. Busby (346 Sunbeam) second and W. A. Jacobs third, at 58.17 and 58.09 mph. Only a fifth-of-a-second separated these last two at the finish.

Kenneth Holden (499 BSA) got away first in Event 3 (Class C—up to 500 cc solo). He was soon passed by Stanley (499 Singer), who won at an average of 63.94 mph. Holden dead-heated with D. R. O'Donovan (490 Norton) for joint second place, at 60.24 mph. This tie was settled at the end of the meeting by a run-off between the two, which resulted in a close race and a win for O'Donovan.

Event four was for Classes D and E. The young seventeen-year-old rider P. J. Wallace (998 Grandex-JAP) who was in trouble at the start, had difficulty in getting away, as did other riders. The start was therefore halted whilst Major Lloyd drove to the Fork enclosure to fetch volunteers to act as pushers for the "big-twin" riders. He soon returned in the BARC Sizaire-Naudin with seven burly helpers.

The result was a win for Charlie Franklin (994 eight-valve Indian) at 71.94 mph, E. F. Remington (986 Matchless-JAP) coming second at 70.90 mph with Oliver Baldwin third on a similar machine at 67.02 mph. Towards the end of the race P. H. T. Hoare (C &

H-JAP), who had a front tyre blown off the rim, cut right across the path of those following and crashed into the inside edge of the track, fortunately without injuring anyone.

Next followed the Senior One-Hour Race. Four teams took part, each consisting of three machines of identical make and of under 1000 cc engine capacity.

This race was noteworthy for the consistent riding of Franklin, who led throughout. Although the smallest machines in the race, because of their consistency, the Enfields achieved the greatest aggregate mileage and carried off the team prize. Of the Indians, B. Alan Hill's was soon out of the running because of a pulled-out chain bolt. J. Manners-Smith (499 Triumph) had trouble early on. He stopped, restarted, and then retired after a few laps. L. Hill and other Rudge team members stopped several times to change their driving belts. Franklin shed his exhaust pipe in his nineteenth lap, and Greaves lost his footrest on his seventeenth circuit. The result was as follows:

SENIOR ONE-HOUR TEAM RACE

		Distance covered	
		miles	yd
1.	H. Greaves (350 Enfield twin)	55	1579
	H. V. Colver (350 Enfield twin)	54	590
	D. Iron (350 Enfield twin)	45	275
	TOTAL MILEAGE	155	684
2.	C. B. Franklin (994 eight-valve Indian)	67	926
	S. George (497 four-valve Indian)	57	38
	B. A. Hill (497 four-valve Indian)	5	766
	TOTAL MILEAGE	129	1730

The Rudge team was third with a total of 120 miles 523 yd, and the Triumph team fourth with 106 miles 199 yd. Archie Fenn (499 Triumph) was the fastest "500", covering 62 miles 1109 yd in the hour.

Freddie Barnes (986 Zenith-Gradua-JAP s/car) and Sidney Garrett (499 Regal-Green-Precision s/car) made up the winning team in the Sidecar Four-Lap Relay Race, which had a Railway-Straight Start and a Fork finish.

In the Ten-Mile Record Race and Sealed Handicap, open to

sidecar outfits (up to 1000 cc) and cyclecars (up to 1100 cc), the order of the first three riders remained unchanged throughout the event.

SIDECAR AND CYCLECAR TEN-MILE RECORD RACE
Railway-Straight start and Fork finish.

		Av. speed (mph)
1.	B. H. Haywood (1096 Singer cyclecar)	69.31
2.	F. W. Barnes (986 Zenith-Gradua-JAP s/car)	57.95
3.	G. W. Hands (1088 Calthorpe cyclecar)	56.25

Haywood also won the sealed handicap. E. B. Ware (748 Zenith-Gradua-JAP s/car) was fourth and also the fastest of the Class H (750 cc) sidecars, with an average of 54.97 mph. Jimmy Cocker (499 Singer s/car), third in the sealed handicap, was the fastest "500" outfit, and averaged 51.65 mph.

The final event of the day was the Press Handicap over a distance of two laps, for members of the motorcycling press. The result was a comfortable win for C. E. Wallace (499 Triumph) with D. Stough (350 Douglas) second, both of *The Motor Cycle;* third was O. T. Stough of *The Auto Cycle* riding a 350 cc Enfield. The winner averaged 52.05 mph.

Start of the record-breaking season

The following Wednesday, September 17th, Kenneth Holden broke the flying-start five-mile 500 cc sidecar record. Riding a 499 cc (85 × 88 mm) belt-driven BSA combination carrying a passenger, he managed to average 52.05 mph. Unfortunately, valve spring breakage interfered with an attempt on the standing-start ten miles distance.

A week later, on Wednesday September 24th, B. H. Haywood was out on the track again and, sharing the controls of his Singer cyclecar with George Baker, set further long-distance records in his class. He covered distances from 250 to 550 miles, and periods of four to nine hours, all at speeds around the 62 to 63 mph mark. On the same day D. R. O'Donovan (490 Norton) set up new Class C and D solo records for the flying-start five miles and standing-start ten miles, with speeds of 71.54 and 68.08 mph.

End of meeting rained off

The two motor cycle events in the otherwise all-car programme at the BARC Brooklands' Race Meeting on Saturday, October 4th were first and seventh on the race card. The second of these two could not be run, however, as a heavy shower caused the second half of the meeting to be abandoned.

The motor cycle race that was held, was the Seventeenth Short Handicap—a two-lap (5¾-mile) event with a Fork start and Long finish, as was usual with BARC-organised meetings. Among the notable absentees was Jack Emerson, who had entered on one of the new 498 cc horizontally-opposed fore-and-aft twin-cylinder ABCs. At the start Jimmy Cocker (499 Singer) arrived late due to a sooted sparking plug after leaving the paddock. All the men got away well except for D. R. O'Donovan (490 Norton), whose engine was decidedly off form. Two interesting entries in the race were those of E. L. Buchanan and F. W. Carryer on 493 cc twin- and single-cylinder Imperials. There were also two 348 cc side-valve AJSs running, in the hands of W. Heaton and Cyril Williams.

E. E. Elwell (350 Douglas) led at the end of the first lap with D. C. Bolton and W. H. Buckeridge, second and third, also on Douglas machines. Williams led by the start of the Finishing Straight on the last lap, but was then passed by Cyril Pullin (499 Rudge) who won by a dozen yards from J. A. B. Hellaby (994 o.h.i.v. Indian). Both of these last two riders were from the 26-sec mark. Cyril Williams came in third on his AJS. Pullin's average speed for the race was 68¾ mph.

The rainy weather continued over into the next week and conditions on the following Saturday, October 11th, were so bad that the scheduled BMCRC Championship Race Meeting had to be postponed until Saturday the 18th.

Bemsee Championship Meeting

As if to make up for the appalling weather of the previous two weeks, that on Saturday, October 18th, was almost Spring-like. Amongst the machines present, Sidney Tessier's single-cylinder water-cooled o.h.v. BAT sidecar outfit, with its large single radiator attached to the down tube of the frame, attracted much attention. E. B. Ware (748 Zenith-Gradua-JAP s/car) had a spare oil tank in the sidecar body, fitted with a pump to replenish the main oil tank and designed for working by the passenger. Cyril Pullin's 499 cc

Rudge had a large rear-mounted oil tank encircling the rear down tube of the frame, in the modern manner, and fitted with a foot-operated pump. Although not competing in any of the races, Jack Stevens the co-founder of the AJS concern was the centre of much interest in view of the fine performances recently put up by machines of his manufacture. He had arrived at the track on one of his 5 hp twin-cylinder models with sidecar attached.

During the first event—the Record Time Trials—Sidney Axford (270 Martin-JAP) collided with a pedal cyclist, who should never have been on the track, and was badly shaken up. Also, to add to his chagrin, he discovered that due to a temporary fault in the timing apparatus his times for the flying-start kilometre and mile had not been recorded.

The fastest performances were as follows:

RECORD TIME TRIALS

	Speed (mph) over:	
Solo classes	fs km	fs ml
B (350 cc) G. E. Stanley (349 Singer)	63.91	64.06
C (500 cc) G. E. Stanley (499 Singer)	74.71	73.60
D (750 cc) C. R. Collier (738 Matchless-JAP)	70.79	69.50
E (1000 cc) E. F. Remington (986 Matchless-JAP)	85.38	83.52
Sidecar classes		
G (500 cc) J. Cocker (499 Singer)	57.07*	57.14*
H (750 cc) E. B. Ware (738 Zenith-Gradua-JAP)	59.18*	60.20*
I (1000 cc) J. Jepson (986 Zenith-Gradua-JAP)	61.12	60.20
Cyclecar class		
K (1100 cc) G. W. Hands (1088 Calthorpe)	77.40*	76.84*

(*New class records)

The next two events, the Hour Cyclecar Race (for cyclecars up to 1100 cc) and the Hour Sidecar Race (for sidecar outfits up to 1000 cc, with passengers of over 140 lb weight), were run off together.

All had started in line except for B. H. Haywood (1096 Singer cyclecar), who had to take a place behind the others, and all got away well with the exception of Howard Newman (499 Ivy-Green-Precision s/car). At the completion of the first lap G. W. Hands

(1088 Calthorpe) was leading, followed closely by Haywood. After an interval came E. B. Ware on his larger capacity (748 cc) outfit well ahead of the others, who followed in the order: Charlie Collier (998 Matchless-JAP s/car), Jimmy Cocker (499 Singer s/car), Cyril Pullin (499 Rudge s/car), Howard Newman (on the Ivy outfit), J. F. Buckingham (746 Buckingham cyclecar), Bert Le Vack (496 Motosacoche s/car), Sidney Tessier (on the BAT outfit), Max Heinzel (830 NSU s/car), Kenneth Holden (BSA s/car), P. H. T. Hoare (986 C & H-JAP s/car), and finally Bert Colver on his small 350 cc Enfield combination. After the first lap Buckingham did not appear again.

The Calthorpe ran magnificently, and gradually increased its lead over the Singer. Among the sidecars, Le Vack retired with a broken inlet valve, Cocker dropped out, while Tessier retired on his ninth lap. Ware, Collier and Hoare held the first three places in the Sidecar Race until lap seven, when Newman took third spot. Pullin seized third place from Hoare in the ninth lap, and this order remained unchanged till the end. The Calthorpe cyclecar, which had run so well, gave up on its sixteenth lap owing to a broken differential housing. Hoare retired with a loose magneto, while Jepson had to give up in his final lap with a cracked cylinder. The results divided up into classes gave the following winners:

HOUR RACE FOR SIDECARS AND CYCLECARS

	Distance covered	
Sidecar classes	miles	yd
F (350 cc) H. V. Colver (350 Enfield)	40	98
G (500 cc) C. G. Pullin (499 Rudge)	52	764*
H (750 cc) E. B. Ware (748 Zenith-Gradua-JAP)	56	542*
I (1000 cc) C. R. Collier (998 Matchless-Gradua-JAP)	54	1053
Cyclecar class		
K (1100 cc) B. H. Haywood (1096 Singer)	62	560

(*New class records)

Racing was adjourned for an hour for lunch, after which the afternoon's programme opened with the Junior One Hour Championship Race (up to 350 cc). The first prize was the *Automotor Journal* Challenge Cup.

In this race A. H. Alexander rode the new o.h.v. Douglas, of which so much had been heard in the motorcycling press. Sidney Axford's Martin-JAP twin was conspicuous for its neat exhaust-pipe arrangement, one pipe from each cylinder. All made a good start, but Alexander nearly collided with fellow Douglas rider E. E. Elwell. First at the end of lap one was G. E. Stanley (349 Singer) followed by Howard Newman (346 Ivy-Green-Precision), Hugh Mason (347 NUT-JAP twin), Alexander, and Cyril Williams (348 AJS). Then after a short interval came Freddie Edmond (350 Humber), Axford, Elwell, H. Greaves (350 Enfield twin), Max Heinzel (349 NSU twin), Bert Colver (350 Enfield twin) and A. M. N. Holzapfel (347 Regal-Green-Precision), whose engine was misfiring and which continued to do so throughout the race.

Axford's luck was out, for a sparking plug and a tyre lacerated by a nail from the track, put him out of the running in the second of his circuits.

Stanley, Newman and Williams held the leading places for the first five laps, and then Alexander assumed third place, while Williams dropped back and finally had to stop in lap seven due to a sticking tappet. Elwell also had to pull up, to change a stretched valve. Alexander hung on to his third place until the twelfth lap, when Newman's retirement placed him second in the running. On his next lap (his unlucky thirteenth), a broken pushrod put him out of the race. Mason now lay second to Stanley, with Edmond third. Then Edmond retired and Greaves, whose machine was running most consistently, lay third. The result was as follows:

JUNIOR ONE-HOUR ACU CHAMPIONSHIP RACE (up to 350 cc) FOR THE "AUTOMOTOR JOURNAL" CHALLENGE CUP.

		Distance covered	
		miles	yd
1.	G. E. Stanley (349 Singer)	62	1199*
2.	H. Mason (347 NUT-JAP)	58	556
3.	H. Greaves (350 Enfield)	54	1042

(*New class record)

Bert Colver (350 Enfield twin), who was fourth, covered 52 miles 885 yd, while fifth man A. M. N. Holzapfel (347 Regal-Green-Precision) covered 51 miles 872 yd.

The next event was the only short-distance race in the afternoon's programme. This was the Five-Lap ACU Championship race for machines of up to 1000 cc, for which the *Motor Car Journal* Challenge Cup was awarded as first prize. It was a scratch event.

All eight competitors were mounted on big twins, except for G. E. Stanley who was riding his 499 cc Singer. All got away well, and as they finished the first lap were almost equally spaced out. The order was: Sidney George (994 eight-valve Indian), E. F. Remington (986 Matchless-JAP), Harry Collier (986 Matchless-JAP), G. E. Stanley, J. A. B. Hellaby (994 o.h.i.v. Indian), E. C. E. Baragwanath (986 Matchless-JAP), W. G. Howard (744 Matchless-JAP) and Oliver Baldwin (986 Matchless-JAP).

In the second and third laps the order of the first three men was unaltered. Baldwin's driving belt came off at the end of the third lap. In the fourth, Remington was leading easily, with Collier second and George third. At the start of the last lap the order was the same, but Collier then broke down and could not finish, and the result was as follows:

FIVE-LAP ACU CHAMPIONSHIP (up to 1000 cc) FOR THE "MOTOR CAR JOURNAL" CHALLENGE CUP. Fork start and finish.

		Av. speed (mph)
1.	E. Remington (986 Matchless-JAP)	76.43
2.	S. George (994 Indian)	72.75
3.	G. E. Stanley (499 Singer)	71.16

The last event of the day, for which the greatest number of entries had been received, was the popular Senior One-Hour ACU Championship Race (up to 500 cc) for *The Motor Cycle* Challenge Cup, which was offered as first prize.

G. E. Stanley did not run in this race, but his stablemate Jimmy Cocker (499 Singer) did, and he led the throng at the end of the first lap, with L. Hill (499 Rudge) second and Cyril Pullin (499 Rudge) third.

Hill led in the second lap with Cocker second and Pullin again third. In lap three, Pullin took the lead, which he held for the next five laps, but D. R. O'Donovan (490 Norton), whose engine "had not seen petrol" prior to the race, was gradually gaining ground. In lap eight O'Donovan lay second and he held this position until a piston seizure caused his retirement in his tenth circuit. Meanwhile,

Pullin kept the lead, and very little distance separated the next two men, Cocker and Hill.

By the end of fifteen laps Hill had made two stops and Irishman Tommy Greene (499 Rudge) was pressing him hard. In the seventeenth round Cyril Pullin stopped for oil, and now Cocker was ahead and kept the lead for four laps. Meanwhile Pullin gradually picked up on and, amidst great excitement amongst the spectators, passed his rival in the twenty-second lap to finish the leader on time as well.

SENIOR ONE-HOUR ACU CHAMPIONSHIP RACE (up to 500 cc) FOR "THE MOTOR CYCLE" CHALLENGE CUP. Fork start.

	Distance covered	
	miles	yd
1. C. G. Pullin (499 Rudge)	64	298
2. J. Cocker (499 Singer)	63	1707
3. T. E. Greene (499 Rudge)	63	1308

There were several other interesting names amongst the finishers, including: F. Carryer (493 Imperial-JAP) who covered 58 miles 1124 yd to finish fifth, Jack Granville Grenfell (490 Norton) who covered 53 miles 689 yd to finish ninth and G. W. Baker (499 Veloce) who was joint eleventh with M. G. Abraham (499 Zenith-Gradua-Green-Precision), both covering 46 miles 353 yd. Hill finished in fourth position, with 60 miles 1034 yd to his credit.

A newcomer who finished tenth in this event, covering 49 miles 1096 yd, was Douglas Hawkes (499 Ixion-Precision). He was to become famous as a driver of racing Morgans at the track during the twenties.

Finishing last, in what was to become an unaccustomed position for him, was the young Bert Le Vack (496 Motosacoche).

500 cc sidecar does sixty

Monday, October 20th, saw Hugh Mason out on the track riding his 499 cc Ivy-Green-Precision with sidecar attached. Timed by Ebbie he covered the flying-start kilometre at 61.45 mph and the flying-start mile at 60.81 mph, thus becoming the first officially to exceed the mile-a-minute on a 500 cc outfit. These were new records for both 500 cc and 750 cc sidecar classes.

After setting up new flying-start five-mile and standing-start ten-mile records, at 53.67 mph and 52.74 mph, he started on an attempt for the hour record. A puncture put him out, however, before he could complete the time, but he was able to set a new fifty-miles' speed with an average of 51.73 mph.

J. F. Buckingham, driving a Buckingham cyclecar of 4.9 hp (RAC rating), 89 × 120 mm bore and stroke, then went out and set up a new standing-start kilometre and mile record for cyclecars at 56.78 mph and 56.6 mph respectively. A broken oil pipe, combined with pouring rain, prevented an attempt on the class hour record.

On the Thursday following, an early thick fog nearly put paid to G. W. Hand's attempts at long-distance records, driving his 1088 cc Calthorpe cyclecar. He succeeded, however, in setting up new records from four to six hours and from 250 to 400 miles.

During October 1913, Norton Motors announced that they would be marketing a special Brooklands' machine whose engine was guaranteed to have powered a motor cycle that had lapped the track at over 65 mph. Within a year, there were two modified versions of the 490 cc s.v., Model 9 Norton available. The BS (Brooklands' Special) which had a dropped frame and was fitted with a Binks "Rat Trap" racing carburetter, was supplied with a BARC certificate guaranteeing that its engine had exceeded 70 mph for a lap or 75 mph for the flying-start kilometre at Brooklands. The BRS (Brooklands' Road Special) was similar to the BS model except that it was fitted with mudguards and a Brown & Barlow carburetter, and in that its engine was guaranteed to have exceeded either 65 mph for a lap or 70 mph for the kilometre—also with an official BARC certificate.

The engines of these machines were so tested in the frame of D. R. O'Donovan's Brooklands' Norton, the choice of speed certificate over kilometre or lap depending upon which timing strip was available at the time. During the periods 1913-15 and 1920-22, O'Donovan, who had a shed at the track, spent most of his time preparing these engines. In 1921 the BRS cost £13 more than the standard Model 9 and the BS £23 more. The latter had a higher compression ratio than the standard touring machine.

Also during October 1913, the FICM (Federation Internationale des Clubs Motocyclistes) met in Paris, and agreed to recommend that the ACU should alter the description of Class A, which was for motor cycles up to 275 cc, to make it read "... for motor cycles up to 250 cc". Later the ACU agreed to this by instituting two new motor cycle classes for records and racing: Class A (up to 250 cc)—as recommended—and Class A1 (up to 275 cc). This arrangement was agreed with by the FICM and made international.

End of season record-breaking

On Saturday, November 1st, the Streatham & District MCC held a 100-mile reliability trial on the public highway. Competitors afterwards arrived at Brooklands for speed tests and a stopping and restarting trial on the Test Hill. Points awarded in these two events were added to the score in the road trial, in order to determine the overall winner.

As usual just before the annual motor cycle show, riders were out on the track after records.

On Thursday, November 6th, R. O. Clark (273 FN) made a fairly clean sweep of the long-distance Class A1 records. He averaged around 44 to 45 mph for periods of from two to six hours, and for distances of from 100 to 250 miles, despite the handicap of weighing more than fourteen stones. The same day Jimmy Cocker (499 Singer s/car) was out with W. Pickering as passenger and set up averages of 56.39 mph and 58.94 mph respectively for the five miles with flying start and the ten miles with standing start, in Class G (for up to 500 cc s/cars).

The following day G. E. Stanley (499 Singer) averaged 73.11 mph and 70.39 mph for the same distances in Class C (for up to 500 cc solos).

The Rudge team were determined not to miss out on any potential record spree and on Thursday, November 20th, Tommy Greene and Cyril Pullin made a successful onslaught on Class C records from five to seven hours and 250 to 400 miles, at average speeds of just under 60 mph.

Then followed a particularly noteworthy achievement, when Lieut. R. N. Stewart, to settle a sporting bet with fellow officers in his regiment, rode for nine hours to set up new Class B (350 cc solo) records on his 349 cc twin-cylinder NSU. He had no trade assistance, it being a purely amateur effort, and he averaged around 41 mph under very windy conditions to set up new eight-hour, nine-hour, and 350-mile records.

Max Heinzel (190 NSU) was out on the track again the following Thursday and set up a new three-hour Class A (250 cc solo) record at 45.21 mph, breaking the Class A1 (275 cc solo) record in the process.

Final race meeting of the year

The last meeting of the year at Brooklands before the track's closure for Winter repairs, was that held by the Public Schools' MCC on Saturday, November 29th. Two events were on the timetable. The first was a speed trial over the flying-start kilometre. The winners were:

SPEED TRIALS
over fs km.

Solo classes	Av. speed (mph)
350 cc A. Nicholson (350 Douglas), Bradfield	50.84
500 cc P. Mathews (499 Rudge), Clifton	66.81
1000 cc E. J. Gibbons (986 Martin-JAP)	71.70

Sidecar classes	
600 cc M. Cremetti (350 Douglas)	40.81
1000 cc L. P. Openshaw (986 Zenith-Gradua-JAP), Eton	56.20

The second event was a three-lap handicap. Scratch man A. J. Luce (986 Zenith-Gradua-JAP), this time running solo, won this despite being baulked somewhat by a large racing car which was circulating the track at the time of the race. Luce was lapping at close on 70 mph throughout the event and averaged 67.20 mph for the distance.

Douglas machines were much in evidence at this final meeting of the year. There were also two 7 hp Indians present, in the hands of Roy Walker and T. R. Browning. Gibbon's Martin-JAP, which won its class in the Speed Trials, was an o.h.v. model that had performed successfully in several hill-climb events during 1913.

8

1914—CALM BEFORE THE STORM

It looked like War in nineteen-thirteen, but war did not come and by early 1914 the European political climate seemed calmer. In England the public seemed unconcerned and things went on much as they had done before. The same was true of activity at Brooklands.

During 1913 several of the new 498 cc o.h.v. ABC machines, with engines disposed à la Douglas, had been made and sold to the public. Jack Emerson, who had shaken up Brooklands' habitués with his Norton exploits, had joined ABC as official works' tester and was busy working on a new project. This came to fruition on Tuesday, January 13th, 1914, when he went out on the track late in the afternoon and beat G. E. Stanley's flying-start mile and kilometre records, becoming the first rider of a half-litre machine to exceed 80 mph—officially. Emerson's speeds were: 80.47 mph for the kilometre and 78.26 mph for the mile.

The author's father, Laurence Hartley, a fifteen-year-old schoolboy at the time, remembered seeing this machine at the track. He had played truant from school that day, and gone down to Brooklands to see the famous track that he had heard and read so much about. He recalled that Emerson had fitted up a conical tail at the rear of his saddle, to prolong his body into a streamline form when lying prone along the tank top at speed. This tail had a light wooden framework and was covered with aeroplane fabric. It was some thirty inches long and of fifteen inches diameter at its broader end, near the saddle.

The 498 cc engine had steel cylinders of 70.45 × 64 mm bore and stroke. Transmission was by chain, countershaft and belt to the back wheel.

The day before, January 12th, a speed of 83 mph had been achieved over the flying kilometre, but unfortunately twenty-four hours' notification was the official minimum time required for record attempts at the track and by the morrow, the weather had turned windy, hence the lower speeds.

Practice for this record attempt was not without its attendant risks, for Jack Emerson was on the track at the same time as L. G. Hornsted. Hornsted was practising for short-distance record attempts in his 200 hp Benz racing car. At one stage, Emerson was climbing up the Members' Banking to attain the necessary speed prior to swooping down on to the Railway Straight. Hornsted higher up on the banking behind Jack, had literally to stand on his brakes to avoid a collision with the ABC rider who, unable to see him, was still ascending the banking. Fortunately a collision was avoided, but in swinging down inside the motor cycle, the big car showered small stones and grit from the track surface into the rider's face.

Emerson's ABC pulled a $3\frac{5}{8}$-to-1 gear, which with its $26 \times 2\frac{1}{4}$ in rear tyre gave an engine speed of 3700 rpm, not allowing for driving-belt and wheel slip. In fact, it was considered that a lot of driving-belt slip had occurred and a possible second machine with all-chain drive had been suggested for future atempts by the ABC designer, Granville Bradshaw.

The record attempts by Emerson had set other people thinking on similar lines, for on Saturday, February 9th, A. C. Starace, driving a 349 cc twin-cylinder NSU sidecar outfit complete with pasenger, set up new records in Class F (350 cc sidecars). These included the flying-start kilometre at 51.07 mph, the flying-start mile at 49.72 mph, the flying-start five miles at 41.82 mph and the standing-start ten miles at 41.34 mph. Hitherto the only 350 cc sidecar record had been Bert Colver's one-hour record on the Enfield. Starace's sidecar was a very neat torpedo-shaped affair in aluminium. Max Heinzel, the well-known NSU rider, assisted during the attempts, and himself made an unsuccessful attempt on Class A1 (275 cc solo) records on Thursday, February 19th, rain forcing a retirement. Riding his 267 cc single-cylinder NSU, Max had another attempt on Saturday, February 28th, and this time was successful. He averaged around 47 mph for over three hours, taking Class A1 100-mile, 150-mile, two-hour and three-hour records in the process.

The same day Starace improved his Class F flying-start five-mile and standing-start ten-mile speeds, with averages of 42.57 mph and

41.82 mph respectively. Attempting the one-hour record, however, he collided with a motorcyclist who should never have been on the track, and this on his eighth circuit forced an end to the proceedings. Fortunately no serious injuries resulted to either party.

Les Bailey, who was now back in Britain from Australia, had taken up his old job with the Douglas concern down at Bristol. Although on crutches, due to an accident earlier in the year, he acted as timekeeper to F. G. Ball, when in February track tests were carried out on the new 350 cc o.h.v. racing Douglas.

The first race meeting of the year, scheduled for Saturday, March 21st, was to have been an Oxford versus Cambridge intervarsity affair. The day started off bright and sunny enough, but by noon had clouded over and the ensuing downpour for the rest of the day forced a cancellation.

Short-distance "250" records

Almost a week later, on Friday, March 27th, the weather was fine and track veteran Harry Martin decided to go for short-distance records in the newly established Class A (250 cc solo) on his 245 cc o.h.v. Martin-JAP. Fitted with belt final drive and a three-speed gear in the rear hub, he cleaned up the principal records as follows: flying-start kilometre at 50.16 mph, flying-start mile at 50.42 mph, flying-start five miles at 47.82 mph, and standing-start ten miles at 48.66 mph.

First Bemsee meeting of the year

The following day, Saturday, March 28th, the weather remained dry, if cold, and all was set for the First BMCRC Brooklands' Race Meeting of the 1914 season.

The first event, starting at 11.00 am, was the Hundred-Mile (actually a 37-lap or 100.55 mile) High-Speed Reliability Trial for Cyclecars. It was run in two classes, Category A (up to 750 cc) and Category B (from 750 cc to 1100 cc), with set minimum average speeds of 30 mph and 35 mph respectively. The winners were to be those vehicles whose fastest and slowest lap times differed by the least amount.

This event resulted in a win for J. T. Wood (1068 GWK) in

Category B, there being no finishers in Category A. He averaged 38.31 mph and had a difference of only three seconds between his fastest and slowest laps. Lionel Martin (1096 Singer cyclecar) was second with a difference of five-and-four-fifths seconds and an average of 40.75 mph.

In Category A, E. B. Ware (740 Morgan-JAP) established new Class J (up to 750 cc three-wheeled cyclecars) records for one hour and fifty miles at averages of 47.26 mph and 47.52 mph.

Whilst the High-Speed Reliability Trial was proceeding, Harry Martin (245 Martin-JAP) once again wheeled his machine out on to the track, with a view to setting up a new Class A (250 cc solo) hour record. After averaging about 45 mph for eight laps, however, he was put out by a tack puncturing his rear tyre.

The afternoon's events consisted of a series of three-lap races with a Fork start and finish, which provided plenty of excitement.

Unfortunately for the first of these races, the 350 cc Scratch Race, there were only two starters: F. G. Ball (349 Douglas) and G. E. Stanley (349 Singer). Ball's Douglas was one of the new racing type, with overhead valves and detachable cylinder heads, while Stanley's machine looked like a standard side-valve Singer except for the fitting of a new Brown & Barlow carburetter with variable jet. Ball's machine was, unfortunately, not pulling well. At the end of lap one, Stanley allowed Ball to be just ahead of him; at the end of the second Stanley led easily, while in the final circuit he won by nearly half-a-mile. He averaged 57.75 mph, while Ball kept up 54.35 mph for the three laps.

Eight starters turned out for the 500 cc Scratch Race. A special air-cooled exhaust valve cap was fitted to Kenneth Holden's 499 cc side-valve BSA for this race. Stanley led in the first lap, with D. R. O'Donovan (490 Norton) second and his team mate Jimmy Cocker third, on the other Singer. Stanley increased his lead in the second lap, the second and third men staying the same. The second-lap leader romped home an easy winner, at 59.29 mph, with O'Donovan and Cocker tying for second place. Cyril Pullin was fourth.

In the next event, the 500 cc Sidecar Scratch Race, there were four starters. Singers again had it all their own way, and Jimmy Cocker (499 Singer s/car) led from the start to finish at an average speed of 49.31 mph. The 499 cc Zenith-Gradua-Green-Precision outfits of A. V. Sumner and E. Smith finished second and third.

Kenneth Holden (499 BSA) after his win in the Senior Brooklands' TT Race on Saturday, April 18th, 1914. He averaged 59.80 mph.

Jimmy Cocker (499 Singer) carrying out track tests early in 1914. Lugs were fitted to the frame of his machine for the rapid fitting of a sidecar.

Bert Haddock (348 s.v. AJS) awaits starter's orders in the two-lap 350 cc Scratch Race at the MCC meeting on July 18th, 1914.

A youthful Bert Le Vack (496 Motosacoche) with his mentor Oliver De Lissa, at the MCC race meeting on Saturday, July 18th, 1914. Le Vack won the 350-560 cc Handicap at 62 mph.

Then followed the 1000 cc Solo Scratch Race, in which there were nine starters. If these, Charlie Franklin and Sidney George rode 994 cc eight-valve Indians, and Sydney Garrett was on Harry Reed's 986 cc DOT-JAP. The first-lap order was: Garrett, Franklin, E. F. Remington (986 NUT-JAP), George, D. Iron and E. C. E. Baragwanath (986 Matchless-JAPs), A. J. Luce (986 Zenith-Gradua-JAP) and J. A. B. Hellaby (994 o.h.i.v. Indian). The driving belt fastener of Oliver Baldwin's 986 Matchless-JAP broke just as he arrived at the Fork for the start, and he could not compete. The second-lap order was: Garrett and Franklin close together, George third and the rest following. On the final lap, Franklin and Garrett had a fine tussle for the lead, Franklin eventually coming in first at an average speed of 79.90 mph, with Garrett second and George third.

A series of handicap races now followed for each of the scratch-race categories run, of which the 350 cc Handicap was the first. Harry Martin (350 cc twin-cylinder Martin-JAP), who always scorned a saddle, was seated on the luggage carrier of his machine. W. A. Jacobs (248 Singer) led at the end of lap one, from the 1-min 57-sec mark, with co-starter Max Heinzel (267 NSU) second, and A. M. N. Holzapfel (347 Regal-Green-Precision) third. In the next lap Holzapfel led easily, with Jacobs second and Heinzel third; scratch man Stanley (349 Singer) moved up rapidly through the field.

The result was a win for Holzapfel at 58.03 mph from the 1-min 58-sec mark. Jacobs was second and G. E. Stanley, despite his heavy handicap, came in third.

In the 500 cc Handicap Race, Stanley (499 Singer) put up a magnificent performance. He moved from scratch to sixth position, in a field of eight, by the end of lap one, was second at the end of lap two and won with a final spurt, at an average speed of 70.79 mph. Second was his team mate Jimmy Cocker (499 Singer) who had 24 sec start, third was D. R. O'Donovan (490 Norton) from the 9-sec mark and fourth Cyril Pullin (499 Rudge) who was at scratch with Stanley.

E. B. Ware (499 Zenith-Gradua-JAP s/car) competed in the 500 cc Sidecar Handicap Race, with an outfit fitted with auxiliary oil and fuel tanks. Jimmy Cocker (499 Singer s/car), who arrived late at the start, had to get away immediately he arrived on the line at the Fork. The result was a win for Cocker at 52 mph. Second man was A. V. Sumner (499 Zenith-Gradua-Green-Precision s/car), and third place was taken by E. Smith (499 Regal-Green-Precision s/car).

The last event of the day was a solo handicap, this time for machines up to 1000 cc. The main feature of this race was the way A. J. Luce's 986 cc Zenith-Gradua-JAP leapt about over the rougher pa ts of the track. In the end Sydney Garrett (986 DOT-JAP) came in an easy winner at 74.01 mph. Luce was second and, Charlie Franklin (co-scratch man with Sidney George) third on his 994 cc eight-valve Indian.

Short-distance 500 cc records go again

D. R. O'Donovan, never one to let the grass grow under his feet, had found some extra speed from his 490 cc side-valve Norton and on Monday, April 6th, timed by Ebbie, he set up new 500 cc solo and sidecar short-distance records,

He first attacked the flying-start kilometre and mile with a Bramble sidecar attached, with averages of 64.65 mph and 62.07 mph.

With the sidecar removed he then made an onslaught on Jack Emerson's recently-established 500 cc solo flying-start kilometre and mile records. He succeeded with speeds of 81.05 mph and 78.60 mph.

All four speeds were also new records in the respective 750 cc classes as well.

Easter Monday racing

Two motor cycle handicaps were staged at the customary BARC Easter Race Meeting, on Monday, April 13th. Both started at the Fork and finished in the Finishing Straight at the Long Finishing Line by the BARC Clubhouse.

The first of these handicaps was the Short Motor Cycle Handicap, over 5¾ miles. Jack Emerson (492 ABC), the scratch man, had a Claudel-Hobson automatic carburetter fitted to his machine and the inlet pipe was neatly jacketed, this jacket being connected by a copper pipe to the exhaust, presumably for easy starting. F. G. Ball and Eddie Kickham were both mounted on 349 cc o.h.v. Douglas machines. Several riders had fitted Senspray carburetters to their engines, including Kickham, W. A. Jacobs (248 Singer), Max Heinzel (267 NSU) the limit man, Victor Horsman (499 Singer) and many others.

Jacobs led at the end of the first lap, with Ball second and Buckeridge (349 s.v. Douglas) third. There was a fairly close finish, J. C. Brooke (994 o.h.i.v. Indian), with a 24-sec start, winning at an average speed of 67½ mph. Ball was second and Jack Emerson on the ABC third. Second to last, came Percy Brewster who rode a 499 cc side-valve Douglas.

The other motor cycle race, the Long Motor Cycle Handicap, was over 8½ miles. Scratch man E. F. Remington (986 NUT-JAP) had a lame leg, and asked to be allowed to have a pusher; since none of the other competitors objected, this was allowed. Despite this, both he and his assistant had their work cut-out getting the engine of his high-geared V-twin to fire.

First time past the Fork, Jacobs (248 Singer) the limit man, led from Buckeridge on the Douglas. J. P. Le Grand (349 Singer) lay third. On the next lap Buckeridge had dropped out and F. G. Ball (349 o.h.v. Douglas) had moved into second spot, with Le Grand third and J. A. B. Hellaby (994 o.h.i.v. Indian) fourth. In the final lap Hellaby passed all three riders ahead of him to win at an average speed of 60¼ mph. Scratch man, Remington, despite his starting difficulties, managed to finish fifth.

More 250 cc short-distance records

W. A. Jacobs' 249 cc Singer had been going so well at the Easter Monday race meeting, that he decided to try for records in the new Class A (250 cc solo), at the earliest opportunity. This presented itself, when on Friday, April 17th, he successfully annexed the flying-start mile at 58.63 mph, the flying-start kilometre at 57.65 mph, the flying-start five miles at 50.00 mph, and the standing-start ten miles at 48.28 mph.

Jacob's first lap in the flying-start five miles' record attempt was covered at 51.34 mph, after which the machine slowed down due, it was afterwards discovered, to a broken piston ring.

Public-School and TT racing

The next day, Saturday, April 18th, saw the BMCRC's Second Race Meeting of 1914. A mixed bag of events had been arranged, including races for members of well-known Public Schools and period races run under Isle of Man TT regulations for **BMCRC** members. To start the ball rolling, however, there was a three-lap Cyclecar Handicap (up to 1100 cc), with a Fork start and finish.

The most interesting of the five entries in the Cyclecar Handicap was probably E. B. Ware's new streamlined 740 cc Morgan-JAP three-wheeler, which was on the 1-min starting mark and proved to be the eventual winner at 54.9 mph.

There now followed four races for Public-School members, each over three laps, again with a Fork start and finish.

The first two past the post at the end of the initial lap of the 350 cc Scratch Race, which was the first of the four, were E. C. Stanley (349 Douglas) and A. B. Watson (347 NUT-JAP). The chief features of this race were the numbers of retirements in the second lap and the fact that the entry consisted of only two makes, Douglas and NUT-JAP. During the event the bookmakers insisted on confusing E. C. Stanley with G. E. Stanley, who was a spectator! He had recently left the employ of Singer Motors as chief development engineer to take up a post in a similar capacity with the Triumph Company, and had not yet a machine available for racing. The eventual 350 cc winner was A. B. Watson, at 48.92 mph.

A number of well-known riders took part in the 1000 cc Scratch Race. The first-lap order was J. C. Brooke (6 hp Zenith-Gradua-JAP), A. J. Luce on an 8 hp machine of the same make, then Powles, whose engine was misfiring. Luce went ahead in the second lap with Brooke close behind. Luce romped home an easy winner at 69.39 mph.

J. Petre (499 Rudge) won the 500 cc Scratch Race at 61.69 mph and A. J. Luce (8 hp Zenith-Gradua-JAP s/car) the 1000 cc Sidecar Scratch Race at 43.40 mph.

In the Brooklands' TT Races the competing machines had to conform to the conditions obtaining in the Isle of Man races, except that touring accessories such as mudguards were not obligatory. The first prize in the Senior (500 cc) event was put up by the proprietors of Shell Motor Spirit (later to become Shell Mex & BP). In addition, BMCRC gold and silver medals were to be awarded to all finishing within 1 hour 20 min of the start of the race.

Some delay was caused by the refusal of several unauthorised individuals to leave the track when requested, and also by Les Bailey's discovery at the last moment that someone had sabotaged his machine by filling his fuel tank with water instead of petrol. All was put to rights, however, and a start was made. F. E. Wasling was riding an experimental 347 cc Royal Enfield fitted with auxiliary exhaust ports and Kenneth Holden was again using air-cooled valve caps.

All made an excellent start. A surprising thing about this race once under way, was how the 350 cc machines managed to more than keep pace with their larger brethren. In the first lap Jimmy Cocker (499 Singer) led the throng, but disappeared from the scene at the end of the third round. Jack Emerson (499 ABC) ran second and Kenneth Holden (499 BSA) was third. In the next lap Holden took first place and kept it to the end of the race. For the next six laps Archie Fenn (499 Triumph) lay second with E. Keyte (344 Royal Enfield) third, while Bailey ran fourth on the Douglas. A broken exhaust valve on his ninth lap and a stop in consequence lost Fenn his second place, leaving the two Junior men second and third overall, with H. Greaves (344 Royal Enfield), Max Heinzel (348 NSU), F. E. Wasling (347 Royal Enfield) and Frank McNab (340 NUT-JAP) following in that order. Emerson stopped several times owing to trouble with his new mechanical oil pump, which tended either to flood the crankcase with lubricant or fail to work at all. Meanwhile Holden was going magnificently on his all-chain drive machine, forging further and further ahead of the field. By the end of the race he was a full four laps ahead of his nearest rival.

Fenn retired on his twenty-third circuit and Holden and Emerson were the only finishers in the Senior Race.

From the third to the twenty-second lap, Les Bailey and H. Greaves stayed in close company, then, for two or three laps Bailey allowed his partner to get ahead of him. But the Douglas rider clearly had the race in his pocket, for in lap seventeen he again took the lead in the Junior event and held it until the end. Results:

BROOKLANDS' TT RACES Fork start and finish.

SENIOR EVENT 350-500 cc) over 26 laps.

		Av. speed (mph)
1.	K. Holden (499 BSA)	59.80
2.	J. L. Emerson (499 ABC)	50.02

JUNIOR EVENT (up to 350 cc) over 26 laps   Av. speed (mph)
1. S. L. Bailey (349 Douglas)   54.29
2. H. Greaves (344 Royal Enfield)   54.17
3. F. E. Wasling (347 Royal Enfield)   48.97

Kenneth Holden covered 60 miles 411 yd in the hour; Bailey, 54 miles 558 yd; and Greaves, 54 miles 201 yd.

There were seven entries in the three-lap Sidecar Handicap. Oliver De Lissa's 496 cc twin-cylinder Motosasoche was again fitted with his patented exhaust valve, which apparently kept the engine remarkably cool. His passenger, incidentally, was the young Bert Le Vack. In the first lap De Lissa (with a 3-min 42-sec start), the limit man, led, with Kenneth Holden (499 BSA s/car) who had a 1-min 51-sec start second; A. J. Luce (986 Zenith-Gradua-JAP s/car), with 1 min start, was third; E. B. Ware (496 Zenith-Gradua-JAP s/car) was fourth; and Freddie Barnes, on a similar machine to Luce, last. In the final lap Luce, who had moved up steadily, came in an easy winner at 52.84 mph, with Holden second at 46.89 mph and Barnes third at 56.12 mph.

The last event, the Public-Schools' Team Championship, in which teams comprising a 350 cc and a 500 cc solo plus a 1000 cc sidecar outfit, was won on points by Rugby. The first man home in this three-lap race was R. L. Keller (499 ABC), who averaged 53.4 mph.

Single-cylinder cyclecar records

Late in the afternoon of Thursday, April 30th, G. L. Holzapfel, driving a 498 cc (90 × 77½ mm, bore and stroke) Carden-JAP cyclecar, annexed the flying-start kilometre and mile records in Class J (up to 750 cc cyclecars) at 61.12 mph and 59.41 mph.

These records secured, J. V. Carden went for the flying-start five-mile and standing-start ten-mile records with a 592 cc Carden-JAP, fitted this time with a single-cylinder 90 × 93 mm engine. His standing-start lap was covered at 50.96 mph, while his last circuit, his fastest, he covered at 58.30 mph. The five-mile record was taken with a speed of 57.91 mph and the ten miles at 55.78 mph.

Collier's kilometre record goes

The sensation of the day at the BMCRC Brooklands' Race Meeting on the following Saturday, May 2nd, was the breaking of Charlie Collier's long-standing Class E (1000 cc solo) flying-start kilometre record by Sidney George (994 eight-valve Indian), at 93.48 mph during the Record Time Trials. The fastest speeds achieved in this event were as follows:

RECORD TIME TRIALS

			Speed (mph) over:	
Solo classes			fs km	fs ml
A	(250 cc)	W. A. Jacobs (248 Singer)	53.77	52.48
		J. P. Le Grand (248 Singer)	57.36	50.16
B	(350 cc)	S. L. Bailey (349 Douglas)	65.41	61.02
C	(500 cc)	D. R. O'Donovan (490 Norton)	76.61	75.31
E	(1000 cc)	S. George (994 Indian)	93.48*	90.82
Sidecar classes				
F	(350 cc)	W. H. Buckeridge (349 Douglas)	44.21	42.96
G	(500 cc)	L. Hill (499 Rudge)	56.49	54.05
I	(1000 cc)	E. B. Ware (986 Zenith-Gradua-JAP)	62.48	61.02
Cyclecar classes				
J	(750 cc)	E. B. Ware (744 Morgan-JAP)	61.95*	61.02*
K	(1100 cc)	L. Martin (1096 Singer)	75.57	74.38

(*New class records).

The remaining seven events consisted of six one-lap sprint races and a final three-lap All-Comers' Handicap.

In the 500 cc Race, although the average speeds were high, the result was an easy win for D. R. O'Donovan (490 Norton) at 67.13 mph with Jack Emerson (499 ABC) second and J. W. Tollady (490 Norton) third.

Seven competitors faced the starter in the 1000 cc Race and very high speeds were expected. Here again the winner, Sidney George (994 eight-valve Indian), had plenty of power to spare, as E. F. Remington (986 NUT-JAP) took second place some considerable way behind him at the finish. George averaged 79.34 mph.

Royal Enfields came in first and second in the 350 cc sprint, E. Keyte winning at 57.89 mph with Greaves following him home.

E. B. Ware (744 Morgan) failed to start in the Cyclecar Race and only four competed. Lionel Martin (1096 Singer cyclecar) won easily at 47.02 mph, with H. Jones (Tweenie cyclecar) second.

Only one entrant failed to start in the 500 cc Sidecar Sprint, and this was D. R. O'Donovan, who apparently had not brought his sidecar down with him to the track. Before the start, L. Hill on one of the new 499 cc TT Rudge-Multis, discovered that he had no oil in his tank. But oil was soon brought, and he made a start, but did not finish due to the breakage of an inlet valve rocker. The winner proved to be G. H. Fry (499 Rudge-Multi s/car), at 47.23 mph with E. B. Ware (499 Zenith-Gradua-JAP s/car) second.

Of the six entrants in the up to 1000 cc Sidecar Race five rode Zenith-Gradua-JAP outfits, the other being a Chater-Lea. Freddie Barnes took first place from E. B. Ware, both on 986 cc Zenith-Gradua-JAP sidecar outfits, at 60.39 mph.

Some time was taken in arranging competitors at the Fork starting line for the three-lap All-Comers' Handicap. H. Greaves (344 Royal Enfield) missed his footrest with his foot on starting off, and fell over with his machine. Apparently no damage resulted, for he soon righted it and got under way. Lionel Martin (1096 Singer cyclecar) proved the winner, at 63.95 mph, with M. G. Abraham (986 Zenith-Gradua-JAP s/car) second and A. J. Luce on a similar outfit, third.

Whitsun racing

As usual, the generous prize money, compared with BMCRC meetings, attracted large entries for the motor cycle races at the BARC Brooklands' Race Meeting on Whit-Monday, June 1st. This, fine weather, and vast crowds of spectators, made for the prospect of a fine meeting. So it proved.

The first motor cycle event, the Nineteenth Short Motor Cycle Handicap over two laps or 5¾ miles, was the third race on the programme. There were forty-three entrants of whom only J. W. Tollady (490 Norton), who had injured his knee, and Les Bailey (349 Douglas), who had a stiff leg, were allowed assistance from pushers at the Fork start.

At the end of the first lap the order of the three race leaders was: A. Lazzell and Eddie Kickham (339 Douglases) first and second with A. M. N. Holzapfel (347 Regal-Green-Precision) third. The two leading men entered the Finishing Straight together at the end of the final lap and Kickham (1 min 30 sec start) just manged to pip Holzapfel at the Long Finishing Line by the judge's box, to win at 58¼ mph. L. Hill (499 Rudge) finished third.

In the Light Car Race, in which Morgans, Cardens, a Winco, a Buckingham and a GWK competed, the winner G. Bullock (9.1 hp Winco), covered the two-lap race distance, again with a Fork start and Long Finishing Line finish, at 60¾ mph.

The other motor cycle event was the ninth race on the programme: the Fifteenth Long Motor Cycle Handicap, over three laps or 8½ miles. Again a Fork start and Long finish were used. There were thirty-six starters including the three placemen in the Short Handicap. Other riders of interest included: Les Bailey (349 Douglas); Oliver Baldwin and E. C. E. Baragwanath (986 Matchless-JAPs)—"Barry" was to achieve much fame with his supercharged Brough-Superior sidecar outfit in the thirties; and the two brothers A. L. and Cyril Pullin (499 Rudges). The latter became famous as the 1914 Senior TT Race winner, in the Isle of Man.

The first-lap leaders were: A. Lazzell (339 Douglas), J. W. Tollady (490 Norton) and J. P. Le Grand (348 Singer). On the next round A. M. N. Holzapfel (347 Regal-Green-Precision) moved to the front, with Tollady and Le Grand still in second and third places. The result was a win for Holzapfel (from the 1-min 57-sec mark) at a speed of 60¾ mph. Second was Oliver Baldwin (986 Matchless-JAP) who was sent off from the 24-sec mark and averaged 73 mph. J. P. Le Grand, who had been third throughout, finished in that position.

During practice before the races, E. F. Remington (986 NUT-JAP) broke his front forks whilst travelling at over 70 mph, but as he was wearing a helmet fortunately escaped with only a grazed forehead. Helmets, though, were not compulsory wear at that time but there was increasing pressure for them to be made official-wear for racing.

Tests on touring machines

On the following Saturday, June 6th, the North-West London Motor Cycle Club staged a special event for touring machines at the track. It was designed to assess speed, petrol consumption, hill-climbing ability, acceleration and braking. Special tests had been devised for each and a number of riders, later well known at Brooklands, took part. Among them were: T. G. Meeten (2 hp OK-Junior) later to become associated with Francis Barnett motor cycles, and R. G. Charlesworth, who became a famous Matchless exponent in the twenties.

Hundred-and-fifty-mile races

Only two events were on the programme of the BMCRC Open Race Meeting on Saturday, June 13th. As each took about three hours to run, however, the day was amply filled. They were the 56-lap (152.19-mile) Junior and Senior Brooklands' TT Races, for machines of up to 350 cc and of 350-500 cc respectively. Each race was run in two categories, one for those riders who had recently competed in the Isle of Man races and the other for any members of the BMCRC who had not done so.

The Junior event began at 10.20 am. All got off the mark well except for E. E. Elwell (339 Douglas) and Smith, whose engines were slow starters.

An interesting rider in this race, from whom much was expected, was Cyril Williams (348 AJS) whose 74 × 81 mm side-valve-engined machine had taken him into second place in the Isle of Man Junior TT Race, only three weeks before.

Owing to the possibility of number plates becoming obscured with oil, one or two riders had their numbers painted on other than the sides of their machines. Les Bailey (349 Douglas), for example, had his on his back. Billy Newsome (another Douglas rider) had his inscribed on the gaiter of his left leg: ideal for the timekeepers, but not much good for anyone else!

On the first lap Bailey led, with E. Keyte (347 Royal Enfield) second and Cyril Williams third. Then followed Billy Newsome, D. G. Prentice, F. E. Wasling and D. Iron (all on Royal Enfields), Tudor Thompson and E. E. Elwell (on 339 Douglases), Frank McNab (340 NUT-JAP), Smith, and H. W. Hands (298 Zenith-Gradua-JAP). At the end of the lap Hands retired with magneto trouble. Keyte took the lead on the second circuit, with Bailey second and Williams third, but in the next round Bailey again took first spot but for the last time in the race.

Keyte led on lap four and held that position until the sixth lap. At this point Wasling stopped with a broken petrol pipe. Prentice, who had been running alternately third and fourth for the last few laps, now took the lead and the order of the first four runners stayed constant for some little while.

The thirteenth lap saw D. Iron (347 Royal Enfield) come in to his pit with the back tyre blown off the rim. After doing seventeen laps Elwell retired with a burst oil pipe and tappet trouble. Meanwhile, Frank McNab was having trouble with belt slip and was losing ground. For the next few laps Keyte held first spot, though once or twice passed by Williams. Newsome alternated between second and third positions which he at times gave up to Prentice, who again led in laps 17 and 18.

Although Prentice or Keyte took the lead occasionally, Cyril Williams seemed to have plenty of speed in hand, and in the twenty-ninth lap he began to forge ahead into first place, which once gained he never afterwards relinquished.

For seven laps Newsome held third place, which he surrendered to Prentice on lap 38. Keyte succeeded in holding second position from lap 31 until the end. Wasling's exhaust valve lifter came adrift on the handlebars and he lost his petrol filler cap, and used a glove instead to block the hole! F. E. Barker (298 Zenith-Gradua-JAP) retired with a broken back wheel bearing and a cracked cylinder, while Frank McNab could not find a sparking plug to stand the pace and had a series of enforced pit stops on this account. Nevertheless, he managed to finish second in the special category. The result was:

BROOKLANDS' JUNIOR TT RACE (up to 350 cc)
over 56 laps or 152.19 miles. Fork start and finish.

		Av. speed (mph)
1.	C. Williams (348 AJS)	53.99
2.	E. Keyte (347 Royal Enfield)	53.18
3.	D. G. Prentice (347 Royal Enfield)	51.83

Special class for BMCRC non-IoM TT competitors

1.	T. Thompson (339 Douglas)	47.68
2.	F. A. McNab (340 NUT-JAP)	43.64

Cyril Williams' machine had all-chain drive and the choice of four gear ratios at the back wheel. This was achieved by using a two-speed gearbox in conjunction with two primary chains and double sprockets. The clutch carried two chain wheels, each having the same numbers of teeth; on the engine shaft—loosely mounted—were two sprockets with unequal numbers of teeth, either of which could be coupled to the shaft by a sliding dog. Twin primary chains coupled the clutch chain wheels to the engine sprockets, the disengaged pair running light. A hand-operated lever controlled the two-speed gearbox and a handlebar control the sliding dog, via a Bowden cable and a system of rods and levers.

It is interesting to note that Avon tyres, then a relatively new brand in racing, were fitted to this machine.

The afternoon event was the 56-lap (152.19 mile) Senior Brooklands' TT Race. The conditions were the same, except for capacity limits of course, as those for the Junior Race. However, there were twenty-five starters as against thirteen in the morning's race. Amongst these was Charlie Collier, making one of his now rare Brooklands' appearances. He rode one of the new 496 cc V-twin (64 × 77 mm) MAG-engined Matchless machines. It had detachable cylinder heads, with inclined (not vertical as on previous Matchless machines) overhead valves, giving a hemi-spherical combustion chamber. The valves were pushrod operated from a camshaft lying in the "V" between the cylinders.

Collier led in the first lap, with Tim Wood (486 Scott two-stroke) second, Graham Dixon (496 Jame-MAG) third and T. McKenna* (490 Norton) fourth. In the third lap McKenna's Norton forged ahead and maintained a lead for the next fifteen laps. Charlie Collier ran second nearly the whole time, but in the eighteenth circuit McKenna slowed; then Collier took the lead and kept it until the end of the race.

Meanwhile things were happening. Both Scotts were put out of action: Wood's by a faulty water union and Frank Applebee's through a seized gear, which caused both chains to break. E. B. Ware (499 Zenith-Gradua-JAP) broke a driving-belt fastener in his first lap; Bert Colver (496 Matchless-MAG) retired with magneto trouble; Sidney George (497 four-valve Indian) came in to his pit with a flat back tyre; Sidney Axford (499 Zenith-Gradua-JAP)

---

* Son of the Rt. Hon. Reginald McKenna MP, Liberal Member of Parliament for N. Monmouthshire, who with Lloyd George vigorously opposed women's suffrage at this time.

suffered sparking plug trouble; and McKenna after putting up a magnificent performance on his Norton, retired with a burst cylinder.

For several laps Robin Bownass (493 NUT-JAP) alternated with Jack Emerson (494 ABC) for second place. But after the twenty-ninth lap, Bownass retired, and Emerson ran on consistently in second spot until the end of the race despite a broken valve.

Charlie Collier, whose machine was functioning well, steadily increased his lead and finished a comfortable winner by nearly eight minutes.

The results were as follows:

BROOKLANDS' SENIOR TT RACE (350-500 cc) over 56 laps or 152.19 miles. Fork start and finish.

	Av. speed (mph)
1. C. R. Collier (496 Matchless-MAG)	60.84
2. J. L. Emerson (494 ABC)	57.55
3. H. G. Dixon (496 James-MAG)	53.94
Special class for BMCRC non-IoM competitors	
1. K. Holden (499 BSA)	56.23
2. E. R. Lloyd (499 Singer)	51.11

So far as incidents during the race were concerned, these were varied and numerous. V. Olsson (493 Zenith-Gradua-JAP) suffered a stretched valve and slipped timing; R. F. Collins (499 Rudge) had a stretched valve and other troubles. Valve troubles also beset Oliver Godfrey (497 four-valve Indian); A. B. Watson's exhaust pipe fell off his 494 cc ABC and the flames burnt the high-tension cable off his magneto!

Sydney Garrett (499 BSA) was stopped by mistake several laps too early, by race officials, and on restarting broke his exhaust valve: not the best of things to happen after a long and tiring race!

Another Indian record

On the Wednesday of the following week, June 17th, Charlie Franklin was out on the track, riding one of Billy Wells' 998 cc eight-valve Indian racers, with a view to breaking Harry Collier's Class E (1000 cc solo) twenty-four-hour record. After three-hours' running, at an average speed of around 63 mph, this attempt was brought to a premature end by the breakage of a petrol pipe. The machine caught fire and enveloped Franklin in flames, which he put out by rolling on the grass verge at the side of the track. But the machine was a complete write-off.

A similar model was brought out and Franklin succeeded with this in breaking the ten-mile standing start record in Class E. This stood to the credit of E. F. Remington at 74.04 mph and was beaten with a new average of 77.95 mph.

An intervarsity meeting

On Sunday, June 28th, at Sarajevo in the Balkans, the event occurred which was to spark off the dreadful holocaust of the First World War: the assassination of the heir apparent to Emperor Franz Joseph of Austria, Archduke Franz Ferdinand and his wife.

It took a while for the import of this news to percolate through to the British public, for this was before the days of radio and television. Meanwhile for a month or so, nineteen-fourteen England continued undisturbed by the turn of events on the continent and Brooklands was no exception. Thus it was that on Tuesday, June 30th, the Oxford and Cambridge Clubs held a race meeting, originally scheduled for earlier in the year, March 21st, but rained off.

Although brilliant sunny weather was the order of the day, poor advertising of the meeting resulted in a meagre attendance, but this was made up for by good sport and high race speeds.

As with BMCRC events, all the races had a Fork start and finish. Also, all the races were handicaps over either two or three laps. The two-lap 500 cc event provided a fine win, at 64.71 mph, for E. H. Lees (494 ABC), with the scratch man T. C. McKenna (490 Norton) second. As was expected, the scratch man Lionel Martin (1096 Singer cyclecar) won the two-lap Passenger Handicap. His average speed was 46.14 mph.

The first of the three-lap handicaps was for up to 500 cc and gave Lees yet another win on his ABC, this time at 63.44 mph. Both of the remaining two events were handicaps for solo machines from 500 to 1000 cc. The first, a two-lapper, was won by J. C. Brooke (994 o.h.i.v. Indian) from scratch, at 61.61 mph. The last event, a three-lap race, was also won from scratch, this time by E. J. Gibbons (986 Matchless-JAP) at 68.80 mph, with Brooke second.

More records for Norton

On Friday, July 17th, D. R. O'Donovan, riding his 490 cc sidevalve Norton, made a successful attempt on the flying start five-mile and standing-start ten-mile records in Class C (500 cc solo). The day was fine and warm, and there was a slight breeze. His machine was in fine fettle and clocked 3 min $57\frac{1}{5}$ sec or 75.88 mph over the five miles, to break the previous record held by G. E. Stanley (499 Singer) by 2.77 mph.

The standing-start ten miles took O'Donovan 8 min $11\frac{1}{5}$ sec. which gave a speed of 73.29 mph, beating Stanley's old record by 2.9 mph. The Norton's fastest lap was covered at 76.07 mph and its equipment included: a Binks carburetter, Ruthardt magneto and a belt—not chain—drive to the rear wheel.

MCC Annual Race Meeting

In contrast to the Intervarsity Race Meeting of three weeks before, quite a large crowd gathered at the Motor Cycling Club's Sixth Annual Meet the following day, Saturday, July 18th.

Despite a large entry and the large number of races, the programme, by virtue of efficient organisation, ran very smoothly right up to the final prize giving ceremony by Charles Jarrott, the club's captain.

Only Gordon Fletcher (339 Douglas) failed to start in the first race, the 350 cc three-lap Handicap. The limit man W. A. Jacobs (348 Singer) led throughout from a 1-min 12-sec start, and won easily at 52.99 mph. Bert Haddock (348 AJS), the scratch man, whose machine was going well, managed to secure second place. J. P. Le Grand, the other Singer rider, had tyre trouble. He managed to start, only to have his driving belt come off the rim.

Several well-known riders failed to make an appearance in the second race, the 350-560 cc three lap Handicap. P. Shaw (499 P & M) led in the first lap, followed by Bert Le Vack (496 Motosacoche) L. Mogridge (499 Rudge), R. Charlesworth (496 Motosacoche) and Dudley Noble (499 Rover). Le Vack took the lead on lap two and held it until the end, to win at 62.39 mph—his first victory at Brooklands. The MAG engine he used was fitted with Oliver De Lissa's patented air-cooled exhaust valves.

Sydney Garrett (994 Indian) won the three-lap up to 1000 cc Handicap at 61.07 mph, with R. Charlesworth (994 Zenith-Gradua-MAG). Whilst A. H. Hewitt was on his second lap in this event, his exhaust pipe came adrift and was soon trailing along the ground. Another retirement was that of Sidney Axford (986 Zenith-Gradua-JAP) with a sooted sparking plug.

A two-lap scratch race for machines up to 350 cc, the fourth event on the race card was won by Bert Haddock (348 AJS). Gordon Fletcher (339 Douglas) dropped out without completing a lap. Bert averaged 55.47 mph.

Charlie Collier (496 Matchless-MAG) won the fifth race—the three-lap, up to 560 cc Solo Scratch Race, at 65.57 mph. D. R. O'Donovan (490 Norton), who finished third, would have won easily but for the stretching of his driving belt, for he had lapped at over 70 mph during the race. The second man was Bert Colver (496 Matchless-MAG) and fourth Bert Le Vack (496 Motosacoche).

The next event, the three-lap 1000 cc Scratch Race, provided another win for Sydney Garrett on his big Indian, though things might have been different if second man Charlie Collier (496 Matchless-MAG) had not been troubled with one cylinder of his twin misfiring. Garrett averaged 74.12 mph for this race. S. A. Rowlandson (499 Rudge-Multi s/car) won the two-lap Passenger Handicap (up to 500 cc) at 50.33 mph, with Bert Haddock (348 AJS s/car) second and Chris Newsome (499 Rover s/car) third. Another contest for sidecar outfits followed, again a handicap, and this time over three laps for combinations of up to 1000 cc engine capacity. Oliver De Lissa (6 hp Motosacoche s/car) took the lead from the start and won this race easily.

Event nine, the Light Car Handicap (up to 1100 cc), was by far the most exciting race of the day and provided an extremely close finish. Run over three laps, it was just won by E. B. Ware (740 Morgan-JAP three wheeler), with A. Mariani (Tweenie) and Lionel Martin (1096 Singer four-wheeler) the scratch man, third, Martin averaged 77.1 mph.

The "Harry Smith" Gold Challenge Cup Race produced a very close finish. The result was a win for Charlie Collier (496 Matchless-MAG) at 68.51 mph, followed by Bert Haddock (348 AJS) and Bert Le Vack (496 Motosacoche).

A team from the Woolwich & Plumstead MCC, comprising: the

V. A. Jacobs (348 s.v. Singer) after winning the 350 cc Handicap at the MCC race meeting on Saturday, July 18th, 1914.

E. B. Ware (740 s.v. Morgan-JAP) has just set up a new flying kilometre record of 65.10 mph in the Record Time Trials on July 25th, 1914

Lieut. A. Lindsay (490 s v. Norton) winner, at 50.80 mph, of the 550 cc class of the Half-Mile Sprint at the First Combined Services' Race Meeting at Brooklands, on Saturday, August 7th, 1915.

Sergeant Arthur Milner (349 Diamond) at the Second Combined Services' Race Meeting at Brooklands on Saturday, September 4th, 1915.

A competitor climbing the Test Hill during a hill-climb competition, at the Royal Aircraft Factory Race Meeting on October 25th, 1915. The last competitive meeting at Brooklands until 1920

Collier brothers and Bert Colver (on 496 Matchless-MAGs), and F. J. Ellis (347 Royal Enfield), won the Invitation Club Despatch Race.

Stanley on a Triumph

Having left the Singer Company, which was going to give up motor cycle production and concentrate on motor cars, G. E. Stanley—and a week or so later his friend Jimmy Cocker—had joined the Triumph concern. It was on Saturday, July 25th, at what was to be the last BMCRC race meeting for six long years, that these two riders made their public appearance on machines of that marque.

The first event on the race card was the Record Time Trials and Stanley successfully demonstrated that a change of employer had done nothing to dim his tuning abilities. He made fastest time in his class and was closely followed by D. R. O'Donovan, whose record-breaking Norton had been re-bushed and was not quite on top form. Cocker was a good third. The only records broken were by E. B. Ware (740 Morgan-JAP three wheeler). This was despite the run-in being taken clockwise, to take advantage of the strong south-westerly breeze blowing up the Railway Straight.

The results were as follows:

RECORD TIME TRIALS

Speed (mph) over:

				fs km	fs ml
Solo classes					
A	(250 cc)	1.	W. A. Jacobs (249 Singer)	55.10	54.38
B	(500 cc)	1.	S. L. Bailey (349 Douglas)	69.90	67.67
C	(500 cc)	1.	G. E. Stanley (499 Triumph)	78.22	75.95
		2.	D. R. O'Donovan (490 Norton)	77.14	74.07
		3.	J. Cocker (499 Triumph)	75.57	73.47
E	(1000 cc)	1.	S. George (994 Indian)	88.07	85.31
		2.	O. M. Baldwin (986 Matchless-JAP)	86.04	83.33
		3.	H. Reed (986 DOT-JAP)	84.73	82.57
Sidecar classes					
F	(350 cc)	1.	S. L. Bailey (349 Douglas)	50.71	48.81
G	(500 cc)	1.	J. Cocker (499 Triumph)	61.45	60.00
I	(1000 cc)	1.	J. Chater-Lea (987 Chater-Lea)	63.91	62.94

Cyclecar classes
J (750 cc) 1. E. B. Ware (740 Morgan-
                    JAP)   65.10* 63.09*
K (1100 cc) 1. L. Martin (1096 Singer)   74.07   71.15
(*New class records).

The actual racing started at 2.00 pm. It included six ten-mile scratch races for the different classes and two three-lap handicaps. Each ten-mile race started at the beginning of the Railway Straight and ended on the fourth circuit at the Fork. The two handicaps each had a Fork start and finish.

G. E. Stanley (499 Triumph) led the Ten-Mile 500 cc Record Race at the end of the first lap. As the riders passed the Fork on the second and third occasions, it was noticed that O'Donovan had drawn up and was riding hard on Stanley's heels. At the finish the Norton rider won by a wheel. This was Stanley's first scratch defeat for two years, other than when he had failed to finish a race through mechanical failure. He commented afterwards that he had believed his pursuer to have been Jimmy Cocker, his stable companion at the Triumph factory. Not until he was passed in the last lap—too late to recover the lead—did he realise his mistake, he said. Graham Dixon (496 James-MAG) was using a new type of carburetter with a flat barrel and what apparently was an expanding choke tube. S. Yano, the Japanese rider, was riding a Triumph built into a very short low frame, but it seemed he had trouble as he did not come round for some time. In this as in all the ten-mile scratch races, the speeds were also taken for the flying-start five miles, starting from a point behind the Members' Hill on the first lap. The results were as follows:

500 CC SOLO TEN-MILE SCRATCH RACE
Railway Straight start and Fork finish.

		Speed (mph) for:	
		Ss 10 ml	Fs 5 ml
1.	D. R. O'Donovan (490 Norton)	70.31	71.29
2.	G. E. Stanley (499 Triumph)	70.28	71.18
3.	J. Cocker (499 Triumph)	68.27	68.88

The next race was over the same distance, but for machines of up to 1000 cc. Once again the event provided great excitement, for

Sidney George (994 eight-valve Indian) and Harry Reed (auxiliary-exhaust-ported 986 DOT-JAP) were in close company throughout the race. Although George held the lead almost the whole time, Reed came off the Members' Banking faster and made the best average speed for the flying-start five miles. Result:

1000 CC SOLO TEN-MILE SCRATCH RACE.
Railway Straight start and Fork finish.

		Speed (mph) over:	
		Ss 10 ml	Fs 5 ml
1.	S. George (994 Indian)	77.56	79.26
2.	H. Reed (986 DOT-JAP)	77.46	79.82
3.	E. C. E. Baragwanath (986 Matchless-JAP)	48.01	72.29

Barry (Baragwanath) had trouble in the earlier stages of this race, hence the good five-mile speed but poor overall average.

The third race was over the same course, for machines up to 350 cc. This was nowhere near so exciting, for though Les Bailey (349 Douglas) at once took the lead, he dropped out in the second lap with a broken valve rocker, and Hugh Mason (350 NUT-JAP) took his place with a good lead from H. Greaves (347 Royal Enfield). E. Keyte (347 Royal Enfield) and Robin Bownass (350 NUT-JAP) followed, and W. A. Jacobs on his little 65 × 75 mm (249 cc) Singer brought up the rear. Travelling well, Jacobs succeeded in breaking Class A records by averaging 51.4 mph and 52.29 mph respectively for the standing-start ten miles and flying-start five miles.

These positions remained unaltered to the finish. Frank McNab's 340 cc NUT-JAP caught fire in the first lap owing to his HT terminal coming off the sparking plug. Fortunately no damage resulted. Result:

350 CC SOLO TEN-MILE SCRATCH RACE
Railway Straight start and Fork finish.

		Speed (mph) over:	
		Ss 10 ml	Fs 5 ml
1.	H. Mason (350 NUT-JAP)	60.20	61.86
2.	H. Greaves (347 Royal Enfield)	58.89	—
3.	E. Keyte (347 Royal Enfield)	56.51	—

Only four starters turned out for the Ten-Mile Cyclecar Race (up to 1100 cc) and Lionel Martin (1096 Singer), and E. B. Ware (740

Morgan-JAP), had it all their own way. Ware's little Morgan travelled magnificently and hung on to the Singer's heels all the way. W. Harriss (10 hp Marlborough) was fairly fast and travelled very smoothly, but Percy Newbold (Warren Lambert) was rather slow. Martin gradually increased his lead, but appeared to miscount the number of laps that he had covered. Just before the finish, he shut off his throttle thinking that the race was over. Ware could have passed him easily, had he not been suffering from the same delusion and cut his engine. In spite of this, Ware's times for the five and ten miles were new class records. Results:

1100 CC CYCLECAR TEN-MILE SCRATCH RACE.
Railway Straight start and Fork finish.

		Speed (mph) over:	
		Ss 10 ml	Fs 5 ml
1.	L. Martin (1096 Singer)	59.70	61.86
2.	E. B. Ware (740 Morgan-JAP)	59.50*	61.22*
3.	W. Harriss (10 hp Marlborough)	54.71	—

(*New Class J 750 cc cyclecar records).

The Ten-Mile Sidecar Scratch Race for machines up to 500 cc provided a win for Jimmy Cocker. His 499 cc Triumph with sidecar attached, travelling in its best form, finished about a mile ahead of Kenneth Holden (499 BSA s/car). He in turn had a long lead over Oliver De Lissa (496 Motosacoche s/car). Cocker's record speeds rather minimised the performance of the other two runners, which would have been quite fair in the usual fields of sidecar racing at that time. Results:

500 CC SIDECAR TEN-MILE SCRATCH RACE.
Railway Straight start and Fork finish.

		Speed (mph) over:	
		Ss 10 ml	Fs 5 ml
1.	J. Cocker (499 Triumph s/car)	56.71*	58.06*
2.	K. Holden (499 BSA s/car)	48.52	50.00
3.	O. De Lissa (496 Motosacoche s/car)	46.12	46.59

(* New Class G 500 cc sidecar records, not applicable to Classes H or I—that is the 750 cc and 1000 cc sidecar classes, due to a newly introduced ruling).

A ten-mile event for 1000 cc Sidecars followed and here again a record fell, albeit at lower speeds than in the 500 cc Sidecar event.

A. V. Sumner (964 Zenith-Gradua-JAP s/car) secured the flying-start five-mile record in Class I (1000 cc sidecars), using one of the new 85 × 85 mm bore and stroke JAP engines. A. J. Luce (986 Zenith-Gradua-JAP s/car) had magneto trouble and did not start, while L. P. Openshaw, with a similar outfit, had sparking-plug trouble which delayed him considerably. J. Chater-Lea (987 Chater-Lea s/car) took up the lead and held it well for the first lap, although afterwards his engine seemed to dry up of oil. Then Sumner and C. R. Taylor (986 Zenith-Gradua-JAP s/car) came to the front, running very close together. P. H. Hoare, on the 986 cc C & H-JAP outfit, a Cornish-produced machine and a relative newcomer to the track, had been travelling well, but then his engine dried up of oil—a habit that engines tended to acquire on the full bore straights at Brooklands! Results:

1000 CC SIDECAR TEN-MILE SCRATCH RACE. Railway Straight start and Fork finish.

	Speed (mph) for:	
	Ss 10 ml	Fs 5 ml
1. A. V. Sumner (964 Zenith-Gradua-JAP s/car)	52.90	53.25*
2. C. R. Taylor (986 Zenith-Gradua-JAP s/car)	52.46	

(*New record for Class I 1000 cc sidecars).

The last two events to be staged were the handicap races over three laps each. Twenty-three riders lined up at the Fork for the start of the All-Comers' Handicap, the first of these. F. Pigot Disney (339 Douglas), Frank McNab (340 NUT-JAP) and W. A. Jacobs (248 Singer) were first away as limit men. But Les Bailey (349 o.h.v. Douglas), starting 39 sec later, was soon in hot pursuit. As the men passed the Fork at the end of lap one, Bailey was travelling well and looked like a potential winner. Soon afterwards, however, both he and McNab dropped out with sparking-plug trouble. G. E. Stanley (499 Triumph), off the 57-sec mark, had crept up several places and Harry Reed (986 DOT-JAP) was improving on his 9-sec start from the scratch man Sidney George (994 eight-valve Indian).

In the second lap Jacobs had run into first place with E. Keyte (347 Royal Enfield) second and Stanley a close third. Hugh Mason (350 NUT-JAP) blew up his rear cylinder and retired, while Stanley surged ahead and came home an easy winner at 70.28 mph. Reed was second at 77.16 mph, and Robin Bownass (492 NUT-JAP) third at 64.62 mph.

The last event of the day, a three-lap Passenger Handicap, was won with ease by H. Greaves (347 Royal Enfield s/car). Starting as limit man, with a 4-min 33-sec start from Lionel Martin (1096 Singer cyclecar) who was at scratch, Greaves was well on his second lap before Martin received the signal to go. He was followed by Oliver De Lissa (496 Motosacoche s/car) who afterwards gave way to T. Brown (740 Zenith-Gradua-JAP s/car) and Kenneth Holden (499 BSA s/car). A. J. Luce (986 Zenith-Gradua-JAP s/car) was working his way up through the field, and Sumner was making a good fight of it with Martin, but both their handicaps proved much too heavy for them. Greaves had bad luck in that although his speed was much better than the record in his class, it could not be accepted as the race was a handicap. His winning speed was 47.58 mph. Holden was second at 50.81 mph and Luce third at 56.37 mph.

So ended an interesting but sparsely attended meeting.

Stanley's racing Singer

When G. E. Stanley joined the Triumph concern, he sold his 499 cc track-racing Singer to Victor Horsman. It was raced by the latter during the first few years after the end of the First World War, under the name VEH. Correspondence between the author and Victor Horsman has revealed some of the more interesting mechanical details of this machine, one of the fastest racing machines in its class for its time.

It had rigid front forks and belt drive to the rear wheel. A special carburetter, made for Stanley by Messrs Brown & Barlow, was used which had no throttle in the accepted sense. A piston valve could nearly shut off all the air and was controlled by the air lever. Another lever operated a taper needle situated in the carburetter on the engine side of this valve. The choke had a $\frac{7}{8}$-in diameter in the region of this needle. Occasionally, however, Stanley would use a Senspray carburetter instead.

A cast-iron piston with a drilled skirt was used, having an internal downward extension from the centre of the piston crown. This bore on the gudgeon pin through an enlarged oil slot in the top of the connecting rod small end. It was intended as a prop or support to stop the much-lightened head of the piston from caving in!

When Horsman later raced Nortons, he gave the Singer to his

1914—CALM BEFORE THE STORM

mechanic Bill ("Curly") Quinn, who later sold it. It ended up in the hands of R. K. Battson, who rode the machine in 1920 in a hill-climb competition organised and run by the now defunct Gipsy MCC, near Leith Hill in Surrey. A subsequent coming adrift of the gudgeon pin and scoring of the cylinder barrel, finally put paid to that fine old engine.

A fateful August

There were rumours on all sides of impending war as the month of July drew to a close. On July 28th, four weeks to the day after the Sarajevo affair, Austria declared war on Serbia—Russia's ally. Russia immediately mobilised her forces. Four days later, Germany, Austria's ally, declared war on Russia and the following day invaded that country's other ally, France. It could not be long now before Britain was dragged into matters.

So it was that on Bank Holiday Monday, August 3rd, 1914, visitors to what was to be the last BARC Race Meeting at Brooklands until 1920, could not help but notice the reality of the situation, as train after train load of troops rolled south along the high embankment overlooking the Railway Straight. Carl Joerns, the German racing-car driver, had already sped back to his native land, leaving behind him forever the Grand Prix Opels.

As with all previous BARC Meetings at the track, the usual two motor cycle handicaps had large entries and the meeting as a whole was very well attended. Unfortunately, a great deal of trouble was experienced with carburation due to the fluctuating temperature during the racing. This was mainly due to a sudden build up of threatening clouds causing temporary sudden drops in temperature, yet without rain actually falling.

In the first motor cycle race, the Long Motor Cycle Handicap, over three laps or $8\frac{1}{2}$ miles, there were thirty-seven starters. Both races started at the Fork and ended at the Long Finishing Line. In this race G. Williamson and L. W. Forinton (994 o.h.i.v. Indians) put up fine performances, but could not catch the first three speedy lightweights with their long starts. The result was a win for Les Bailey (349 o.h.v. Douglas) at $61\frac{1}{2}$ mph, with E. J. Webster (350 NUT-JAP) second and Eddie Kickham (339 Douglas) third.

During the interval between the races A. L. Pullin (499 Rudge), who had suffered considerable carburation trouble, decided to change the float in his carburetter. J. P. Le Grand (348 Singer) experienced similar troubles. He had come off worse though, with a cracked piston.

A still larger field of forty-four riders made up the second motor cycle event, the Short Motor Cycle Handicap, over two laps or 5½ miles. This again proved a triumph for the Douglas marque, Eddie Kickham coming in first at 62 mph, with E. J. Webster on the NUT-JAP again second. This time L. W. Forinton was rewarded for his efforts with a third place.

It's war!

The following day, August 4th, with Germany's invasion of Belgium, Britain declared war, the British Army having mobilised the previous day. Major Lindsay Lloyd was already with his regiment, and the remaining BMCRC meetings, the September BARC meeting and another Essex meeting were cancelled. Although these were the days before the passing by Parliament of the *Defence of the Realm Act*, Mr Locke-King unreservedly and without any pressure being brought to bear upon him offered his brainchild—Brooklands —for use by the military authorities. Thus, on August 5th, the Royal Flying Corps took possession of the Flying Ground, the famous Blue Bird café being turned into the officers' mess.

Despite all this, providing the military requirements of security at the Flying Ground were observed, it was still possible to use the track. D. R. O'Donovan was still checking out his BR and BRS Norton engines against the watch. Even record attempts could still be made, and were. On Friday, August 14th, H. Alan Rhodes and Bert Haddock, alternately driving a 348 cc side-valve AJS with NSC sidecar attached, set out after Class F (350 cc sidecar) records.

Rhodes opened the proceedings by attacking the 350 cc sidecar short-distance flying-start records, and succeeded with figures of 52.27 mph, 50.70 mph and 46.60 mph for the kilometre, mile and five miles respectively.

The next attempt was that of Bert Haddock on the one-hour 350 cc sidecar record, riding the same outfit. Before starting he exchanged the Amac carburetter used by Rhodes for a Senspray. *En route* he beat the standing-start ten-mile record in this class, and almost up to the end of the hour was lapping regularly at around 42½ mph, when he unluckily burst a petrol pipe, which knocked a mile-an-hour off his average speed. The standing-start ten miles were covered at 42.55 mph and 41 miles 757 yd were covered in the hour, both of which were new records.

On Tuesday, September 22nd, these figures were knocked for six by Les Bailey driving a 349 cc o.h.v. Douglas sidecar outfit. With a standing lap at 48.10 mph and a fastest flying-lap at 50.64 mph, he set up the following records in Class F (350 cc sidecars):

	Speed (mph)
Flying-start kilometre	53.00
Flying-start mile	52.79
Flying-start five miles	52.02
Standing-start ten miles	49.64

But for a stop with a broken valve rocker in the last eight minutes of the attempt on the one-hour record, he might have completed over fifty miles in that time. As it was he took the record with a distance of 43 miles 1730 yd.

Things now became tighter at the track from a security point of view and as from Wednesday, September 30th, members of the general public were banned from Brooklands. BARC and BMCRC members were still to be admitted, however. As most racing men were now actively engaged in one branch or another of the armed forces, there seemed little prospect of any competitions being organised at the track for some little while, to say the least. This was despite an optimistic invitation for applications from clubs wishing to run speed trials at the track, made by the BARC secretary in the motorcycling press during the later months of the year.

There was to be some racing at the track during the war, but that had to wait until the following year.

9

1915—THE MILITARY TAKE OVER

OPTIMISTICALLY the British Motor Cycle Racing Club, in January, 1915, issued a list of provisional dates for some seven proposed race meetings for the coming year. The prospect of Outer Circuit racing at Brooklands in the foreseeable future was, however, becoming increasingly remote: firstly, because the continual running of solid-tyred Leyland and Thornycroft RFC lorries across the track was playing havoc with its surface, and producing such deep ruts as to make it unsafe for vehicles at speed; secondly, because the prevalent public feeling regarding the war would not countenance such trivial matters as motor or motor cycle racing. At least not at present.

The only real activity at the track during the first half of 1915 was the passing out of BS and BRS Norton engines by the redoubtable D. R. O'Donovan. Even he, tough and as good a rider as he undoubtedly was, by virtue of the roughness of the track had to confine his high-speed activities to the relatively smooth Railway Straight. The engine of a BS Norton at this time would be one that had been certified to exceed 75 mph and that of a BRS to exceed 70 mph, each over the flying-start kilometre—the full lap not being available for the reasons mentioned. O'Donovan continued this Brooklands testing until at least the end of the year.

By early May, the track had become so badly damaged by RFC lorries, that they were banned from making use of it by the Brooklands Track Authorities. Furthermore it took some little time for the War Office to live up to its undertakings to repair this damage, which was a condition of its use by the RFC. By early June, however, repairs started to proceed and thoughts began to be given to the possibility of staging, not a civilian, but a Combined Armed Services' Race Meeting, that Summer. This idea was originally mooted in the corespondence columns of *The Motor Cycle* by a Lieut. F. M. C.

Houghton, of the 25th Divisional Cyclist Company, stationed at Aldershot.

500 cc Class records go

The Railway Straight was not in too bad a surface condition, so on Monday, June 14th, D. R. O'Donovan decided to have a crack at his own records for the flying-start kilometre and mile, in Class C (500 cc solo), which he held at 81.5 mph and 78.6 mph. Again his machine was to be his fixed-head 490 cc side-valve (79 × 100 mm) Norton single, with single-geared final drive by belt, which had served him so well in the past. Set up with a gear ratio of $3\frac{11}{16}$-to-1 and pulling a claimed maximum power output of 16 bhp at over 4000 rpm, he easily surpassed his earlier speeds by covering the flying-start kilometre at 82.85 mph and the flying-start mile at 78.95 mph.

The First Combined Services' Race Meeting

"Wizard" O'Donovan, as he had become known on account of his prowess at tuning engines, had amply demonstrated the feasibility of using the Railway Straight for high speeds, despite the parlous state of other portions of Brooklands Track. The BMCRC therefore decided to make use of it and go ahead with the organisation of a Combined Armed Services' Race Meeting for serving personnel, in conjunction with the military, as a morale boosting operation. A preliminary programme of events was drawn up and Saturday, July 31st proposed as the race day. But this was too soon for the repairs to the Paddock and the Railway Straight to be completed, so the meeting date eventually agreed upon was Saturday, August 7th.

On the day everything ran off without a hitch, despite a monster entry of 172 riders and machines, and the weather was fine and sunny throughout. As a special concession the public was allowed in, and this created certain safety problems, as the Railway Straight had no special enclosures for spectators. Timing was carried out from the "Bathing Machine", a special timing cabin on wheels used for timing record attempts in the pre-war days. All the competitors were in uniform and were drawn from all branches of the armed forces.

There were eleven events on the day's programme, five half-mile standing-start sprint scratch races on the Railway Straight, three hill-climb events up the Test Hill, and two gymkhana events: one a "quick-change-plug" race, and the other a serpentine "slow" race, this last being staged in the Paddock.

The sprint results gave the following winners:

HALF-MILE SPRINT SCRATCH RACES
from a standing start on the Railway Straight.

Classes	Speed (mph)
Up to 270 cc 2 strokes: Cpl A. Ward (211 New Hudson)	35.80
Race for 2¾ hp Douglas machines: Lt. L. A. Felden	41.47
550 cc Touring: Lt. G. Barnard (499 Sunbeam)	48.01
550 cc Racing: Lt. A. Lindsay (490 Norton)	50.80
1000 cc solos: Pte. A. McColl (994 Matchless-JAP)	52.63
Passenger machines (1100 cc) : Cpl. F. E. Barker (Zenith-Gradua-JAP s/car)	46.15

All the half-mile sprint winners were in the Army.

The races in the Hill-Climb Event, which were run on a scratch basis, each had a twenty-five yard run-in before reaching the base of the Test Hill. Corporal F. E. Barker, riding a 349 cc V-twin Zenith-Gradua-JAP, won the 350 cc Hill Climb Race at 26.69 mph. The 550 cc class of this event was won by a Private G. Kendall (490 Norton), of the Duke of Lancs Own Yeomanry, at 33.36 mph. In the up to 1000 cc solo class, two riders, 2nd Lieut. G. Barnard (499 Sunbeam) and Private H. F. Edwards (994 Zenith-Gradua-JAP) tied for first place, also at 33.36 mph.

John Alcock (349 Douglas), a Flight Warrant Officer in the Royal Naval Air Service, scored fourth place in the up to 550 cc racing class of the half-mile sprint. He became famous in 1919, when in association with Lieut. A. W. Brown he made the first flight across the Atlantic Ocean from North America in a Vicker's Vimy bomber. Heading the flight controls section of the ground staff in Newfoundland in this attempt, was Bob Dicker, another well-known Brooklands' rider of the immediate pre- and post-World War I period.

Lieut. A. Lindsay, who won the 550 cc racing-machine sprint, rode T. McKenna's old racing Norton, which at the last BMCRC official race meeting on Saturday, July 25th, 1914, almost a year before, came fourth behind Jimmy Cocker in the 500 cc class of the Record Time Trials. On that occasion the machine had averaged 70.79 mph and 68.44 mph respectively for the flying-start kilometre and mile.

Several well-known racing men, now in uniform, were present at the Combined Armed Services Meeting. Gordon McMinnies, a Chief Petty Officer in the RNAS, won his heat of the Passenger Sprint event and came second in the final, at 45.92 mph. He drove an 1100 cc eight-valve MAG-engined Morgan three-wheeler cyclecar. F. E. Barker was of course well known as a Brooklands' habitué, as were also Oliver Baldwin, now a Corporal in the Army Service Corps, and Sam Wright.

At the end of the afternoon the prizes were awarded, the Aggregate Cup, presented by *The Motor Cycle*, being won by G. **Barnard**. Barker won the second prize.

Hundred miles-an-hour in the offing?

With the successful breaking of records on a somewhat bumpy Railway Straight and repairs on it proceeding apace, several interested parties were thinking in terms of attempting the Class E (1000 cc solo) short-distance records. Being the first motorcyclist to do 100 mph in Britain was a particularly attractive prospect. Billy Wells, the agent for Indian Motor Cycles in Britain, suggested that he might allow Charlie Franklin or Sidney George to have a crack on his 994 cc eight-valve Indians. Harry Martin was mentioned by some as a possible contender for the 100-mph stakes. Nothing came of these conjectures, and the first officially recorded 100 mph by a motor cyclist in Britain had to wait until the post-war period.

The Second Combined Services' Race Meeting

No less than 195 entries were received for the Second Combined Armed Services' Race Meeting held at Brooklands on Saturday, September 4th, 1915. Eleven events had been organised as on the previous occasion and were run off with no less efficiency.

This time crowd control and organisation were simplified by holding the standing-start half-mile sprint scratch races on the Finishing Straight near the BARC Clubhouse and the Paddock. It also enabled the Hill-Climb event to be expedited as competitors did not have to travel all the way from the Railway Straight to get to the base of the Test Hill.

Once again several well-known ex-Brooklands' riders were taking part in the proceedings, including: Lieut. Sidney Axford RNAS, Sub-Lieut. L. P. Openshaw RN, the recently commissioned Lieut. Frank McNab RNVR, Corp. Sam Wright ASC MT, Lance-Corp. Tudor Thompson RE, and many others.

HALF-MILE SPRINT SCRATCH RACES
from a standing start on the Finishing Straight.

Class	Speed (mph)
250 cc (two-strokes): Sergt. A. Milner (198 Levis)	38.70
350 cc: Sergt. A. Milner (349 Diamond)	42.86
550 cc (touring): Corp. H. G. Hodgson (492 ABC)	44.78
550 cc (racing): Pte. G. Kendall (490 Norton)	49.70
1000 cc (solo): Pte. G. Kendall (490 Norton)	50.28
1000 cc (sidecars): Flt. Sub-Lieut. L. P. Openshaw (Zenith-Gradua-JAP s/car)	46.15

The star of this meeting proved to be Sergeant Arthur Milner, who on his 349 cc Diamond also won the 350 cc class of the Hill-Climb Event. The 550 cc class of the Hill-Climb resulted in a tie for first place between Corporal Hodgson and Captain G. W. Huntbach (499 Premier). Flight Sub-Lieutenant Openshaw won the unlimited (1000 cc) solo class on his big Zenith, with sidecar detached.

Corporal Graham Johnson won *The Motor Cycle* Cup for the maximum number of points gained from places achieved in the various events held that day.

More Norton activity at the track

During September D. R. O'Donovan had a new chain-driven 490 cc Norton undergoing tests at Brooklands. It was provided with a dummy gearbox shell, which merely served to support the bearings of a countershaft. The avowed intention was to develop it for record-breaking.

On September 22nd, a Wednesday, O'Donovan riding a 490 cc Norton with sidecar attached was able—due to improved track conditions—to set up a new flying-start five-mile record in Class G (for sidecar outfits up to 500 cc). His average speed was 58.78 mph, which was high enough to break the equivalent records in Classes H (750 cc sidecars) and I (1000 cc sidecars) as well.

Whether the machine was the chain-driven model or his older belt-driven one is not clear from Press reports of the event at the time.

An Aircraft Workers' Race Meeting

The two Combined Services' Race Meetings, run earlier in the year, had been so successful that a similar meeting was organised to provide a morale booster for the workers at the Royal Aircraft Factory at Farnborough. Held on Saturday, October 23rd, some 245 motor cycle entries had been received by race day, and spectators turned up in large numbers.

Once again the Finishing Straight was used for the various half-mile standing-start sprint races, which were this time all handicaps, as were the hill-climb races.

HALF-MILE SPRINT HANDICAP RACES
from a standing start on the Finishing Straight.

Class	Speed (mph)
300 cc (solo): N. A. Champion (270 Sun-Vitesse)	37.10
1000 cc (passenger vehicles): F. G. Kennard (737 Matchless s/car)	43.80
350 cc (touring solos): S. O. Turner (349 Douglas)	51.10
1000 cc (touring solos): P. Davey (965 Matchless)	56.12

C. Doczy (270 Sun-Vitesse) won the 300 cc class of the Hill-Climb Event on the Test Hill, W. F. Guiver (499 Ariel) and E. G. Perrott (349 Douglas) won the 550 cc and 1000 cc classes, and Guiver finished second to Perrott in the larger class.

The passenger event resulted in a win for C. S. Horsfield (746 Humber s/car).

Two gymkhana events, the "quick-change-plug" race and a serpentine "slow" race, concluded matters. Then the weather, which had been dull and cold throughout the afternoon, broke up altogether and it began to rain. The meeting was now over and no one could say when the next one would be.

With the war in France now at its height, the British public had its attention focussed on things other than Brooklands. This and the increasing demands of the military for greater security at the Flying Ground made any further track racing out of the question, and brought to a close the pioneering stage of Brooklands' history. But this was not the end of the story, for the great track was only slumbering, until its awakening after hostilities had ceased.

INDEX

Abbott, A. Ray., 46, 66, 93
ABC, 196, 205, 206, 210, 211, 213-215, 221, 222, 238
Abercromby, Sir G. W., 47
Abraham, M. G., 201, 216
AC cyclecar, 135
Agadir incident, 126
Ainslie, M. L., 105
Air Springs Ltd., 56
Aircraft Workers' Race Meeting (1915), 239
Aitken, 33
AJS, 190, 196, 197, 218-220, 224, 232-233
"Albert Brown" Challenge Trophy, 182
Alcock, John, 236
Alcyon, 107, 122, 128
"Alec Ross" Cup, 136
Alexander, A. H., 198, 199
All British Engine Company (ABC) Ltd., 161
Amac carburetter, 109, 232
Applebee, Frank A., 29, 43, 57, 174, 183, 185, 220
Arbuthnot, Sir Robert K., 51, 78, 79, 169, 175, 176, 178-180
Ariel, 66, 142, 239
Armstrong, F. P., 140
Arnott, F. H., 67, 72, 73, 74, 76, 148
Ashtead, H. E., 33
Ashworth, J., 33
ASL-JAP, 53, 56, 71
Astley, H. J. D., 47
Auto Cycle Club, 20
Auto Cycle Union (ACU), 20, 49, 72, 75, 77, 115, 146
Annual race meetings of: (1910), 75-78; (1911), 101-104; (1912), 153-155; (1913), 196-201
Inter-Team Race, 115
"Lamp Trials", 85
"Silencer Trials", 163
Automobile Club de France, 13
Automotor Journal Challenge Cup, 75, 101, 198, 199
Autotrix-JAP cyclecar, 132
Avon tyres, 220
Axford, Sidney R., 128, 134, 145, 150, 168, 171, 172, 184, 186, 187, 197, 199, 220, 224, 238
Ayres, N. A., 131, 135, 136

Baddeley, L. A., 81, 107
Bailey, S. L. (Les): wins 150-mile Junior Brooklands' TT (1912), 148-150; first to exceed 70 mph on 350 cc (1912), 161-162, 207; wins Junior Brooklands' TT (1914), 212-214; achieves 53 mph on 350 cc sidecar, 233
Baker, Frank E., 141, 160
Baker, George W., 170, 185, 190, 192, 195, 201
Baldwin, Oliver M., 176, 191, 193, 200, 209, 217, 225, 237
Ball, F. G., 207, 208, 210, 211
Baragwanath, E. C. E. ("Barry"), 143, 145, 171, 191, 192, 200, 209, 217, 227
Barker, F. E., 75, 219, 236, 237
Barnard, G., 236, 237

INDEX 241

Barnes, F. W. (Freddie): Test Hill records by, 28, 53, 82; Long-distance records by, 82, 89; wins Junior Brooklands' TT (1911), 91, 127, 128, 141, 154, 157, 158, 165; achieves 70 mph with sidecar (1913), 171, 173, 177, 178, 184, 192, 194, 195, 214

Barnes, George, 97

Bashall, Aubrey, 125, 149, 150

Bashall, J. T. ("Bizzy"): riding Triumphs, 29, 30, 41; riding BAT-JAPs, 63, 66, 68, 69, 74, 102, 124, 125; sets 750 cc hour record (1910), 69; sets 1000 cc sidecar hour record (1911), 125

Bashall, W. Harry: 24, 28, 31-32, 37, 38, 46, 47, 48, 50, 66-68, 159, 160; second in TT (1908), 30; wins first 1000 cc solo hour race (1909), 35; 16-20 hp twin of, 40, 82; Junior TT winner (1912), 155

Bateman, Frank, 158, 163, 164, 168, 170-172, 183

BAT-JAP: TT second (1908), 30; First win by twin, 35; First win by single cylinder, 44; 500 cc hour record by, 48; team in 60-lap race, 66-69; 16-20 hp twin, 82; wins Senior Brooklands' TT (1911), 87-88; Sidecar hour record by, 125; Water-cooled V-twin, 175; Water-cooled single-cylinder, 196

Battson, R. K., 231

Beasley, H. P., 146, 147

Bedelia cyclecar, 134, 143, 154

Bedford car, 138, 148

Bell, C. Gordon, 92, 94, 113, 114, 120

Bell, R. J., 25, 99, 179, 181, 183, 184, 189

Bellinger, L. W., 50

Bennett, Charlie E., 46, 54-56, 58, 60-62, 71, 75, 77-79

Bentley cars, 29

Bentley, Walter O., 29, 45, 48, 49, 54, 55, 58, 59

Benz car, 90, 206

Benzole, 176, 178, 179

Benzole Handicap, 178

Bickford, Oscar L., 22, 23

Billings, Mrs., 83

Binks carburetter, 168, 223
 "Rat Trap", 202

Bird, C. H., 148

Bischoff, P. W., 38, 80

Blondeau, Monsieur, 77

"Blue Bird" café, 83-84, 232

Blunt, 40

Bolton, D. C., 89, 93, 94, 130-132, 196

Bookmakers, 43, 59, 60, 61-62, 112, 174

Bosch, 46, 74

Bourbeau, R., 154

Bowen, Harold H., 29-33, 35, 36, 41, 42, 44, 52, 55, 59, 60, 94
 exceeds 65 mph on 500 cc BAT-JAP (1909), 45
 sets new 500 cc hour record (1909), 48
 wins One-Hour Brooklands' TT (1910), 57-58
 second in Multi class of 60-lap race (1910), 67, 69

Bownass, Robin, 221, 227, 229

Bradbury, Dan., 117
 motor cycles, 83, 93, 157, 180, 185, 187, 188

Bradshaw, Granville, 161, 166, 206

Bramble sidecar, 210

Brewin, A. J., 189

Brewster, Percy, 145, 150, 151, 158, 159, 185, 189-191, 211
 exceeds 73 mph on Norton (1912), 143-144

British Motor Cycle Racing Club (BMCRC or "Bemsee"),
 Formation of (1909), 28
 First race meeting of (1909), 31-33

Brittain, A. W., 106, 107

INDEX

Brooke, J. C., 211, 212, 222
Brooklands Automobile Racing Club (BARC),
  First race meeting of (1907), 19
  First motor cycle race held by (1908), 23-24
Broom, F. E., 63
Brough, George, 51, 141
  motor cycle, 141, 142
Brown, 107
Brown, A. W., 236
Brown, Barry, 74
Brown, L. G., 173, 174
Brown, T., 230
Brown & Barlow (B & B) carburetter, 98, 156, 202, 208, 230
Browning, T. R., 204
Brunton, A., 65, 66
BSA, 89, 163, 170, 174, 177, 178, 189, 192, 193, 195, 198, 208, 213, 214, 221, 228, 230
Buchanan, E. L., 196
Buckingham, J. F., 170, 198, 202
  cyclecar, 198, 202, 217
Bucquet, Monsieur, 19
Bullock, G., 217
Burney, C. S., 82, 86, 88, 92
Busby, V., 193
Butler, Percy, 103

C & H-JAP, 193-194, 198, 229
Calthorpe, 65, 137
  cyclecar, 164, 173, 184-188, 195, 197, 198, 202
Cambridge University MCC, 26, 33, 69, 222
Cameron car, 138
Canning Town track, 20, 35, 75
CAP carburetter, 120, 144
Carden, J. V., 214
Carden-JAP cyclecar, 214, 217
Carryer, F. W., 196, 201
Carter, T. A., 32, 151, 152
  cyclecar, 145
CAV coil, 25
Champion, N. A., 239
Chapman, J., 174

Charlesworth, R. G., 140, 218, 223, 224
Chater-Lea, J., 225, 229
  motor cycles, 23, 24, 59, 67, 74 225, 229
Chitty, W. D., 50, 51, 57, 65, 73-75, 77, 78, 94, 101, 103, 117, 118
  First 60 mph on 350 cc solo by (1910), 70
Chota cyclecar, 170
Cissac, Henri, 20, 40, 51, 108
Clark, R. O., 25, 28, 29, 48, 67, 118, 203
Clarke, D. R., 58, 66, 71
Claudel-Hobson carburetter, 210
Coatalen, Louis, 129, 148
Cocker, Jimmy, 118, 143, 183, 186, 193, 195-198, 200, 201, 208, 209, 213, 225, 228, 236
Collier brothers. See Collier, Harry, A., and Charlie, R.
Collier, Charlie R.: 20, 23; breaks 1000 cc hour record (1908), 25-26; First Brooklands win by (1910), 31; rides 20 hp Matchless 40; exceeds 75 mph for lap (1910), 65; exceeds 80 mph (1910), 70; versus de Rosier (1911), 108-113; exceeds 90 mph (1911), 116; wins Brooklands' Senior TT (1914), 221
Collier, Harry A.: First Brooklands win by (1909), 33; exceeds 70 mph for race (1909), 49; wins sidecar race (1910), 77; wins MCC Championship (1913), 182
Collier, senior, H. H., 20, 28, 35, 115
Collier-de Rosier Match Races (1911), 108-113
Colliver, E. A., 106
Coloured sashes, 37, 62
Colricke-Herne, E. D., 65-68, 73
Colver, H. V. (Bert.): Hour record by (1907), 35; First Brooklands win by (1910), 62; exceeds 70 mph on 750 cc (1910), 70; wins

INDEX

Brooklands' Junior TT (1911), 87; second in 350 cc class of Six-Hour Race (1913), 188; wins one-hour 350 cc sidecar race (1913), 198
Cook, Will. E., 24, 30, 32, 38-43, 51, 63, 66, 73, 81
   wins first BARC motor cycle race, 23
Cookson, J. J., 81, 183, 184, 187, 188
Corah-JAP, 131, 134-136, 173, 174
Cox, Harold, 119, 144
Crawley, S., 174
Cremetti, M., 204
Creyton, W. (Billy), 66, 68
Croucher, R., 142
Crundall, J. F., 30, 31, 59, 62
Cushman, Leon, 190

Daily Express, 178
Dart-JAP, 75
Davey, P., 239
Dayrell, Frank W., 38, 48, 51, 52, 60, 65
De Dion spray carburetter, 37
de la Ferte brothers, 85
De Lissa, Oliver, 107, 180, 181, 214, 223, 224, 228, 230
De Peyrecave, L. F., 157, 185, 187, 188
de Rodakowski, E., 14, 19, 23, 27
de Rosier, Jake, 85, 103, 106, 108-116
Deacock, A. V., 51, 67
Dee, F. C., 35
Dew, H. E., 189
DEW cyclecar, 189
Dewar, W., 64, 66, 72, 137
Diamond, 238
Dicker, R. E. (Bob), 59, 236
Dickson, E. D., 26, 34, 64, 69
Dickson, F. P., 34
Disney, F. Pigot, 229
Dixon, A. J., 129, 174
Dixon, H. Graham, 220, 221, 226
Doczy, C., 239

Donaldson, 14
DOT-JAP, 67, 103, 147, 159, 160, 165, 172, 173, 209, 210, 225, 227, 229
DOT-Peugeot, 23, 38
Douglas: First Brooklands appearance of (1909), 29; First Brooklands win by (1912), 145; Details of 72 mph "350", 161-162; 350 cc o.h.v., 207, 208, 210, 227, 229, 231, 233; 499 cc s.v., 211
Drury, Noel E., 67
Dunlop beaded-edge tyres, 26, 98
Duocar. *See* Duo cyclecar.
Duo cyclecar, 157, 185, 187, 188
Duralumin connecting rod, 144
Dutton, T. D., 64

Ebblewhite, A. V. ("Ebbie"), 28, 36, 64, 109, 119, 160, 193, 201, 210
Edge, S. F., 14, 19, 24
Edmond, F. G. (Freddie), 139, 140, 149, 150, 167, 170, 179, 186, 199
Edward VII, Death of, 63
Edwards, H. F., 236
Eland, 45
Elce, E. H. (Billy), 97, 103, 120, 121, 135, 136, 140, 148, 152, 153, 159
Electrical timing, 18, 22, 51
Elliott Bros., 18
Ellis, Bill, 116
Ellis, F. J., 225
Elphinstone, 18
Elwell, E. E., 167, 184, 189, 196, 199, 218, 219
Emerson, J. L. (Jack), 160, 161, 196, 211, 213, 215, 221
   wins Senior 150-mile Brooklands' TT (1912), 150-152
   wins *The Motor Cycle* Challenge Cup (1912), 155
   achieves first 80 mph on 500 cc solo (1914), 205-206
Enfield, 99, 118, 119, 149, 155, 159, 167, 186, 188, 190, 194, 198, 199,

206, 213-216, 218, 219, 225, 227, 229, 230
Essex MC, 173, 174, 232
Ethyl alcohol fuel, 57
Evans, Guy Lee, 36, 38-41, 44-48, 50, 52, 54, 55, 57-61, 64-67, 75, 76, 79, 82
Evans, P. J., 123
Exshaw, R. T., 32

Fabbrici Automobili Itala, 15
Farman biplane, 77, 83
"La Gypaète", 83
Fenn, A. G. (Archie), 30, 31, 41, 42, 45, 54, 57, 58, 66, 169, 194, 213
Ferdinand, Archduke Franz, 222
FICM, 202, 203
First Combined Services' Race Meeting (1915), 235-237
FitzHerbert, E. C. W., 35, 56, 67, 69
Fletcher, Gordon, 32, 36, 41, 42, 45, 60, 126, 223, 224
Flook, Percy, 170
FN, 23, 25, 29, 32, 48, 56, 63, 67, 69, 118, 181, 203
Folwell, E., 177, 178
Forgan-Potts, J., 105
Forinton, L. W., 231, 232
Forster, A. G., 28
Forward, 93, 94, 119
Francis, A., 185, 188
Francis, Prince of Teck, 54
Franklin, Charlie B., 66, 68, 69, 101-103, 140, 141, 158-160, 163, 193, 194, 209, 210, 221, 222, 237
Frasetti, E. 52, 76, 77
Frays-JAP, 50, 70, 71, 74, 75, 77, 78, 94, 101, 117, 118
with twin-port cylinder head (1910), 65
Frazer-Nash, A. (Archie), 170, 173, 175, 178
car, 29
Friedlander, S. M., 137

Garrett, Sydney F., 109, 142, 145-147, 150, 151, 154, 157, 158, 160, 161, 177, 181, 194, 209, 210, 221, 224
Gaskell, Dr. H. S., 90, 93, 94, 98
Geddes, J. Stewart, 29
Geiger, Martin, 32, 57, 58, 62, 67, 70, 71, 77
Genn, W. W., 45
George V, 54, 104
George, Lloyd. *See* Lloyd George
George, Sidney, 176-178, 189, 191, 192, 200, 209, 210, 225, 227, 229, 237
exceeds 93 mph (1914), 215
Gibbons, E. J., 204, 222
Gibson, Gordon, 25
Gibson, Hugh, 161, 185, 187, 188
Gibson, John, 58, 60, 62, 66, 95
Gipsy MCC, 231
Giuppone, J., 21, 26
Givaudan, 57, 70, 73
Glover, P. F., 165, 166
GN cyclecar, 170, 175, 178
Godfrey, H. R. (Ron), 29, 173
Godfrey, Oliver C., 57, 83, 86-90, 93, 94, 98-100, 102, 103, 105, 111, 112, 117, 118, 120, 122, 150-152, 155, 158-161, 180, 181, 183, 184, 221
covers almost 60 miles in hour on Rex (1909), 52
Goodacre, F. Lister, 66
"Gradua" variable-gear, 28-29, 83
Grandex-JAP, 193
Gray, G. T., 173, 174
Gray, Norman, 77
Greaves, H., 159, 188, 194, 199, 213-216, 227, 230
Greene, T. E. (Tommy), 201, 203
Grenfell, Jack Granville, 192, 201
Grey, Spencer, 66
Griesbach, R. C., 38, 48
Griffiths, G., 128
Guest, R. E., 141, 142, 146, 180, 185
Guiver, W. F., 239
GWK cyclecar, 135, 138, 143, 153,

154, 161, 164, 175, 177, 178, 207, 217
  Infinitely-variable gear of, 135
Gwynne, E., 35, 62, 66, 68, 186, 187

Haddock, B. (Bert), 223, 224, 232
Halsall, Chris., 181
Halsall, S., 184
Handasyde, G. H., 83
Hands, G. W., 148, 164, 185, 187, 188, 195, 197, 202
Hands, H. W., 122, 218
Hardy, F. A., 29, 76
Harkness, P. Y., 93, 104, 105
Harriss, W., 228
"Harry Smith" Cup, 107, 142, 180, 182, 224
Hartley, Laurence W. E., 205
Haswell, J. R. (Jack), 87, 88, 94, 100, 104, 105, 113, 114, 115, 117, 118, 120, 124, 136, 150, 151, 152, 184, 185, 186, 187, 188
Hawkes, Douglas, 201
Hayward, C. O., 169
Haywood, B. H., 170, 171, 173, 175, 177, 178, 189, 192, 195, 197, 198
Heales, S., 164, 165, 168, 172, 173
Heaton, W., 196
Hedström, Oscar, 59, 103
  carburetter, 37
Hellaby, J. A. B., 177, 196, 200, 209, 211
Hellesen-Hunt/Nilmelior ignition, 29, 120
Helmets, 43, 109, 217
Henry, Prince of Prussia, 114
Hewitt, A. H., 224
High-Speed Reliability Trial, 79-81, 164, 207-208
Hill, B. Alan, 132, 174, 194
Hill, F., 135
Hill, L., 150, 151, 153, 158, 163, 165, 166, 168, 172, 190, 191, 194, 200, 201, 215, 216, 217
Hoare, P. H. T., 193-194, 198, 229
Hobart, 81

Hodgson, H. G., 238
Holden, Colonel, 14, 18
  motor cycle, 14
Holden, Kenneth, 89, 163, 170, 189, 192, 193, 195, 198, 208, 213, 214, 221, 228, 230
Holder, N. F., 185, 187, 188
Holroyd, Jack, 86, 107, 185, 186, 188
Holzapfel, A. M. N., 172, 199, 209
Holzapfel, G. L., 214
Hornsted, L. G., 206
Horsfield, C. S., 239
Horsman, V. E. ("Victor"), 133, 150, 168, 173, 186-191, 210, 230
Houghton, F. M. C., 234, 235
Howard, W. G., 183, 185, 191, 192, 200
Huckle, H., 151
Humber, 30, 33, 55,
  198 cc, 81, 97, 140
  340 cc twin, 119, 123, 129, 132, 139, 144, 149, 150
  499 cc single-cylinder, 58, 59, 62, 66, 67, 81
  746 cc, 239
  "Humberette" cyclecar, 174
Huntbach, G. W., 238
Hunter, A. R., 38, 115
Hunter, G. F., 64, 131, 134, 139, 143, 154, 175
Hunter, H., 114, 131, 134-136, 155, 159, 171
Hutchinson tyres, 109

Imperial, 196, 201
Indian: First appearance at Brooklands of (1909), 36; o.h.i.v. (i.o.e.) V-twins and singles, 36-37; 1-2-3 win One-Hour TT Race (1910), 55; first in Brooklands, 60-lap TT Race (1910), 69; Details of de Rosier's racing, 108-109; Details of four- and eight-valve (1912), 157
International Cup Races: First

(1904), 19-20; Second (1905), 20, 24; Third (1906), 20
Iron, D., 190, 194, 209, 218, 219
Ivy-Green-Precision, 149, 171, 172, 184, 185, 190, 197-199
Ixion-Precision, 201

Jacobs, W. A., 29, 140, 149, 179, 180, 182, 193, 209-211, 215, 223, 225, 227, 229
James-MAG, 220, 221, 226
JAP engine, "90-bore", 91, 100, 101, 128, 137, 180
16-20 hp, 40, 51, 81-82
JAP-Specials, 31, 33, 51, 60
Jarrott, Charles, 14, 223
Jenkins, A. J., 150
Jepson, H., 189, 197, 198
Joerns, Carl, 231
Johnson, F. P., 76, 78, 91, 98
Johnson, Graham, 238
Johnson, W., 105
Jones, F. C., 147
Jones, Henry, 174, 216
Jones, Vickers, 67
Joseph, Emperor Franz, 222

Karslake, Harold, 181
KD, 24
Keller, R. L., 214
Kendall, G., 236, 238
Kennard, F. G., 239
Kennedy, J., 37
Kerry Abingdon, 79, 142
Keyte, E., 188, 213, 215, 218, 219, 227, 229
Kickham, Eddie, 23, 29, 137, 139, 140, 155, 167, 210, 216, 217
Kingfisher-JAP, 78, 89, 99, 104
King's Own-JAP, 59
Knight, Albert A., 173, 184
Krause, M., 35, 44

Lambert, A. W., 158, 164, 174, 177, 178
Lambie, A., 138
Langston, Miss Beatrice, 80, 81

Laurin et Klement, 20, 23, 24
Lazzell, A., 216, 217
Le Grand, J. P., 29, 56, 107, 174, 178, 180, 182, 211, 215, 217, 223, 232
Le Vack, Herbert (Bert), 141, 185, 187, 188, 190, 201, 214, 223, 224
Leader-Peugeot, 23
Lees, E. H., 26, 33, 34, 174, 222
Legh, R., 33
Leicester and District MCC, 64
Levis, 238
Leyland and Thornycroft lorries, 234
Lindsay, A., 236
Lloyd, E. R., 221
Lloyd, F. Lindsay, 27, 28, 36, 60, 183, 193, 232
Lloyd George, 220
Lloyd, H. T., 124
LMC, 83, 86
Locke-King, H. J., 14, 24, 27, 123, 232
"Long Tom". *See* Tyler, Tom
Longuemare carburetter, 25, 40
Loughborough, T. W. (Tommy), 32, 53
Luce, A. J., 95, 99-102, 105, 113, 120, 169, 189, 204, 209, 210, 212, 214, 216, 229, 230
Lyso belt, 95

McArthur, J., 157
McColl, A., 236
McDonagh, A. J., 165, 170, 172, 190
McKenna, Reginald, 220
McKenna, T. C., 220-222, 236
Mackenzie, A. K., 33
Mackenzie, M. K., 27
McLeod, L., 176
McMinnies, W. Gordon, 30, 33, 38, 169, 237
wins first Brooklands motor cycle race, 22-23
McNab, Frank A.: establishes 500 cc hour record (1909), 35; 500 cc

class winner of 60-lap Brooklands' TT (1910), 66-69; wins race against aeroplane (1910), 77; covers 60 miles in hour (1911), 104; 750 cc class winner of Six-Hour Race (1913), 184-188
Mago, A., 157
Maitland, Angus C., 63, 64, 66, 67, 70, 71, 75, 77, 82, 86
Manners-Smith, J. A., 130, 178, 194
March, Vernon, 165, 172, 178
Marchant, Dougal, 22
Marians, B. M., 107
Mariani, A., 181, 224
Marlborough cyclecar, 228
Marshall, Jack, 53, 66-69
Martin, C. R., 150, 151, 155
Martin, Harry ("Wizard"), first Brooklands win by, 54
   achieves 68 mph on 350 cc (1910), 73
   wins *Automotor Journal* Challenge Cup: (1910), 75; (1911), 101
   exceeds 62 mph on 275 cc (1911), 96
   does 73 mph on 500 cc (1911), 117
   covers 54 miles in hour on 275 cc (1911), 119
   wins first cyclecar race (1912), 128-129
   takes 250 cc kilometre at 50 mph (1914), 207
Martin, H. P., 83
Martin, Lionel, 208, 215, 216, 224, 226, 227, 228, 230
Martin-ASL-JAP, 61, 71, 73, 75, 78, 79
Martin-JAP: First Brooklands win by, 48; wins 350 cc class of Two-Hour Race (1909), 50; "over-square" 340 cc o.h.v., 54; 498 cc V-twin, 117; powered Morgan, 129; 268 cc with petrol "vaporiser", 139; 245 cc o.h.v. three-speed, 207
Martin-Precision, 168, 172
Martin-Zedel, 86, 87, 91

Mason, Hugh, 150, 159, 164, 167, 184, 186-188, 190, 199, 201, 227, 229
Matchless-JAP: 20, 23; 1908 TT machine, 25-26; First Brooklands win by (1909), 31; "90-bore" single-cylinder, 91; for Collier-de Rosier races, 109; chain-driven racer, 120, 122; six-speed, 165
Matchless-MAG, 176, 180, 181, 182, 183, 185, 220, 221, 224, 225
Matchless monoplane, 40
Matchless Motors, 20, 26, 29, 35, 40, 115
Mathews, P., 204
Maw, T. F., 51
Mead, G. G., 35, 44, 45
Meeten, T. G., 97, 218
Meeten-JAP, 97
Mercédès car, 139
Mere, C. L., 33, 34
Meredith, C. W., 180
Merfait, J. ,24
Miller, A. G., 128, 168, 169, 176
Mills, H. C., 141, 142, 145, 147, 151, 165, 171, 177
Milner, Arthur, 238
Minerva, 23, 43, 65, 72
MMC-Chater-Lea, 35
Mogridge, L., 223
Moorhouse, Arthur J., 56, 60, 66-69, 107, 118, 119, 127, 130-133
Morgan, A. E., 44, 71
Morgan, H. F. S., 158, 161
Morgan-Blumfield cyclecar, 185, 187, 188
Morgan-JAP cyclecar, 128-129, 132, 135, 158, 161, 164, 174, 177, 178, 208, 212, 215, 217, 224, 225, 226, 227, 228
Morgan-MAG, cyclecar, 237
Moss-Blundell, Dr. C. B., 64
Motor Car Act (1896), 13
Motor Car Act (1903), 13
Motor Car Journal Challenge Cup, 76, 101-102, 155, 200

Motor Cycle Show, 82, 203
  Olympia, 122
  Stanley, 26
Motor Cycling Club (MCC), 37, 51, 64, 106, 107, 141, 142, 179, 180, 182, 223
Moto Rêve, 32, 35, 36, 41, 42, 45, 54, 74, 87, 99, 101, 159
Motosacoche, 86, 107, 141, 174, 180, 181, 185-188, 190, 198, 201, 214, 223, 224, 228, 230
Moxey, E. L., 168, 169
Mullett, F. H., 64
"Multi" variable gear, 166, 169, 170
Mundy, Rex, 66, 140
Munro, L. C., 39, 45, 46, 47
Myers, Eric, 59

Napier Aero Engines, 128
Napier car, 47
New Century-Givaudan, 65
New Hudson, 93, 236
Newbold, Percy, 176, 184, 190, 228
Newman, Howard, 149, 171, 172, 184, 185, 187, 190, 197-199
Newsome, Chris. T., 142, 163, 180, 224
Newsome, W. F. (Billy), 53, 66, 68, 89, 91, 92, 96, 154, 155, 159, 167, 170, 175, 176, 218, 219
Nicholson, A., 204
Nicholson, J. P., 190
Nikodem, Ed., 20
NLG-JAP, 40, 51, 66, 81, 90, 91, 190
NLG Motors, 28
NLG-Peugeot, 23, 24, 30, 32, 38-41, 42, 43, 44, 73, 76
Noble, Dudley H., 141, 142, 181, 182, 223
"Noise Nuisance" and silencing, 14, 24-25, 91, 123, 124
North, F. C., 142
North-West London MCC, 217
Norton, James ("Pa"), 143
  motor cycles, 79, 86, 89, 92, 93, 150-152
  First appearance at Brooklands, of, 29
  Brewster's record-breaking (1912), 143-144
  BS and BRS, 202, 232, 234
  Chain-driven 490 cc, 238
Nottingham MCC's Clipstone Speed Trials, 117
NSU, 23, 25, 38, 39, 59, 63
  7 hp V-twin racer, 32
  takes records, 203, 204, 206, 207
NUT-JAP, 149, 150, 159, 164, 167, 184, 186, 188, 190, 199, 211-213, 215, 217-219, 221, 227, 229, 232

Oberländer, A., 55, 59, 62, 63, 65
O'Donovan, D. R., 143, 167, 172, 178, 179, 193, 196, 200, 202, 215, 232, 234
  First Brooklands win on Norton by, 193
  Record breaking by, 195, 210, 223, 235, 238
Oil pumps, mechanical, 52, 54, 86, 108, 157, 213
OK-Junior, 218
Oldman, W. O., 104, 110, 115, 132
Oliver, V. F. M., 34
Olsson, V., 31, 33, 35, 107, 221
Opel cars, Grand Prix, 231
Openshaw, L. P., 204, 229, 238
Ordnance Surveys, Director of, 15, 34
Oxford University MCC, 69, 222
Oxted-JAP, 107

Palmer, L. N., 134
Palmer Tyre Company's Silver Cup, 97
Parc des Princes circuit, 21
Paris-Madrid Race (1903), 19
Paris-Vienna Race (1902), 19
Parker, H. E., 44, 66, 76
Parker, R. G., 178
Partridge, H. G., 24, 38, 43, 46, 63, 72

INDEX

Patteson, Cyril, 54, 74, 79, 87
Paulhan, Louis, 83
Peach, C. E., 65, 72
Peachy, Tom, 141
Peerless, 185, 192
Pennington, A., 44
Percival, C., 106
Perrott, E. G., 239
Petit, H., 138
Petre, J., 212
Petty, Harold, 150
Peugeot motor cycle, 21, 26, 63
    engine, 23
Phillips, G. A., 30
Phillpott, S. W., 149
Pickering, W., 203
Picric acid, 58
Pither, Frank E., 121, 122, 146
P. & M., 107, 180, 223
    two-speed gear, 59
Pollard, W., 38, 43, 50
Portland sidecar, 121
Powles, 212
Pratt, W., 28
Pratts Motor Spirit, 25
Precision engine, 141, 168, 179
Premier, 66, 67, 89, 141, 238
Prentice, D. G., 218, 219
Prestwich & Company, J. A., 19, 40, 134
Printz, H., 143
Printz, R. L., 135, 138
Public Schools' MCC, 204, 214
"Puffing Billy", 22
Pugh, John Vernon, 163
Pullen, G. C., 138
Pullin, A. L., 217, 231
Pullin, Cyril G., 98, 154, 163, 178-182, 186, 188, 196, 198, 200, 201, 203, 208, 209, 217

Quadrant, 38, 50
Quinn, W. (Bill or "Curly"), 231

Readwin, F. E., 158
Record Time Trials: (1909), 42, 45, 48; (1910), 57, 70, 73; (1911), 96, 117; (1912), 131, 143-144, 157-158; (1913), 171, 192-193, 197; (1914), 214-215, 225-226
Reed, Harry, 67, 147, 159, 160, 165, 172, 173, 209, 225, 227, 229
Regal-Green-Precision, 141, 142 145-147, 150, 151, 154, 157-161, 164, 165, 171, 172, 176, 177, 199, 209, 210, 216, 217
Remington, E. F., 137, 152, 159, 160, 176, 177, 179, 191-193, 197, 200, 209, 211, 215, 217, 222
Rex, 23, 29, 30, 36, 43-46, 48, 49, 51, 52, 56, 57, 65, 69, 107, 140
Reynolds, George, 28, 47, 53, 77, 160
Ricardo, Sir Harry, 103
Rhodes, H. Alan, 232
Riddell, Howard, 177, 179, 183, 187, 188
Rhys, W. L. T., 96, 97, 121, 124, 135, 136
Roberts, B., 71, 97
Roberts, F., 174
Robinson, J., 129
Rogers, T., 159
R.O.M. tyres, 46
Rover, 141, 142, 163, 180-182, 223, 224
Rowlandson, S. A., 181, 182, 224
Royal Enfield. *See* Enfield
Royal Flying Corps (RFC), 84, 232, 234
Rudge: First appearance at track of (1910), 82; First track race of, 86; wins Palmer Trophy, 97; First 60 mph in hour on 500 cc by (1911), 97-98; exceeds 72 mph at Clipstone, 117; exceeds 65 mph for hour, 121; sets first 500 cc sidecar record, 121; 750 cc single-cylinder, 165, 173
Rudge-Multi, 165, 170, 172, 186, 188, 216
Rudge-Whitworth. *See* Rudge and Rudge-Multi.
Rudge-Whitworth Company, 101

Ruthardt magneto, 223

Sabella-JAP cyclecar, 129, 154, 158
Sale, Tony, 51
Samson, F. R., 138, 139
Sarajevo assassination, 222, 231
Savory, F., 67
SCAR car, 148
Schmidt, P., 105, 122
Schmutz, A., 38
Schulte, M. J., 54
Scott, Alfred, 185
  motor cycles, 59, 183, 184, 185, 220
Second Combined Services' Race Meeting (1915), 237-238
Senspray carburetter, 175, 210, 230, 232
Shamrock-Gloria belt, 26
Shanks, H., 24, 35, 78, 89, 99, 104
Shanks, R. J., 39
Sharpe, W. H. S., 44
Shaw, H. D., 88, 93, 94
Shaw, P., 180, 223
Shell Mex & BP, 212
Shell Motor Spirit, 212
Sheppard, A. E., 107
SIAMT, 136
Singer, 100, 104, 110, 130-135, 139, 144, 145, 155, 156, 168, 170-180, 188, 190, 192, 195, 197, 199, 211
  cyclecar first Brooklands' win, 173
  Details of G. E. Stanley's, 230
  Four-valve racing, 129-130
  motor cycle first win, 99
Singer & Company Ltd., 156, 168, 172, 184, 212
Singer Motors. *See* Singer & Company Ltd.
Six-Hour Race (1913), 182-188
Sizaire-Naudin car, 36, 40, 193
Slatter, Norman D., 107, 122, 128
Slaughter, J. H., 31, 32, 33, 35, 36, 41, 66, 83, 86
Smith, E., 208, 210, 218
Smith, Geoffrey, 114

Smith, S. C. W., 136
Smith, W., 32, 35, 39, 42
Smyth, J. C., 30, 45
Soresby, N. O., 141, 180
Spencer, W. Stanhope, 115, 117, 120, 121, 123, 132, 135, 146, 148, 156, 159
Splitdorf magneto, 37
Sproston, A. J., 97, 100, 115
"Squish" effect, 103
Stanley, E. C., 212
Stanley, G. E. ("Wizard"): riding Premier, 66; First Brooklands win by (1911), 99; exceeds 75 mph on 500 cc s.v. Singer (1912), 134; sets 500 cc hour record at 67 mph (1912), 156; first to cover 60 miles in hour on 350cc (1913), 185; exceeds 78 mph on 500 cc s.v. Triumph (1914), 225
Starace, A. C., 206
Stevens, Jack, 197
Stewart, R. N., 87, 92, 113-115, 203
Stoewer car, 148
Stough, D., 195
Straight, Fred, 77
Straight, L. N., 148
Streatham & District MCC, 115, 147, 203
Summers, O. L., 28
Sumner, A. V., 181, 182, 184, 189, 208, 229, 230
Sunbeam, 193, 236
  car, 129, 148
Sun-Vitesse, 239
Surridge, Victor J., 82, 86, 88, 92-96, 100, 101, 104-106, 121
  first to cover 60 miles in hour on 500 cc, 97-98
Swift, 142

Tapley, A. G., 65
Tate, E. D., 69, 129
Taylor, C. R., 229
Teague, H. D., 32
Temple, L., 159
Tessier, Sidney T., 86-88, 95-97,

INDEX

100, 103, 107, 113-115, 117, 120, 127, 128, 131, 132, 147, 154, 158, 196, 198
Test Hill, 27, 28, 53, 60, 64, 85, 93, 127, 145, 203, 236, 237
The Auto Cycle, 195
The Motor Cycle, 25, 77, 146, 155, 195, 200, 201, 234, 237
Thomas, D., 38
Thompson, Tudor, 165, 186, 218, 238
Timson, S. Day, 143
Tollady, J. W., 189, 215, 216
Torrey, C. E., 33
Townsend, C., 148
Triumph, 27, 30-36, 38, 42, 45, 46, 53, 96, 100, 118, 120, 124, 137, 150, 152, 184, 186, 188, 225, 226, 228
  First race win by (1908), 22-23
  First win of an official race by (1908), 25
  "Imperial" (1910), 54
  499 cc o.h.i.v. (1912), 150
Triumph Company, 19, 54, 88, 212, 225, 230
Trump-JAP, 29, 30, 31, 35, 42, 51, 58, 61, 62, 64, 66, 69, 70, 71, 73, 82, 104, 105, 110, 111, 113, 114, 115, 120, 184, 187, 188
Turner, S. O., 239
Turner-Smith, 148
Tyler, Tom, 61-62
Tweenie cyclecar, 216, 224
Twin carburetters, 116, 164, 165

VEH, 230
Veloce, 184, 201
Vickers Ltd., 15, 144
  Vimy bomber, 236
"Victor, E. H." *See* Horsman, V. E. ("Victor")
Vindec-Special, 22, 23, 26, 27, 31-35, 44-45, 57, 58, 62, 67, 70, 72-74, 76, 77

Wadden, G., 132
Wadham, V., 89
Walker, A. G., 140, 143
Walker, Roy, 93, 204
Wallace, C. E., 195
Wallace, P. J., 128, 193
War Office Speed Tests, 126-127
Wanderer, 51, 67
Ward, A., 236
Ward, H., 143
Ward, W., 82
Ware, E. B., 59, 142, 192, 197, 198, 208, 215, 220, 224, 226, 228
  Hundred-Mile Race winner on Rudge (1912), 127
  wins 750 cc sidecar class of Six-Hour Race (1913), 185, 187, 188
  drives streamlined Morgan, 212
Warren Lambert cyclecar, 228
Wasling, F. E., 213, 214, 218, 219
Watawata belt, 58
Watney, Gordon, 139
Watson, A. B., 212, 221
Watson, F. J., 142
Watson, J. Harrison, 77, 78, 82, 83, 105
Weatherilt, Peter, 85, 98-101, 119, 122, 137, 151, 152, 154, 157, 159
Webster, A., 81
Webster, E. J., 102, 231, 232
Wells, W. H. (Billy), 23, 28, 36, 41, 42, 44, 52, 82, 102, 154, 221, 237
  wins first Brooklands sidecar race (1910), 70-71
Werner, 19
West, T. V., 165, 166
White, A. Baker, 31, 86, 93, 94, 96, 97, 100, 104, 105, 106, 110, 113
Whitehead, C. M., 170
Whitlark, J. H., 33, 140
Whittet, A. W., 32
Wilberforce, Victor, 81, 90, 91, 149, 168, 169, 180, 182
Wilkie, A. H., 33, 37
Williams, Cyril, 190, 191, 196, 199
  wins Brooklands' Junior TT Race (1914), 218-219
Williamson, G., 90, 231
Wilton cyclecar, 181

Winco cyclecar, 217
Winit-JAP, 143, 145
Witham, S. A. M. (Sam), 58, 66-68, 70, 83, 173
Wondrick, C. V., 20
Wood, H. O. (Tim), 183-188, 220
Wood, J. T., 135, 138, 143, 153, 154, 158, 161, 164, 175, 178, 207
Woodhouse, Jack, 150, 151, 159, 165
Woodman, Alan E., 59, 60, 63, 119, 132, 139, 144, 149
Woolwich & Plumstead MCC, 224
Wright, A. C., 24
Wright, F., 82
Wright, Sam, 66, 67, 81, 99, 119, 123, 127, 129, 180, 182, 237, 238

Yano, K., 134, 148
Yano, S., 179, 226
Yates, Bert, 58, 59, 66, 67, 81, 97

Zenette-JAP, 28, 31
Zenith-ABC, 166
Zenith-Gradua-Green-Precision, 177, 179, 183, 184, 187-189, 194, 201, 208, 209
Zenith-Gradua-JAP, 33, 36, 38, 53, 82, 83, 85, 89
  "barred gate" motif, 28
  350 cc solo, 91, 98-100, 119, 122, 157, 192
  500 cc solo, 110, 137, 142
  750 cc sidecar, 171, 185, 187, 188, 196, 197, 198, 212, 230
  1000 cc sidecars, 127, 128, 131, 134, 143, 164, 165, 171, 173, 177, 181, 184, 198, 204, 212, 214, 215, 216, 229, 230
Zenith-Gradua-MAG, 224
Zenith Motor Works, 28